Suicidal Behaviour in Europe

Results from the WHO/EURO Multicentre Study on Suicidal Behaviour

Edited by
Armin Schmidtke
Unni Bille-Brahe
Diego DeLeo
Ad Kerkhof

Hogrefe & Huber

Library of Congress Cataloging-in-Publication Data

is available via the Library of Congress Marc Database under the
LC Control Number 2001096203

National Library of Canada Cataloguing in Publication Data

Main entry under title:

Suicidal behaviour in Europe: results from the WHO/Euro multicentre study on suicidal
behaviour

Includes bibliographical references.

ISBN 0-88937-249-7

1. Suicidal behaviour-Europe.   I. Schmidtke, Armin

HV6548.E9S85   2001   362.28'094   C2001-903165-3

 Published with the support of the European Commission 5th Framework Programme for
RTD – "Quality of Life and Management of Living Resources"

PUBLISHING OFFICES
USA: Hogrefe & Huber Publishers, 875 Massachusetts Avenue, 7th Floor,
                    Cambridge, MA 02139
                    Phone (866) 823-4726, Fax (617) 354-6875, E-mail info@hhpub.com
EUROPE: Hogrefe & Huber Publishers, Rohnsweg 25, D-37085 Göttingen, Germany,
                    Phone +49 551 49609-0, Fax +49 551 49609-88, E-mail hh@hhpub.com

SALES & DISTRIBUTION
USA: Hogrefe & Huber Publishers, Customer Service Department,
                    30 Amberwood Parkway, Ashland, OH 44805,
                    Phone (800) 228-3749, Fax (419) 281-6883, E-mail custserv@hhpub.com
EUROPE: Hogrefe & Huber Publishers, Rohnsweg 25, D-37085 Göttingen, Germany,
                    Phone +49 551 49609-0, Fax +49 551 49609-88, E-mail hh@hhpub.com

OTHER OFFICES
CANADA: Hogrefe & Huber Publishers, 1543 Bayview Avenue, Toronto, Ontario M4G 3B5
SWITZERLAND: Hogrefe & Huber Publishers, Länggass-Strasse 76, CH-3000 Bern 9

Hogrefe & Huber Publishers
Incorporated and Registered in the State of Washington, USA, and in Göttingen, Lower Saxony,
Germany

Printed and bound in Germany
ISBN 0-88937-249-7

Foreword

Suicide is probably the most personal act anyone can perform. There are few acts that have such deep roots in social and human conditions, or have such far reaching consequences. Suicide affects the single individual who takes his/her life, it affects those persons in his/her immediate circle and it affects the local community as well as the wider community. We know of no culture in which suicide does not occur.

Suicides have been registered in Europe since the beginning of the nineteenth century, in some countries even longer. However, definitions and measurements have differed very much between the countries, and even between different geographical areas within the same country. Suicidal attempts have not been registered on a national level.

A great step forward was made when the WHO/Euro Multicentre Study on Suicidal Behaviour was established. In the monitoring part of the project, 1989-1999 a total of 25 centres in 19 countries were or are participating (1989-1993: 16 centres in 13 European countries, 1995-1999: 20 centres in 16 European countries, as well as Israel and Turkey). The catchment areas comprise nearly 5,7 million inhabitants. Leading experts in European suicidology have taken part in this unique investigation, so systematically planned, performed and coordinated. The results are convincing. There are great differences between the countries, great changes have taken place both as to suicide and suicidal attempts – as great changes have taken place also in European communities, not least in Eastern Europe during the last decade.

However, this book is not only of statistical interest. It will be of great importance for establishing suicide prevention programs, which we hopefully will see established in most, if not all, European countries. Thus it gives hopes for saving many lives and prepares the ground for better lives for those surviving suicide attempts. Final conclusions are given as to National Suicide Prevention Strategies (an overview) and WHO Strategies, and the WHO/Euro Network on Suicide Prevention is presented.

This book is not only of a high scientific level, and should be read by professional suicidologists, researchers and clinicans, but also has important messages to the many interdisciplinary members of staff whose work involves dealing with people at risk of suicide. It is a unique example of European scientific cooperation. This book will be a milestone in the history of suicidology.

Nils Retterstøl
Professor emeritus, University of Oslo
Previous President of the International Association for Suicide Prevention
(1989-1991)

Table of Contents

Part II: Results in the Individual Countries

Northern Europe

Central Europe

Invited Papers

Part III: Future Perspectives

Appendices

Preface

In the spring of 1985, a small group of five people (Dr. John Henderson, WHO Copenhagen, Denmark; Prof. Heinz Häfner and Dr. Armin Schmidtke, Central Institute for Mental Health Mannheim, Germany; Prof. René Diekstra, University of Leiden, The Netherlands; and Dr. Peter Kennedy, York, UK) met in the WHO building in Copenhagen and, in the days before a European conference on social psychiatry, discussed the possibilities of suicide prevention in the European region of WHO in the frame of target 12 of the European strategy "Health for All by the Year 2000". Nobody in this group could imagine the long-lasting results of this discussion. Later in the year, on behalf of this group, a small working group in Leiden (comprising in addition Prof. Niels Juel-Nielsen, Odense, Denmark, and Dr. S. Platt, Edinburgh, UK) then prepared a meeting for a bigger European conference in York, UK, with the aim of discussing and preparing European suicide prevention research and strategies.

One of the outcomes of the meeting in York in 1986 was a common working definition of "suicide attempt" (then "parasuicide") and the decision to start a WHO multicentre and multinational European study to get a "real" picture of the magnitude of suicidal behaviour in Europe, to obtain epidemiological data, and to identify groups at risk. In the following years, several meetings took place to prepare the material to describe and assess the various catchment areas in different countries, to develop the monitoring forms and the material for the interviews etc. (e. g. in Leiden, Edinburgh, Wuerzburg, and Copenhagen). Someone who has never participated in a multinational multicentre study cannot imagine the amount of work involved in preparing and performing an epidemiological multilingual study with the same research frame, time schedule and instruments, on the one hand taking into account the huge varieties of the individual centres and on the other hand not neglecting and forgetting the common goals.

The study officially started in January 1989 after some months of test runs with 15 centres from 12 countries. Some members of the Steering Group in the first years were more or less sales representatives for the project, presenting it to governments and local authorities in the various countries and in the catchment areas, helping the centres in getting funds and in performing the huge task of educating researchers, interviewers, and helping with the data analyses.

The study immediately became well-known in Europe, the first results were presented soon in congresses not only in Europe but also overseas and in many papers. The first comprehensive results were published in the so-called Wassenaar Book (Kerkhof, A. J. F. M., Schmidtke, A., Bille-Brahe, U., DeLeo, D. & Lönnqvist, J. (Eds.). *Attempted suicide in Europe*. Leiden: DSWO Press).

Due to the increasing fame of the study, other researchers became more and more interested in joining the study. Therefore, the original Steering Group was enlarged and the responsibilities split within it. Over the years, many new centres joined the study, some of course also left. Wuerzburg became responsible for the monitoring part of the study, the part which collected data on suicide attempts, and the common data collection and analyses.

In December 2001, the study became part of the WHO/European Network on Suicide Research and Prevention. The monitoring part now comprises 36 centres from 27 countries (including Turkey and Israel). It is now one of the largest and longest continuing monitoring studies on a mental health problem in Europe. Other countries and states are sometimes envious of this long-term cooperation and the magnitude of data, whose value can hardly be estimated.

The study, however, also had some agreeable side effects. It not only collected data and a picture of suicidal individuals in Europe but also built a network of suicidologists in Europe. Many young researchers got an insight into international cooperation and research methods, were educated in epidemiological methodology and suicidology, and numerous master theses and dissertations resulted. During the study, many researchers became friends over the years and, therefore, also contributed to European cooperation.

The present book (internally called Wassenaar 2 Book) is the comprehensive publication of the results of the monitoring part of the study from the beginning up to now. It presents the results of data collection over 14 years. When we planned this work, we could not imagine the workload involved in preparing such a book, and the task of editing chapters with such a large amount of information and numerous figures. Of course, the book would not have been possible without the help and support of many people. From the beginning, the WHO staff (the regional advisors Dr. J. Henderson, Dr. J. Sampaio-Faria, and Prof. Dr. W. Rutz from the European WHO Region) always supported the study and helped to encourage people. The editors also have to thank many people, who helped in the common data analyses, the checking and the editing, as well as with the layout. First of all, our thanks go to the first secretary of the group, Prof. Dr. Stephen Platt, Edinburgh, UK, whose work and help was in the first years unpayable. Dr. Bettina Weinacker, Wuerzburg, Germany, was the driving force behind the data collection over a number of years, checking and analysing. Dr. Cordula Löhr and DP Katrin Benkelmann, both also from Wuerzburg, took over this task with the same enthusiasm. Prof. Dr. Diego DeLeo helped with the English editing of the chapters, Unni Bille-Brahe also assisted with the editing and the layout, as well as cand. psych. Wieser.

We also have to thank Robert Dimbleby from Hogrefe & Huber Publishers, Göttingen, for the possibility to publish the book in this prestigious publishing house, and for his patience with us since it was not possible to always keep the deadlines.

We hope that this book will be of interest for all European suicidologists as well as for other disciplines and will help to fulfil one of the originally planned tasks: "To achieve a sustained and continuing reduction of suicidal behaviour in Europe."

A. Schmidtke, D. DeLeo, U. Bille-Brahe and A. Kerkhof

Part I

Introduction

Chapter 1

The Suicide Situation in Europe and Suicide Prevention Within the Framework of the WHO Programme "Health for All by the Year 2000"

W. Rutz

The suicide situation in Europe is diverse. In some countries, suicide figures are decreasing – reflecting a stable social situation and economical well being. In other countries, suicidality is stable or even decreasing, in spite of continued social instability, unemployment and an increasing prevalence of depression. In the third category of countries, one can find high prevalence of both depression and suicidality, especially in the countries of Eastern Europe, over the previous decade or more, where dramatic societal transition and changes have taken place, and where mental health services are underdeveloped. The crucial and discriminating aspect of suicidality in European countries relates to a respectable and increasing improvement in the recognition of, and access to the treatment and monitoring of depression.

There have been many attempts – successfully in some research environments – to relate suicidality to unemployment, age, gender, social connectedness, family status and economic determinants of health. Even if findings were consistent and statistically significant in some countries, it is difficult to find a consistent pattern in a global or even European realm. For example, while unemployment in one country may lead to isolation, shame, loss of dignity and self-confidence, and contribute to and aggravate a suicidal process, this may not be the case in an other society.

Family and social connectedness may mean more to women than to men in many societies. On the other hand, loss of social status, identity as family provider or other traditional roles may have a stronger effect on male individuals.

The inconsistent findings in this research highlight the complexity of factors leading to suicide: They show a multifactoriality where an interactive causation can be found in the social, psychological, existential and even the biological/genetical dimensions of human life.

Other consistent findings suggest that the vast majority of all suicides are not committed in a situation of free will or philosophical autonomy, but in a condition of psychiatric disorder, mostly depression and/or heavy alcohol abuse. What we have learned, is that the suicidal process often goes through a presuicidal phase of clinical depression, distorting in a depressive way the cognitive perception of reality and self-value. In most cases, depression may be caused by a multifactoriality of biological, psychosocial and existential variables, leading in interaction and mutual reinforcement to depression and later in many cases, if untreated, to suicide.

From this research we have to learn that suicide prevention should be multifaceted and comprehensive and that one of the feasible ways in most societies to prevent suicide is through improved social and professional recognition of depression, greater access to treatment and better monitoring of depression, including a long term follow up.

In suicidology, there no longer seems to be time for disputes between qualitative and quantitative researchers, between representatives of sociological, psychological, theological or biological reductionism or for getting stuck finding different cultural patterns behind suicidality and an incompatibility of theses patterns between countries.

Today it is time for comprehensive approaches and multidimensional process thinking, with respect to cultural peculiarities and spiritual differences. One of the groups which has made important contributions to the state of art and knowledge in suicidology today is the Network represented in the WHO/EURO Multicentre Study on Suicidal Behaviour, which has existed, worked, gathered information and produced scientifically significant evidence over many years and in many important publications.

One of the most important outcomes of this group's work to date, is demonstrated through findings that show the suicidal diversity throughout Europe. As well as this, evidence points to some common factors underlying the process of suicidality and frequent presuicidal depression:

- A loss of identity, dignity and self respect due to transition and social changes;
- A loss of social connectedness and sense of coherence, to be seen by and to see others, to be involved in a network of social communication and reinforcement;
- A loss of feeling of being integrated in a meaningful social context;
- A loss of having control of what is happening in one's own life and how to react to this – a loss of feeling of not being helpless (a feeling of hopelessness).

Depression and suicidality have to be seen against a background of biological vulnerabilities which may even be genetically and hereditarily expressed in the family background and the individual life history. Our knowledge about

- the multidimensional and multifactoral causal process behind the development of depression, suicidality and later committed suicide,
- the importance of social connectedness, sense of coherence, identity and helplessness as causative factors in the suicidal process,
- biological predetermination concerning suicide and depression

today provides us with the possibility to develop a variety of effective approaches to suicide prevention.

Most of the approaches have been founded upon scientific research and hardly any of them stand in contradiction to each other. It seems unrealistic to expect that further research looking at monocausally linked background factors of suicidality will deliver better scientific knowledge. What we need today is to go beyond the collecting of data and move towards the research linked to it; from a focus on monocausalities to comprehensive and integrative action. The evidence exists, but has to be disseminated and implemented. Comprehensive strategies have already been developed, but have to be improved, tested in pilot projects and disseminated to the countries of Europe where suicidality in many cases is still, and sometimes dramatically, an increasing problem.

This does not mean, however, that the collection of evidence and data has become superfluous. On the contrary, the knowledge existing today about the complexity and multifactoriality of suicidality and suicide prevention and the linkage of suicides to transition and societal change, creates an unquestionable need to continuously and carefully monitor suicidality and suicide related causal factors in the societies of a changing Europe. At present we see dramatic transitions in the countries of Eastern Europe. We still expect more transitions in the countries accessing the European Union in a process which will come to demand adaptation especially in the rural areas and in subpopulations at risk. For example, farmers in England and Ireland, adolescents in France, Portugal and Spain and women in Scandinavia as well as elderly in Central Europe have already changed their life in a sometimes dramatic way.

This data analysis has to comprend the analysis of not only noxic but also protective factors. For example, what makes males in Eastern Europe so exposed to suicidality and what protects women in the same situation? Male alexithymia and incapacity to show weakness and ask for help may play a negative role. Women's greater capacities to create and maintain social networks, to develop a feeling of social significancy and to find meaning in life seem to be some of the protective factors which have to be investigated further. Maybe spiritual dimensions, still existing in some of the countries of Eastern Europe, can again help Western European cultures to fight anomia and feelings of existential emptiness. Probably suicidality is only one part of a more comprehensive complex of self-destructive and risk-taking behaviour. Continued research is needed.

To monitor data on this and to develop a comprehensive approach to suicide prevention is a task of the WHO and its collaborating Network on Suicide Prevention.

In this context, the knowledge presented in this book as well as the partial restructuring and reorientation of the WHO's collaborative Network on Suicide Prevention in Europe is an important step in the WHO's suicide preventional activities in a still dramatic European reality.

This book links to earlier WHO publications on suicidality in Europe and is the first one of two books, giving evidence, calling for action and pointing out feasible possibilities for prevention. It is a part of WHO's activities linked to the year 2001, dedicated by the United Nations and the World Health Organisation to Mental Health. Topics actualised during the World Mental Health day in April, the World Health Assembly in May and in the World Health Report in October 2001 include:

• The burden, the costs and the suffering related to mental disorder;
• The generality of mental ill health and death related to it;
• The stigma inhibiting people to ask for help in time and facilitate early intervention; and
• The treatment gap between what is today possible to do and what really is done due to lack of resources but also stigma and discrimination.

In all these areas, suicide research as presented here and carried out by the WHO Network, has to make important contributions.

This book reflects the current state of knowledge in suicidology and contributes to developing evidence-based possibilities to prevent suicide. It will be followed up by all European member states of the World Health Organisation through activities in education, awareness rising and engaging all sectors of society to reverse high or rising suicide trends in many countries and many populations at risk in Europe.

Chapter 2

The WHO/EURO Multicentre Study on Suicidal Behaviour

History and Aims of the Study

A. Schmidtke, U. Bille-Brahe, D. DeLeo & A. Kerkhof

Introduction

In many European countries, suicidal behaviour constitutes a major public and mental health problem and a considerable drain on resources in both primary and secondary health care settings (Schmidtke et al., 1993). Therefore, in implementing the WHO programme, "Health for All by the Year 2000 (HFA 2000)", the European region of WHO identified prevention of suicidal behaviour as a main task (WHO, 1992). As part of the action in the implementation of target 12 of the WHO European strategy and to develop indicators for this target, comparative data on rates and trends in attempted suicide in European countries were required. However, due to cross-cultural differences in the medical treatment of suicide attempters and in research methodology, it has proven almost impossible to make valid comparisons about any aspect of suicidal behaviour between different European countries. In the absence of national data, researchers have been forced to rely on local surveys, which vary considerably in terms of their operational definitions of suicide attempts, the representativeness of the samples, the time span covered, the amount of information gathered, etc. In addition, local studies have not always been adequate from an epidemiological standpoint. Therefore, the WHO/EURO Multicentre Study on Parasuicide had a significant role in relation to the action plan to implement target 12 and in the development of indicators for this target.

History of the study

In 1985, a small group of five international experts (Dr. J. Henderson, WHO Copenhagen, Prof. Dr. H. Häfner and Dr. A. Schmidtke, Central Institute for Mental Health Mannheim, Germany, Prof. Dr. R. Diekstra, University of Leiden, The Netherlands, and Dr. P. Kennedy, York, UK) met in the WHO building in Copenhagen and discussed the possibilities of suicide prevention in the European region of WHO in the frame of target 12 of the European strategies. In 1985 a small working group in Leiden (with additionally Prof. Dr. N. Juel-Nielsen, Odense, Denmark, and Dr. S. Platt, Edinburgh, UK) then prepared on behalf of WHO a meeting for a bigger European WHO conference in York, UK, with the aim of discussing and preparing common European suicide prevention research and strategies. The meeting in York, UK, was organized by Dr. P. Kennedy and gathered all at this time leading researchers in suicidology in Europe. For the first time also participants from the former USSR and some other Eastern states were present. One of the outcomes of the meeting in York was the decision to start a multicentre and multinational European study to get a "real" picture of the magnitude of the problem in Europe and to generate epidemiological information about attempted suicide as well as to gather information about special groups at risk.

In order to avoid the errors made in previous studies as much as possible, a common working definition of "suicide attempt" was discussed and this common definition of suicidal behaviour had to be used by all participating centres. This definition was the proposed ICD-10 definition. Originally parasuicide (later changed to suicide attempt) was defined as "An act with nonfatal outcome, in which an individual deliberately initiates a non-habitual behaviour that, without intervention from others, will cause self-harm, or deliberately ingests a substance in excess of the prescribed or generally recognized therapeutic dosage, and which is aimed at realizing changes which the subject desired via the actual or expected physical consequences".

In York the structure of the study was also set up. The study was to be guided by a Steering Group (originally: Dr. J. Henderson, WHO, Prof. R. Diekstra, Leiden, Dr. A. Schmidtke, Wuerzburg, Dr. S. Platt, Edinburgh, and U. Bille-Brahe, replacing Prof. Juel-Nielsen). The background and the organization of the study have previously been described in detail by Platt et al. (1992), Bille-Brahe et al. (1993), Schmidtke (1989), Schmidtke et al. (1993) and Kerkhof et al. (1994).

In the coming years, several meetings took place to prepare the material to describe and assess the various possible catchment areas. The data collection was to be identical in all centres, using common methods of sampling and a common monitoring sheet. During these meetings the material for the other parts of the study (the material for the interviews, etc.) was also prepared, e. g. in Leiden, Edinburgh, Wuerzburg, and Copenhagen). The place of Prof. Diekstra in the Steering Group was taken over by Dr. Ad Kerkhof, University of Leiden, The Netherlands.

The study started officially in January 1989 after some months of test runs with fifteen centres from 12 countries (Sør-Trøndelag, Norway; Helsinki, Finland; Umea and Stockholm, Sweden; Odense, Denmark; Leiden, The Netherlands; Berne, Switzerland; Bordeaux and Cergy-Pointoise, France; Guipuzcoa, Spain; Wuerzburg, Germany; Innsbruck, Austria; Szeged, Hungary; Emilia-Romagna and Padua, Italy. Oxford, UK, joined later, as did another 11 centres located in Ireland, Belgium, Lithuania, Slovenia, Yugoslavia, the Ukraine, Estonia, Latvia, Greece, Turkey, and Israel. Some members of the Steering Group were in the first years more or less representatives for the project, presenting it to governments and local authorities in various countries and in the catchment areas and helping the centres in performing the huge task of educating researchers, interviewers, and with the data analyses.

The catchment areas for the monitoring part included at the beginning of the study in total nearly 6 million inhabitants (population 15+: nearly 4 million).

When the technical coordinator, Dr. S. Platt, Edinburgh, left the Steering Group, as new member Dr. De Leo, from Padua, Italy, was appointed, and Unni Bille-Brahe,

Odense, Denmark, took over the position of the technical coordinator. The centre in Wuerzburg became responsible for the Monitoring part of the study, the part which collected data on suicide attempts, and the common data collection and analyses, and the centre in Odense became responsible for the Repetition part.

The study immediately became well known in Europe, the first results were presented soon in congresses not only in Europe but also overseas and in many papers. The first comprehensive results were published in the so called Wassernaaar Book (Kerkhof, A., Schmidtke, A., Bille-Brahe, U., DeLeo, D. & Lönnqvist, J. (Eds.). *Attempted suicide in Europe*. Leiden: DSWO Press.

During the course of the study, some centres dropped out, mainly due to financial problems, and some dropped out of part of the study, either the Monitoring part or the Repetition part. Other centres – encouraged by the enormous spreading of the results of the study and its increasing fame - continuously applied to join. During these processes, the Steering Group, in collaboration with WHO, decided to enlarge the study.

However, one of the main problems for the new centres was, of course, to learn and to adapt very quickly to the level of knowledge which the old centres have. Here, WHO/EURO, the Steering Group, the centres which are responsible for the two parts of the study, and the WHO collaborating centres provided support in training and education.

Once a year, a so-called technical meeting, organized mainly by the Wuerzburg group, provided an occasion to learn about technical problems and to analyze methods. The centres were informed about new developments and new techniques of collecting and analyzing the data. During the meeting, an effort was made to solve problems which had arisen during the previous year. Also once a year, the main investigators met to decide on the political aspects within the study, mainly in connection with international congresses.

The WHO/Euro Multicentre Study on Suicidal Behaviour became part of the WHO/EURO Network on Suicide Prevention and Research in December 2001. At that point, the Monitoring Study comprised 27 centres from 24 countries, and it had been one of the most comprehensive and longest-running continuous monitoring studies of suicidal behaviour in Europe. This long-term cooperation and the amount of data are sometimes regarded with envy. The value of the data can hardly be estimated. Therefore, we also invite other researchers to use this data pool.

The WHO European Regional Office launched a new project, entitled the WHO/European Network on Suicide Prevention and Research, in December 2001. In this frame, the former WHO Multicentre Study now comprises the Monitoring and Evaluation Part. This now includes 37 centres in 27 countries (see chapter 32).

References

Bille-Brahe U, Schmidtke A, Kerkhof A, DeLeo D, Lönnqvist, J & Platt, S (1994). Background and introduction to the study. In: Kerkhof A, Schmidtke A, Bille-Brahe U, DeLeo D & Lönnqvist J (Eds.). *Attempted suicide in Europe*. Leiden: DSWO Press, 3-15.

Bille-Brahe U, Andersen K, Wasserman D, Schmidtke A, Bjerke T, Crepet P, DeLeo D, Haring C, Hawton K, Kerkhof A, Lönnqvist J, Michel K, Philippe A, Querejeta I, Salander Renberg

E & Temesvary B (1996). The WHO-EURO Multicentre Study: Risk of parasuicide and the comparability of the areas under study. *Crisis,* 17, 32-42.

Bille-Brahe U, Bjerke T, Crepet P, DeLeo D, Haring C, Hawton K, Lönnqvist J, Michel K, Philippe A, Pommereau X, Querejeta I, Salander Renberg E, Schmidtke A, Temesvary B, Wasserman D & Sampaio-Faria JG (1993). *WHO/EURO Multicentre study on parasuicide. Facts and Figures.* Copenhagen: World Health Organization.

Kerkhof A, Platt S, Bille-Brahe U & Schmidtke A (1992). Parasuicide in Europe. In: Lester D. (Ed.) *Suicide '92.* Proceedings Silver Anniversary Conference, Denver: American Association of Suicidology, 190-192.

Platt S, Bille-Brahe U, Kerkhof A, Schmidtke A et al. (1992). Parasuicide in Europe: The WHO/EURO multicentre study on parasuicide. I. Introduction and preliminary analysis for 1989. *Acta Psychiatrica Scandinavica,* 85, 97-104.

Schmidtke A. (1989). *WHO (Euro) Multicentre study of parasuicide.* Working paper for the WHO Consultation on Strategies for reducing suicidal behaviour in the European Region, Szeged, Hungary, ICP/PSF 024/18.

Schmidtke A, Bille-Brahe U, Kerkhof A, De Leo D, Platt S, Sampaio-Faria J, Henderson J & Pototzky W (1993). The WHO/EURO Multicentre Project on Parasuicide – State of the art. *Italian Journal of Suicidology,* 3, 83-95.

WHO. (1986). Summary Report. Working group on preventive practices in suicide and attempted suicide. York, UK, ICP/PSF 017 (s).

Chapter 3

Definitions and Terminology Used in the WHO/EURO Multicentre Study

U. Bille-Brahe, A. Kerkhof, D. DeLeo & A. Schmidtke

Mors voluntaris, self-killing or self-murder have been some of the words used to describe the cause-of-death when somebody has taken his own life. The word *suicida* (self-slayer) was used already by the end of the 11th century and later, during the 17th century, the word *suicide* (said to be derived from Latin *sui caedere*), was a commonly accepted term (van Hooff, 1990).

The word suicide does not, however, define the *concept* of suicide, and through the years scientists and clinicians have been discussing how to construct definitions fit for everyday work and for research. More than one hundred years ago, Émile Durkheim wrote that the word suicide refers to all deaths that directly or indirectly are the outcome of a positive or negative act carried out by the deceased, who knew that the act would have a fatal outcome (Durkheim, 1897/1951). Half a century later, Erwin Stengel (1967) in his work on differentiating between completed and attempted suicide, defined suicide as a conscious and deliberate act carried out by a person who wanted to harm himself and the self-harm was fatal. Retterstøl (1990, p.10) agreed to this definition, but added that suicide can also be defined as a self-inflicted life-threatening act resulting in death – a definition that is close to the one given in Encyclopaedia Britannica (1974): "Suicide is the human act of self-inflicted, self intentioned cessation." Suicidologists working within a sociological framework argue that suicide is an activity comprising acts based on societal, concrete historical motives, the aim and the end being the individual's own biological death (e.g. Hammerlin & Enerstvedt, 1988). Finally, Shneidman (1994) concluded in his book 'Definition of Suicide' that "Suicide is a conscious act of self-induced annihilation, best understood as a multidimensional malaise in a needful individual who defines an issue for which the suicide is perceived as the best solution."

All these definitions have the main important elements in common, namely that the self-destructive act has to be conscious and deliberate. However, the question whether motives, causes, or concepts such as 'wishing to die' should be part of the definition, is still in debate. In 'Operational Criteria for the Determination of Suicide' published by the US Centers for Disease Control (Rosenberg et al., 1988), three criteria have to be met: 1) death as the result of injury of some sort which is 2) self-inflicted and 3) intentionally inflicted. In their discussion on definitions of suicidal behaviour on the need for a new nomenclature, O'Carroll and co-workers argue that the nomenclature for suicide-related behaviour has to be based on terms of outcome and intent to die (O'Carroll et al., 1996).

The main argument against incorporating motives such as the wish to die, is that it may be difficult or in fact impossible posthumously to prove any reason or motive behind the act, or any presence or strength of the wish to die. Another problem is that, as a manner of death, suicide can be perceived both as a means and as a goal. Many researchers argue that in practically all suicides one will find elements of ambivalence, and that in most cases the motive was not a wish to die (i.e. death as a goal), but a wish to cease living – or more specifically, cessation of consciousness (i.e. death as a means).

In the definition of suicide worked out in 1986 by the Regional Office Working Group on Preventive Practices in Suicide and Attempted Suicide (WHO Regional Office for Europe, 1986) these points of view are taken into consideration:

> "Suicide is an act with fatal outcome which the deceased, knowing or expecting a fatal outcome had initiated and carried out with the purpose of provoking the changes that he desired".

It is important to note that the definition contains no criteria regarding suicidal intention, neither regarding the danger or fatality of the act. On the other hand, persons that for some reason are unable to understand the potential danger of the act (e.g. because they are psychotic or retarded) are excluded.

When trying to define non-fatal suicidal acts, the problems are even more complicated, the reason being that not all non-fatal suicidal acts are 'unsuccessful' suicides. In particular, this became evident in the decades after the 2nd World War, when the frequency of so-called 'suicide attempts' increased with an almost epidemic haste. Studies proved that these self-inflicted injuries not necessarily were motivated by a wish to die, but rather by a 'wish to live'. In some cases, the person could see no other way out of his problems, but in other cases the intention was to provoke changes that would make life (again) worth living or at least tolerable, or simply to avoid negative conditions at least for a while. A suicide attempt, therefore, could also be seen as manipulation or 'a cry for help' (Stengel, 1967). Feuerlein (1971) suggested that suicidal acts could be classified according to the intent in three groups: '*serious attempted suicide*', '*suicidal gesture*' and '*suicidal break (pause)*'. But still, the term attempted suicide was felt inadequate because in most cases the suicide attempter in fact had no intention to die. The problem was then to work out a definition that would cover all deliberate, conscious non-fatal suicidal acts, whether the intention to die had been strong, ambivalent or non-existent. By the end of the 1960s, a confusing number of terms designed to cover these kind of suicidal acts was in use. In 1969, Kreitman and his co-workers, therefore, proposed the new term *parasuicide* to replace them all. Kreitman argued that suicidal acts can have various motives, varying from a wish to die to a cry for help or attention; they may be well planned or carried out impulsively; they may be potentially fatal or without any serious danger, and what was needed, therefore, was a term that could act as a kind of umbrella for all these types of non-fatal suicidal acts.

When initiating the WHO/Euro Multicentre Study, the working group agreed at the meeting in York in 1986 to adopt the term parasuicide for the study, and the following definition was worked out:

> "... an act with non-fatal outcome, in which an individual deliberately initiates a non-habitual behaviour that, without intervention from others, will cause self-harm, or deliberately ingests a substance in excess of the prescribed or generally recognized therapeutic dosage, and which is aimed at realizing

changes which the subject desired via the actual or expected physical consequences."

Again, accepting that assessing the 'real' motivation behind the act is almost impossible, the definition leaves open the question of suicidal intent. The definition includes acts that are interrupted before the actual self-harm occurs (e.g. the person is removed from the tracks before the train arrives) but excludes self-harmful acts by mentally retarded or disturbed people who do not understand the meaning or consequences of their act.

The use of the term parasuicide has its advantages and its disadvantages. During the first part of the study the definition and its operationalisation was critically questioned.The use of the term parasuicide helped in making it more clear to the staff that they should not make any distinction based on inferred intention between suicidal patients. On the other hand, it turned out to be difficult to explain the term parasuicide without referring to the term attempted suicide, and in addition there would in some countries be language problems, as the word parasuicide may be difficult to translate. However, paradoxically, the major problem seems to be the definition of the term itself.

Currently at least four points of view exist:

1) Parasuicide is a special subcategory restricted to attempts with low intention to die, of the larger class of attempted suicide.

2) Attempted suicide is a limited subdivision of the overall term parasuicide used for the full-range of non-fatal suicidal behaviour, attempted suicide being restricted to attempts with a strong intention to die (unsuccessful suicide),

3) Parasuicide and attempted suicide are mutually exclusive terms based on the distinction high-low suicidal intent: the term parasuicide being restricted to attempts with low suicidal intent, while the term attempted suicide is restricted to attempts with a definite or unambiguous intent,

4) Parasuicide and attempted suicide should be used interchangeably (because intention is extremely difficult to assess).

Therefore, in 1994 the participants of the study decided to change the title of the study to WHO/Euro Multicentre Study on Attempted Suicide.

As to the definitions of fatal and non-fatal suicidal acts in general, there seems to be some support to the definitions worked out by the WHO/Euro group – but the problem of constructing a proper, unambiguous and operational term for non-fatal suicidal acts remains unsolved, until empirically based standards for measuring suicidal intent can be worked out. It is the hope of the participants of the WHO/Euro Multicentre Study that by analysing data from the second part of our project, namely the Repetition-Prediction Study, it will be possible to come up with some proposals as to the general use of the terms.

In the studies on suicidal behaviour one has, however, to keep in mind that while unambiguous and operational definitions are indispensable tools in epidemiological research, they do not in themselves explain or help to understand suicidal behaviour. Cultural differences and attitudes towards suicidal behaviour in force in the various areas under study are elements that have to be taken into consideration too. Probably few, indeed, if any person standing with a rope or a bottle of pills in his hand will think of his suicidal ideation as a 'philosophical' question (Camus, 1991), or in terms of definitions – but somehow his motivation or intent behind the suicidal act is related to the perception in force of the meaning of (and thereby the attitudes towards) suicidal behaviour (Boldt, 1988). Whether working within a sociological, psychiatric, psychological or other frames of reference, it is important to keep this in mind when discussing definitions of suicidal behaviour.

References

Boldt M (1988). The meaning of suicide: implication for research. *Crisis* 9/2:93-108.
Camus A (1991). *The Myth of Sisiphus.* London: Penguin.
O'Carrol PW, Berman AL, Maris EW, Moscicki E, Tanney BL, Silverman M (1996). Beyond the tower of Babel. *Suicide & Life-Threatening Behavior.* 26/3:237-252.
Durkheim É (1897). *Suicide: A study in sociology.* New York: Free Press, 1951
Encyclopaedia Britannica 15 ed. Micropaedia vol. 9.p.316, Chicago, Ill. 1974.
Feuerlein W (1971). Selbstmordversuch oder parasuizidale Handlung? *Nervenarzt* 42:127-130
Hammerlin Y & Engerstvedt RT (1988). *Selvmord.* Oslo: Falken.
Van Hoooff AJL (1990). A longer life for "suicide". *Romanische Forschungen*, 102, 255-259.
Rosenberg ML, Davidson LE, Smith JC, Berman AL, Buzbee H et al. (1988). Operational Criteria for the Determination of Suicide. *Journal of Forensic Sciences* 32/6: 1445-1455.
Shneidman E (1984). *Definition of Suicide.* Northvale NJ: Jason Aronson.
Stengel E (1967). *Suicide and attempted suicide.* London: Penguin.
World Health Organization. (1986). Summary Report, Working Group on Preventive Practices in Suicide and Attempted Suicide. Copenhagen: WHO Regional Office for Europe.

Chapter 4

Suicide and Suicide Attempts in Europe

An Overview

A. Schmidtke[1], B. Weinacker, C. Löhr, U. Bille-Brahe[1], D. DeLeo[1], A. Kerkhof[1], A. Apter, A. Batt, P. Crepet, S. Fekete, O. Grad, C. Haring, K. Hawton, C. van Heeringen, H. Hjelmeland, M. Kelleher, J. Lönnquist, K. Michel, X. Pommereau, I. Querejeta, A. Philippe, E. Salander Renberg, I. Sayil, B. Temesvary, A. Värnik, D. Wasserman & W. Rutz[2]

Introduction

In many European countries suicidal behaviour constitutes a major public and mental health problem and a considerable drain on resources in both primary and secondary health care settings (Schmidtke, 1997, Bille-Brahe, 1994). In numerous countries, the number of suicides is significantly higher than the number of deaths due to traffic accidents. In some countries suicides among youngsters are among the top three causes of death. Due to the changing age pyramids in some countries (increasing percentage of older persons) the problem of suicidal behaviour among the elderly is also increasing (Gulbinat, 1996).

Despite the common burden, the suicide situation in Europe differs between the various countries. In recent years, especially in East-Europe, the rank order of suicide rates among the various countries has changed dramatically. This is partially due to the splitting up of countries. On the other hand, some countries have published official suicide rates for the first time in their history.

In some of the countries very high suicide figures can be found, even within some countries the rates for different regions vary significantly. In some countries the suicide figures are decreasing, covarying with a stable social situation and a good economic status. In other countries suicidality is increasing covarying with social changes and instability, unemployment and an increasing prevalence of psychiatric illnesses.

The burden due to lost years for the community is immense. Every suicide also effects on the average at least 6 other persons (WHO, 2000). Therefore, suicide prevention is seen by the WHO as a major target.

To implement effective suicide prevention programmes reliable data about the magnitude of the problem and time series of these data are needed. Suicides are reported

---

[1] Steering Group of the WHO/EURO Multicentre Study of Suicidal Behaviour

[2] WHO/EURO Office, Copenhagen

from most European countries to the WHO by the national governments. The sources of the data are mainly the statistical Bureaus of the individual countries.

The situation concerning suicide attempts is more unclear. Due to cross-cultural differences in the medical treatment of suicide attempters and in research methodologies, it has proven almost impossible to make valid comparisons about any aspect of suicidal behaviour between different European countries up to the mid-eighties. In the absence of national data, researchers have been forced to rely on local surveys, which vary markedly in terms of their nominal and operational definitions of suicide attempts, the representativeness of the samples, the time span covered, the amount of information gathered and so on. In addition, local studies have not always been adequate from an epidemiological standpoint (e.g. failing to identify risk factors for suicide attempts) or from the perspective of health-service referral (e.g. failing to identify the pattern of treatment following suicide attempt).

Therefore, as part of the WHO/Europe strategy to delevop preventive programmes and to develop indicators for this goal, comparative data of the magnitude and trends in attempted suicide in the European countries were required.

Data

The suicide data were received partly by the data bank of the WHO, the latest data mostly from the Statistical Bureaus of the individual countries, collaborating centres, and researchers.

In the absence of national data, the WHO launched the described research project to assess the "real" suicide attempt rates of a country. In the monitoring part of the project, 1989-1999, a total of 25 centres in 19 European countries were or are participating (1989-1993: 16 centres in 13 European countries; 1995-1999: 20 centres in 16 European countries, as well as Israel and Turkey). The catchment areas comprise nearly 5,700,000 inhabitants (population 15+: 5,000,000; see Figure 1).

In order to avoid the errors of previous studies and to rule out inadequacies from an epidemiological standpoint, each centre participating in the project is required to provide standardized information about the catchment area in question and to use a common definition of suicidal behaviour.

Methods

Instruments

For comparability reasons, a common definition of "suicide attempt", the proposed definition of the ICD-10 version, was used in this project (see chapter 3). In order to ensure that data collection was identical throughout the project, a monitoring sheet to be used by all participants was designed.

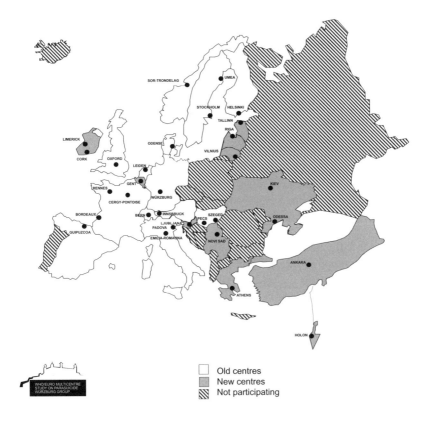

Figure 1. Area with the Participating Centres

This contains data concerning age, sex, place, date and time of the suicide, the method of suicide attempt according to the new ICD-10-code, data about previous suicide attempts, and various sociodemographic variables (see also Chapter 3; Platt et al., 1992, Schmidtke et al., 1993).

Computation of Rates

The individual centres estimated their total rates 15+ and the rates for the individual age bands using their monitoring data. For estimation of the "real" rates, "estimation factors" for each year were used: these factors were computed with regard to the size of the sample of institutions, general practitioners, and psychiatrists, and whether annual or sample time periods were covered. In order to enhance reliability, the rates for the individual age groups were calculated using broader age bands. This procedure was chosen to avoid small differences in the raw figures in the 5-year age bands (which might only be due to unreliability of the sampling procedures or to chance) resulting in incorrect rank orders of the rates for the individual age groups which could then lead to misinterpretation of the true situation. The following age bands were used: 15-24 years, 25-34 years, 35-44 years, 45-54 years, and 55+ (Platt et al., 1992).

The rates were calculated for each individual centre, and for the entire maximum period (up to the year 1999) for each centre.

Age Standardization

Because of the different age structures in the individual centres, comparisons between the total rates do not usually reflect the real situation. Oxford and Wuerzburg, for example, which represent large university cities, have an increased percentage of younger age groups: these age groups have an increased risk of suicide attempts. Therefore, for comparisons, it is absolutely necessary to test whether age adjustments may lead to other results.

To check the influence of various age distributions between the centres, for the first period also the method of direct age standardization was used, based on figures of the "World Population Prospects, 1992 Revision", edited by the United Nations (1993a,b). The "medium variant" of these estimations was used. This "standard European" population was used first to calculate the "average percentages" of each age band. For the individual age groups of each country's population, their percentage of the entire population of that country was then calculated as if all countries had identical age distributions. Subsequently, for these population figures the number of suicide attempts was estimated using the real suicide attempt rates per 100,000 for each age group of the individual country. The adjusted rates for persons aged 15+ years were then computed by using the sum of these estimated numbers of suicide attempts and the real population figures for the individual countries.

Results

Suicide

Figure 2 shows the latest available suicide figures for the European countries. The highest rank for male suicide rates was obtained by Lithuania with 76.5 per 100,000, and the lowest obtained by Turkey with 3.9 per 100,000. The highest rank for female suicide rate could also be found for Lithuania with 12.6 per 100,000, the lowest with 1.5 per 100,000 for Greece.

Therefore, the ratio between the highest and lowest suicide rate in Europe is 1:20 for males and 1:8 for females.

In all countries the male rates are higher than the female rates. The average male female ratio is 1:4, the range being 1:1 (Turkey; Bosnia-Herzegovina has a female suicide rate of 0, therefore, a ratio cannot be calculated) and 1:7 (Belarus).

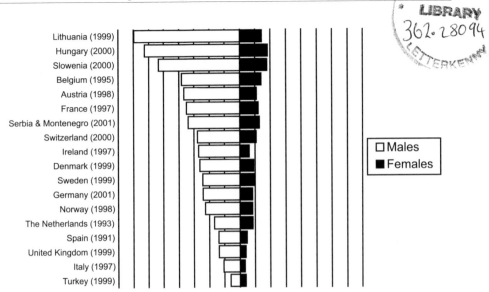

Figure 2. Suicide rates of different European countries, latest available year

If one calculates an average "European" suicide rate, this rate would be 28 per 100,000 for males and 7 per 100,000 for females.

Suicide attempts

In the first period of observation, the highest average male person rate was found for Helsinki (Finland: 327 per 100,000), and the lowest (46 per 100,000) for Guipuzcoa (Spain); this represents more than a sevenfold difference (7.1:1). The highest (average) female rate was found for Cergy-Pontoise (France: 542 per 100,000), the lowest (72 per 100,000) again for Guipuzcoa, which was also more than a sevenfold difference (7.5:1). With only one exception (Helsinki), the person based suicide attempt rates were higher among women than men (15 of 16 centres). The average person based ratio of male: female suicide attempt rates for persons aged 15+ years was 1:1.5, the range being 1:2.2 (Cergy-Pontoise, France) – 1:0.8 (Helsinki, Finland).

In the second period of observation, the highest average male person rate was again found for Helsinki (Finland: 327 per 100,000), and the lowest (35 per 100,000) for Ankara (Turkey); this representing more than a ninefold difference (9:1). The highest (average) female rate was found for a French centre, Rennes, (504 per 100,000), and the lowest (81 per 100,000) also for Ankara, which is more than a six-fold difference (6:1).

Figure 3 shows the latest available suicide attempt figures for each centre participating in the WHO Study.

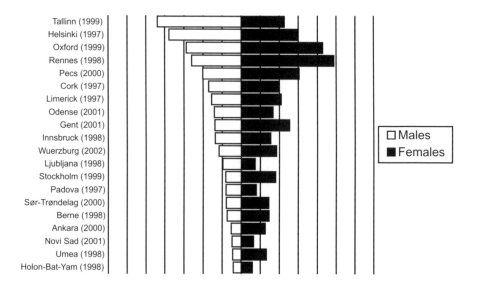

Figure 3. Latest available person – based suicide attempt figures for each centre participating in the WHO Study

With four exceptions (Helsinki, Innsbruck, Ljubljana, Tallinn), the person based suicide attempt rates were higher among women than men (15 of 19 centres). The average person based ratio of male: female suicide attempt rates for persons aged 15+ years is 1:1.2, the range being 1:2.3 (Ankara, Turkey, and Umea, Sweden) – 1:0.7 (Tallinn, Estonia).

Table 1 shows the person-based suicide attempt figures for people aged 15+ years for the individual centres for the period 1995-1999. Figure 2 shows the rates for persons aged 15+ years for the latest available year (mostly 1999), also including the centres which left the study in previous years.

If one calculates an average "European" suicide attempt rate for persons aged 15+ years for the years 1989-1993, this rate would be 140 per 100,000 for males and 193 per 100,000 for females.

For the period 1995-1999 the average European suicide attempt rate would be for males 170 per 100,000 and for females 209 per 100,000. (The rate of the Israelian centre for the year 1997 is 67 per 100,000 for males and 130 per 100,000 for females)

Table 2 shows the average rates for the individual age groups for second period (1995–1999).

In nearly all of the centres, the highest person rates were found in the 15-24 year-old-age female group (17 of 19 centres; average rate of all centres 370 per 100,000; the highest average rate in Rennes, France, 832 per 100,000), the lowest in Ljubljana, Slovenia (139 per 100,000). The highest person rate for any age group (male or female) and year was 917 per 100,000 for the 15-24-year-old females in Rennes in 1996. Among males, the age group 25-34 was the age group with the highest rates in 10 of 19 centres. The highest male rate was found in Helsinki with 607 per 100,000 for the 35-44 year-old age group in 1997.

In the majority of the centres, the rates among people aged 55 years or more were the lowest (males 17 of 19 centres, females in all 19 centres). The greatest difference between the different age groups was found for females in Limerick (15-24 years vs. 55+ years 13:1; Ankara had no suicides in persons aged 55+ years, therefore a ratio was not calculated) and for males again in Limerick (15-24 years vs. 55+ years with a ratio of 10:1). The highest average person-based ratio of male suicide attempt rates : female suicide attempt rates was found in the age group 15-24 years (1:1.7), the next highest in the age group 35-44 years (1:1.3). This ratio diminishes in the age group 55+ to 1:1.1, with a range from 1:1.9 (Pecs and Rennes) - 1:0.6 (Gent, Helsinki and Ljubljana).

Table 1. Person-based suicide attempt figures for the individual centres for the period 1995 – 1999, age 15+

Centres	Males					Females				
	1995	1996	1997	1998	1999	1995	1996	1997	1998	1999
Ankara				32	39				85	77
Berne	87	76	77	74		153	112	111	145	
Cork	192	148	170			197	150	201		
Gent	411	355	320	243		425	356	315	293	
Helsinki	272	329	378			232	281	294		
Holon-Bat-Yam	71	67	67			118	126	130		
Innsbruck	168	133	156	136		163	122	156	153	
Limerick	219	192	155			277	226	208		
Ljubljana	69	80	74	97		71	65	72	72	
Odense	124	128	116	111	108	177	151	164	180	151
Oxford	356	351	354	342	287	439	412	451	436	428
Padova	51	69	80			86	84	79		
Pecs			277	239	273			424	375	333
Rennes	346	340	277	259		548	535	558	381	
Sør-Trøndelag	92	87	102	94	77	117	124	135	135	134
Stockholm	106	88	90	82		161	190	172	181	
Tallinn	281	229	356			190	187	188		
Umea	61	47	57	45		97	137	118	131	
Wuerzburg	77	122	96	78	91	127	147	126	133	116

Age-standardized Rates

The age-standardization led only to some changes in a few centres (cf. Schmidtke et al., 1994). However, the rank order of the centres did not change dramatically. The centres with the highest male rates were still Helsinki, Cergy-Pontoise, Oxford, Szeged, and Odense. Guipuzcoa remains with the lowest male rate.

The highest ranks for the female rates are still found for Cergy-Pontoise, Oxford, Helsinki, Stockholm, Szeged, and Odense. Again, Guipuzcoa is the centre with the lowest female rate.

Therefore, if one calculates average-adjusted "European" suicide attempt rates for people aged 15+ years, these rates would be only slightly lower than the crude rates.

Table 2. Average rates for the individual age groups for second period (1995 – latest available year, latest 1999).

Centres	Males					Females				
	age groups in years									
	15-24	25-34	35-44	45-54	55+	15-24	25-34	35-44	45-54	55+
Ankara	43	39	32	33	7	168	72	30	7	0
Berne	93	137	89	49	33	258	227	114	107	40
Cork	285	262	178	101	33	356	228	221	116	36
Gent	401	544	407	350	94	693	490	449	297	58
Helsinki	300	435	467	281	148	306	366	427	303	85
Holon-Bat-Yam	73	95	65	43	64	244	115	103	93	78
Innsbruck	181	203	164	124	78	166	197	222	119	82
Limerick	326	317	183	78	34	526	293	234	112	40
Ljubljana	112	116	60	52	64	139	84	68	52	40
Odense	124	172	186	102	48	273	170	256	162	74
Oxford	418	487	371	260	94	750	569	488	279	91
Padova	56	93	101	74	33	191	88	95	73	53
Pecs	374	402	333	193	85	575	472	657	268	159
Rennes	355	456	440	279	71	832	668	745	428	133
Sør-Trøndelag	107	124	120	91	33	228	172	181	109	39
Stockholm	80	123	97	105	59	271	236	199	191	73
Tallinn	473	333	339	214	109	438	230	209	141	78
Umea	73	78	66	42	26	307	155	128	100	27
Wuerzburg	180	106	95	65	51	315	163	122	114	53

Changes over time

Even though all centres did not cover some years, where comparisons were possible the rank order of the different centres did not change drastically over the period covered. Helsinki, Oxford, and Gent were consistently the centres with the highest rates for males over the period 1989-1999. Padova was the centre which had mostly the lowest rates. The centres with the highest female rates were always Oxford, Gent and Helsinki, and Padua was again the centre with the lowest rates (see table 2).

During the period covered by the majority of the centres, the average male rates for persons aged 15+ years for the periods 1989/1993-1995/1999, decreased more than 5% for six centres (Table 3 and Figure 4a and 4b) with an average decrease of 13%. The centre with the greatest change over time was Innsbruck, where the male rate for people 15+ years increased by 70%. In Stockholm, the male rates showed a decrease of 40%.

Table 3. Changes in person-based suicide attempt rates in the centres included in the WHO/ EURO Study on Suicide Attempts participating from 1989 until present

Centres	Males			Females		
	1989-1993	1995-1999	Change in %	1989-1993	1995-1999	Change in %
Berne	111	79	-29	142	130	-9
Gent	371	333	-10	321	346	8
Helsinki	315	327	4	240	269	12
Innsbruck	87	148	70	108	149	38
Odense	168	118	-30	197	165	-16
Oxford	263	337	28	356	433	22
Padova	58	67	16	95	83	-13
Sør-Trøndelag	140	90	-36	186	129	-31
Stockholm	153	91	-41	230	176	-23
Umea	85	53	-38	140	121	-14
Wuerzburg	70	92	31	110	129	17

For the female rates, the average decrease was 4%, and 6 centres showed a decrease of more than 5% (see Table 3). The centre with the greatest decrease was Sør-Trøndelag (31%). However, the female rates in Innsbruck also showed major increases (38%).

Decreases in rates were found in most of the individual age groups[1]. The highest average decrease was found in males aged 35-44 years (-16%) and in females aged 55 years or older (-16%).

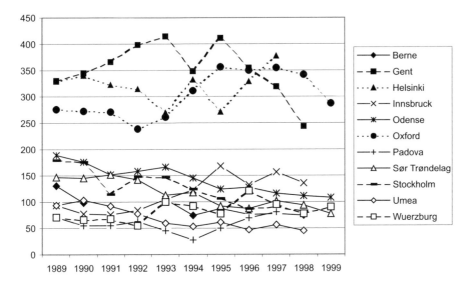

Figure 4a. Female suicide attempt rates over time for the different centres, from 1989 on

---

[1] For these computations, Gent was not included, since age and sex separated data were only available for the second observation period.

In contrast, younger females aged 15-24 years, showed an increase of 17%.

To examine whether the decreasing trends in attempted suicide could be attributed to a "fading out" of the monitoring in the various centres, the trends in the rates for persons aged 15 years or older over the two observation periods in the individual centres were also compared. During the period covered, the trends were not uniform. A continuous decrease could not be found; rather, in most of the centres, an increase over the years observed could be found.

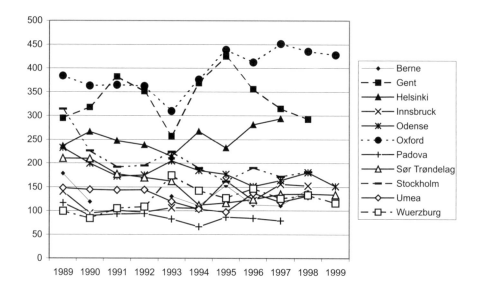

Figure 4b. Male suicide attempt rates over time for the different centres, from 1989 on

Discussion

The differences between the suicide and suicide attempt rates of the various European countries are enormous. Since the beginning of the official registration, Hungary has been the country with the highest suicide rates in Europe, if not in the World. However, Hungary is now surpassed by some of the new Russian and Baltic states. The highest male rates are found for Lithuania, the Russian Federation, Belarus, Estonia, Latvia, Hungary, and Ukraine. The highest female rates were also found for Lithuania, Hungary, and Slovenia.

Nordic and Eastern European countries also have somewhat higher suicide rates, while the southern parts of Europe have comparatively low suicide rates. In comparison America and Asia generally have lower rates than most of the European countries (Schmidtke et al., 1993).

In all European countries, even those countries with very low rates, male suicide rates are higher than the female rates.

The results show that these differences in suicide rates between the countries are not equally distributed for all age groups. Most differences (even for the states or areas within one country) are only significant for the older age groups (cf. Moksony, 1995; Schmidtke, 1995).

With regard to suicide attempts as previously stated (Platt et al., 1992), cross-sectional and longitudinal analyses of suicide attempt rates in Europe have been previously hampered by the virtual absence of appropriate national data. Therefore, previous attempts to examine the epidemiology of suicide attempts in Europe (Diekstra, 1982, 1985) were restricted in that information was gathered in different centres with neither uniform definitions nor standardized case-finding criteria. Consequently, one major objective of the WHO/EURO Multicentre Study on Suicidal Behaviour was to gather sufficiently reliable and valid data to obtain a credible picture of suicide attempts in the region (both cross-sectional and longitudinal; Schmidtke et al., 1993). As a result of the Steering Group's efforts and the high level of expertise and training experience now available at the local level, one can be reasonably confident that the comparisons between centres and the computation of trends which are presented here are valid. As Platt et al. (1992, p. 102) stated «... like is being compared with like».

In the majority of the centres, it has been estimated that all adult suicide attempts admitted to any health institution in the catchment area have been monitored; and in the other centres, as the various estimation factors show, very few cases appear to have been missed. Due to the near impossibility of establishing a "true" suicide attempt rate in the population, concentration on ensuring the complete coverage of medically treated suicide attempts in the various centres seemed to be the most advantageous method. The various special analyses in individual centres illustrate the validity of this decision. For example, in Wuerzburg, all cases first seen by private practitioners or non-medical health institutions (e.g. crisis lines, counselling services etc.) were eventually also seen by a medical institution after the index suicide attempt.

The first publications of Part I of the project, the monitoring part, only presented preliminary data for 1989 (Kerkhof et al., 1992; Platt et al., 1992). However, in these publications it was already clear that major differences existed between participating European centres. Helsinki, Cergy-Pontoise and Odense documented the highest male suicide rates, and Cergy-Pontoise, Stockholm and Bordeaux the highest female rates. During the study, some centres withdrew from the study, and numerous new centres were included. Therefore, the rank order of the centres changed. However, when considering the entire period studied, Gent, Helsinki and Oxford still remained the centres with the highest male attempted suicide rates. In contrast to all the other centres, the male rates in Helsinki are even higher than female rates.

Oxford, Gent, and Helsinki have the highest female rates, especially in the age group 15-24 years. In Oxford, this may be attributable to the high percentage of students. Often, students are regarded as a population with a higher risk of suicidal behaviour (cf. Lungershausen, 1968; Kuda & Kuda-Ebert, 1981; Kuda, 1984; Uno, Ando & Ishikawa, 1987). However, the incidence of attempted suicide among students in the United Kingdom has also been found to be lower than among other persons of the same age (Hawton et al., 1978; Platt 1986; Hawton et al., 1995).

The rank order of the individual countries change only slightly after age adjustment (as in previous publications; Ballesteros & Querejeta, 1992), which indicates that the age structure of the individual centres is not so different. The crude rates for those aged 15 years and older for centres with a younger population (e.g. Oxford) overestimate the risk of suicide attempts in that region a little bit, whereas centres with an older population underestimate the real situation.

The person-based suicide attempt rates for persons aged 15 years and older in 8 centres were more than 50% higher among women, and in 11 centres more than 30%, whereas in only one centre (Helsinki) the male rate was higher. The average difference was 47%. Similar results could also be found for most of the individual age groups. The greatest differences were found in the younger age groups, whereas the difference diminishes with increasing age. The age group 55 years and older in Cergy-Pontoise was the only exception, though this might be due to the small raw figures. However, since the highest male:female ratio for people aged 15+ years was only 1:2.2, the previously mentioned hypothesis that the sex ratio recently has become markedly lower than that found in the seventies (Diekstra, 1982; Platt et al., 1992) seems to be true over a longer period with more reliable data. Further research is required, however, to determine if this is an effect of increasing or stable male rates and/or a general trend of decreasing female rates. So far, the results of the four-year period indicate that the rates of both sexes are now decreasing in the majority of the centres, but that in some centres (Cergy-Pontoise and Wuerzburg), the female rates actually increased.

In contrast to the previously published data in 1989, the highest age-specific rates were usually found in the age group 15-24 years, especially for females. This confirms the often published data and opinion that suicide attempts, especially more demonstrative acts, are more commonly found among teenagers and young adults. However, this simple inverse relation between age and suicide attempts appears to lose its validity for males. Nevertheless, the lowest rates were most often found for the age group 55 years and older of both sexes.

The question remains whether these comparisons between the centres are meaningful and valid and whether the results justify statements about similarities and differences in profiles of suicide attempters and trends in suicide attempt rates. With regard to investigations and the task of the WHO to monitor trends, it appears unlikely that trends and changes in a centre do not reflect general trends in the country, although the level of the rates themselves might be different elsewhere.

In studies over longer periods of monitoring, when decreasing trends were reported, often the hypothesis is suggested that this might partly be due to an effect of a "fading out" of the monitoring (e.g. that the monitoring system gets "fatigued" due to an increasing unwillingness to fill out the monitoring forms). The comparisons of the trends of the rates for persons aged 15 years and older over the four-year period in the individual centres showed that the trends were not uniform. There was a continuous decrease in only one centre. In most of the centres, there were also years with increases.

Therefore, it can be assumed that the decreasing trends could not be attributed to this "fading out" but are at least partly "true" trends. Therefore, the results show that one of the previous goals of the WHO, to reduce the suicide and suicide attempt rates by at least 20 percent (WHO, 1986), has nearly been reached with regard to attempted suicide. Of course further research efforts are required to establish whether this trend is stable.

Variations in ascertainment procedures and methodological artifacts due to different age structures and percentages of immigrants cannot account for the major part of these variances. Also, economic hypotheses cannot explain these differences (Bille-Brahe et al., 1996). In addition, different values do not explain the difference in suicidal behavior (Aish-van Vaerenberg, 1996). However, one of the methodological problems in comparing such international data is that cross-sectional comparisons of national figures on socio-demographic parameters (e.g. unemployment, divorce rates, health facilities etc.) are relatively inadequate in describing and comparing people's every day lives and the degree of their alienation and hopelessness, which are usually seen as factors causing suicidal behaviour (Bille-Brahe et al., 1996). Therefore, to date, besides some ethnic hypotheses, the most convincing hypotheses are those based on different attitudes toward suicidal behavior.

The methodologically adequate way to investigate the influence of cultural factors on suicidal behavior seems to be by performing long term time series analyses and determining over time the covariations of the different cultural and economical variables with the suicide and suicide attempt figures.

References

Ballesteros J & Querejeta I (1992). *Suicide attempt in 14 catchment areas in 1989.* Findings from the WHO-EURO sponsored Multicentre Study on Suicide attempt. Paper presented at the 4th European Conference on Suicide. Odense.

Bille-Brahe U, Bjerke T, Crepet P, DeLeo D, Haring C, Hawton K, Kerkhof A, Lönnquist J, Michel K, Philippe A, Pommereau X, Querejeta I, Salander Renberg E, Schmidtke A, Temesvary B, Wasserman D & Sampaio-Faria JG (1993). *WHO/EURO Multicentre study on suicide attempt.* Facts and figures. Copenhagen.

Bille-Brahe U, Schmidtke A, Kerkhof A, DeLeo D, Lönnqvist J & Platt S (1994). Background and introduction to the study. In: Kerkhof A, Schmidtke A, Bille-Brahe U, DeLeo D, Lönnqvist J (Eds.). *Attempted suicide in Europe.* Leiden: DSWO Press, 3-15.

Bille-Brahe U, Andersen K, Wasserman D, Schmidtke A, Bjerke T, Crepet P, DeLeo D, Haring C, Hawton K, Kerkhof A, Lönnqvist J, Michel K, Phillippe A, Querejeta I, Salander-Renberg E & Temesvary B (1996). The WHO/EURO Multicentre Study: risk of parasuicide and the comparability of the areas under study. *Crisis,* 17, 32-42.

Diekstra RFW (1982). Epidemiology of attempted suicide in the EEC. In: Wilmotte J & Mendlewicz J. (Eds.). *New trends in suicide prevention.* Basel: Karger, 1-16.

Diekstra RFW (1985). Suicide and suicide attempts in the European Economic Community: an analysis of trends, with special emphasis upon trends among the young. *Suicide and Life Threatening Behavior,* 15, 27-42.

Gulbinat W (1996). The epidemiology of suicide in old age. *Archives of Suicide Research,* 2, 31-42.

Hawton K, Crowle J, Simkin S & Bancroft J (1978). Attempted suicide and suicide among Oxford University students. *British Journal of Psychiatry,* 132, 506-509.

Hawton K, Haigh R, Simkin S & Fagg J (1995). Attempted suicide in Oxford University students, 1976-1990. *Psychological Medicine,* 25, 179-188.

Kerkhof A, Platt S, Bille-Brahe U & Schmidtke A (1992). Suicide attempt in Europe. In: Lester D. (Ed.) *Suicide '92.* Proceedings Silver Anniversary Conference, Denver: American Association of Suicidology, 190-192.

Kuda M (1984). Suizidalität bei Studierenden. Zur Genese und Psychopathologie. *Medizin, Mensch, Gesellschaft,* 4, 234-244.

Kuda M & Kuda-Ebert M (1981). *Zur Vorhersage der Selbstmordgefährdung bei Studierenden und Drogenabhängigen.* Bern: Huber.

Lungershausen E (1968). *Selbstmorde und Selbstmordversuche bei Studenten.* Heidelberg: Huthig.

Moksony F (1995). The age pattern of suicide in Hungary. *Archives of Suicide Research,* 1, 217-227.

Platt S (1986). Suicide and suicide attempt among further education students in Edinburgh. *British Journal of Psychiatry,* 150, 183-188.

Platt S, Bille-Brahe U, Kerkhof A, Schmidtke A et al. (1992). *Suicide attempt in Europe: The WHO/EURO multicentre study on suicide attempt.* I. Introduction and preliminary analysis for 1989. *Acta Psychiatrica Scandinavica,* 85, 97-104.

Platt S, Hawton K, Kreitman N, Fagg J & Foster J (1988). Recent clinical and epidemiological trends in suicide attempt in Edinburgh and Oxford: a tale of two cities. *Psychological Medicine,* 18, 405-418

Schmidtke A (1989). WHO (Euro) *Multicentre study of suicide attempt.* Working paper for the WHO Consultation on Strategies for reducing suicidal behaviour in the European Region, Szeged, Hungary, ICP/PSF 024/18.

Schmidtke A (1995). Suizid- und Suizidversuchsraten in Deutschland. In: Wolferdorf M & Kaschka W (Eds.). *Suizidalität. Die biologische Dimension.* Heidelberg: Springer, 17-32.

Schmidtke A (1997). Perspective: Suicide in Europe. *Suicide and Life-Threatening Behavior,* 27, 127-136.

Schmidtke A, Bille-Brahe U, Kerkhof A, DeLeo D, Platt S, Sampaio-Faria J, Henderson J & Pototzky W (1993).The WHO/EURO Multicentre Project on Suicide attempt – State of the art. *Italian Journal of Suicidology,* 3, 83-95.

United Nations (Ed.) (1993a). *The sex and age distribution of the World populations, The 1992 Revision.* New York: United Nations, Department of Economic and Social Information.

United Nations (Ed.) (1993b).*World Population Prospects, The 1992 Revision.* New York: United Nations, Department of Economic and Social Information and Policy Analysis.

Uno M, Ando E & Ishikawa K (1987). Ein Beitrag zum Problem des Studentensuizids. *Fortschritte der Neurologie und Psychiatrie,* 55, 273-278.

WHO. (1986). *Summary Report, Working Group on Preventive Practices in Suicide and Attempted Suicide.* Copenhagen: WHO Regional Office for Europe.

WHO. (2000). *Preventing suicide: a resource for primary health care workers.* Geneva: World Health Organization (= WHO/MNH/MBD/00.4).

Chapter 5

Sociodemographic Characteristics of Suicide Attempters in Europe

Combined Results of the Monitoring Part of the WHO/EURO Multicentre Study on Suicidal Behaviour

A. Schmidtke, U. Bille-Brahe*, D. DeLeo*, A. Kerkhof*, C. Löhr, B. Weinacker, A. Batt,
P. Crepet, S. Fekete, O. Grad, C. Haring, K. Hawton, C. van Heeringen,
H. Hjemeland, J. Lönnquist, K. Michel, X. Pommereau, I. Querejeta,
E. Salander Renberg, B. Temesvary, A. Värnik, D. Wasserman & W. Rutz*

Introduction

The WHO/EURO Multicentre Study on Sucidal Behaviour has played a significant role in the actions to implement one of the main targets of the WHO to reduce suicidal behaviour in Europe and in the development of indicators for this target. Therefore, within this project one aim was also to generate an epidemiological picture of suicide attempters in the European Region as well as to gather information about special risk groups.

In order to avoid the errors of earlier studies and to rule out inadequacies from an epidemiological point of view, each participating centre in the project had to provide standardized information (see also Chapter 2). The data of all centres were collected, checked and corrected in connection with the individual centres by the Wuerzburg centre. The Wuerzburg centre also was given by the WHO and the Steering Group of the project the responsibility of analysing the data.

Data basis

In order to ensure uniformity in the method of obtaining data across the various centres, a monitoring form to be used by all participating centres was drawn up. This monitoring form contained questions about age and sex, place, date and time of the suicide attempt, the method of the suicide attempt according to the new ICD-10 X-code, and about previous suicide attempts. Within this form information was also recorded about various sociodemographic variables, such as current marital status, household composition, religious denomination, level of education (based on the appropriate national standards), level of vocational training, economic situation at the time of the

* Members of the Steering Group

suicide attempt, change of address during the past year and the treatment offered after the suicide attempt (Platt et al., 1992, Schmidtke et al., 1993).

Data from 27 centres in 19 European countries were available: Sør-Trøndelag, Norway; Helsinki, Finland; Stockholm and Umea, Sweden; Tallinn, Estonia; Odense, Denmark; Oxford, U.K.; Leiden, The Netherlands; Gent, Belgium; Wuerzburg, Germany; Bordeaux and Rennes, France; Berne, Switzerland; Innsbruck, Austria; Ljubljana, Slovenia; Guipuzcoa, Spain; Emilia and Padova, Italy; Pecs and Szeged, Hungary. For some centres the sociodemographic part of the form has not yet been through the correction procedure: Ankara, Turkey; Athens, Greece; Cork-Limerick, Ireland. Table 1 gives an overview about the centres participating in the monitoring part and on the time period covered by the individual centres.

Table 1. Centres participating in the study

Centre	Time period covered
Ankara	1998-1999
Berne	1989-1990; 1993-1998
Bordeaux	1989
Cork	1995-1999
Êmilia-Romagna	1989-1994
Gent	1996-1999
Guipuzcoa	1989-1991
Helsinki	1989-1997
Holon	1995-1999
Innsbruck	1989-1998
Leiden	1989-1992
Ljubljana	1995-1998
Novi Sad	1998-1999
Odense	1989-1999
Oxford	1989-1999
Padova	1989-1996
Pecs	1997-1998
Rennes	1995-1996
Sør-Trøndelag	1989-1999
Stockholm	1989-1998
Szeged	1989-1991
Tallinn	1995-1996
Umea	1989-1995
Wuerzburg	1989-1999

Statistical analyses

To compare trends and developments over time, two time periods were chosen: the first five years of the study, 1989-1993 and the last available five years, 1995-1999. For all centres, the maximally available and checked information for both periods was used. During the second period, data were no longer available from some centres, and consequently due to various reasons, Guipuzcoa (Spain), Bordeaux and Cergy-Pointoise (France) and Emilia (Italy) left the study. For the second period, only data for shorter periods were available from some of the centres. The reasons were mostly related to the fact that the centres joined the study at a later stage, or that they could only collect data for some years due to financial problems. No data were available for Padua and Tallinn (1997-1999), Helsinki (1998-1999), Ljubljana, Stockholm and Innsbruck (1999), Gent, Belgium (1995), Pecs, Hungary (1995-1996). For each variable, an average of the percentages in each centre was computed. This should prevent centres with a high number of suicide attempters (e.g. Helsinki or Odense) from distorting the percentages in the direction of their population. For some variables (e.g. repeaters), the total number of persons was used for the computation.

To test significant differences of the frequencies of the various variables, Chi-Square tests and tests of significance of proportions were used.

Reliability of data

The reliability of the monitoring data varies because of many missing values. This seems to be especially the case in relation to questions regarding level of education, vocational training, level of last/actual job and religion. For the variable "Level of educational qualifications", missing variables counted for 44% of all answers, and in 34% of all cases for "Nominal religious denomination" there was no specification. The variable "Job at time of suicide attempt" had missing values in 27% of all cases. For the variable "Household composition – usual situation" there were no data in 21% of all cases. For most variables, an average of 10% and 20% of the episodes included missing values. Another reason for these percentages of missing values is that several centres were not able to provide the information requested for, for example, "Level of vocational training", which was not recorded in Emilia, Helsinki, Leiden, and Oxford; "Job at time of suicide attempt" was not recorded in Bordeaux, Emilia, Innsbruck and Oxford. No data were available for the "Household situation before the suicide attempt" in Oxford and Helsinki. Age and sex seemed to be most reliably assessed; for example, for age only in 0.4% of all cases and for sex only in 4 out of 22,655 episodes for the period 1989-1993 values were missing.

Results

For the period 1989-1993, 22,672 episodes of attempted suicide were analysed. These attempts were made by 17,486 persons. For the period 1995–1999, 19,727 episodes of attempted suicides could be analysed, these attempts were made by 13,427 persons. At present, this is the largest pool of specific data about suicide attempts in the world.

The analyses are primarily based on the specified reporting of individual cases.

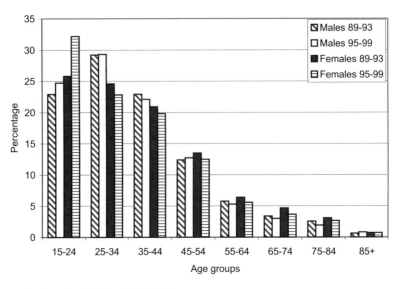

Figure 1. Age distribution 1989-1999

Figure 1 shows the average proportion of each age group of suicide attempters. In two-thirds (10/15) of the centres that collected data in the first period (1989–1993) the highest person-based percentages for men was found among the 25-34-year-olds, with an average person-based percentage of 29%. All other age groups had markedly lower percentages. Similar results were found for the second period. In 1989–1993, in more than half of the centres (8/15), females in the age group 25-34 years also had similarily high percentages (average person-based percentage of 25%). This rate slightly decreased for the second period to 23%. In the first period, in 6/15 centres, females in the age group 15-24 years had the highest percentages, in the second period 12 of 15 centres had the highest rates for this age and sex group. Due to extreme percentages in some centres (e.g. Oxford with 45% for the first period and 50% for the second period, and Umea with 47% for the second period), the average person-based percentage in this age group was even higher (26% for the first period and 32% in the second period) than in the 25-34-year age group. The percentages in the age groups 55 years and older were the lowest in all of the centres, indicating that the older the age groups, the lower the percentage.

These results were stable over the entire investigation period. The age distribution did not change remarkably neither within nor between the time periods.

Figure 2 shows the average percentages of the various methods of attempted suicides. Generally, the methods used for the suicide attempt were most often "soft". For the soft methods a slight increase over time was detectable. During 1989-1993, 65% of the males and 82% of the females used these methods. Cutting (mostly wrist cutting) was the most frequently used method (males 16%, females 9%). During 1995-1999, the proportion of persons who used cutting was similar, (males 16% and females 8%) and for this method, no significant changes over time could be observed. Due to the new ICD-X-classification of methods it was also possible to record special methods.

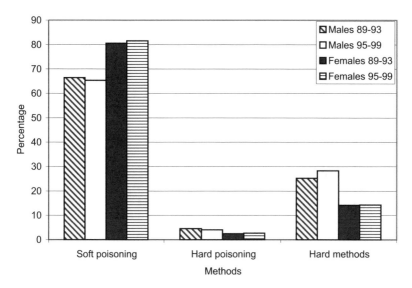

Figure 2. Methods used for the suicide attempts

During 1989-1993, 1.8% of males and 1.3% of females used "alcohol" (X 65) alone as method of attempted suicide. For males, this method increased significantly (3.2%), whereas for females this method remained stable (1.4%).Therefore, this subgroup should not be overlooked. In addition, the method "car accident" (X 82) was not negligible (1989-1993: 0.5% of males and 0.1% of females). The same results were found for the second period.

The frequencies of the different methods of attempted suicide in the various centres were more or less the same; however, exceptions were found. For example, in the first period in Szeged, poisoning with pesticides, herbicides, or other toxic agricultural chemicals (X 68) was relatively common (18% of males and 15% of females), while in the other centres, these percentages ranged between 0-3%. In the first period, Innsbruck, Wuerzburg and Guipuzcoa reported high percentages of cutting among males (30%, 29%, 25% respectively). In the second period, Tallinn, Ljubljana, Innsbruck and Odense had similarly high percentages (50%, 30%, 26%, 22%). In comparison to the other centres, in the first period Sør-Trøndelag had higher percentages of the "alcohol method" (males 6.8% and females 4.7%). During the second period, these differences disappeared.

For all centres, the methods used for the suicide attempts did not covary significantly with age. "Soft" methods were prevalent in all age groups. There were some exceptions for special methods, for example, poisoning diminished with increasing age among females (but only by about 10%), and older rather than younger men attempted suicide by "jumping or lying before moving object". Only one male person older than 55 years used the "car accident method". However, because of the extensive range of possible categories for method classification (25 in all), there were very small frequencies reported for particular methods.

As far as it could be assessed, the distribution of religious types within individual centres did not differ from that of the general population. A common analysis without

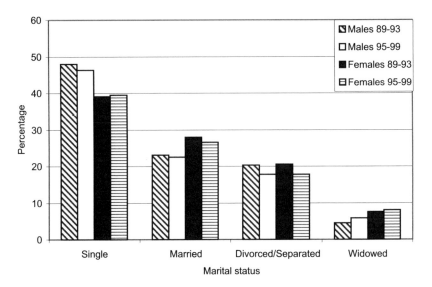

Figure 3. Marital status

regard of the population figures would not be meaningful since the distributions of the populations according to religion are quite different from centre to centre (compare Bille-Brahe et al., 1993).

The analysis according to marital status showed that the category with the highest average percentage was that of single persons (Figure 3). This finding was stable over the study period. Nearly half (1989-1993: 48%; 1995-1999: 46%) of all males and 38% in the first period and 39% in the second period of all females were never married. Only 24% and 23% of the males and 28% and 27% of the females were married; 20% and 17% of the males and 21% and 17% of the females were divorced or separated, one exception being Odense with 36% married people and 28% single. Considering the hypothesis that the probability of being married and consequently being divorced is lower among younger age groups, a separate analysis for persons older than 25 years was performed. This analysis showed that the general results were age dependent and that an interaction effect exists. That is, the proportion of single persons diminished with increasing age, whereby only 35% and 34% of the males, and 22% and 20% of the females older than 25 years were single. However, the rates of broken partnerships increased with age, where 23% of the males and 26% females older than 25 years were divorced or separated. Therefore, in general in the second period, the proportion of single and married persons who made suicide attempts, was less pronounced.

In the Multicentre Study there is, for the first time, available information on both the usual, normal living situation and household composition, and on the situation as it was prior to the suicidal act. An average of 33% and 25% of males and 23% and 18% of females were usually living alone (Figure 4). Of the males, 2.7% and 2.7%, and 9.4% and 10.2% of the females were living alone with child(ren). Sixty percent and 65% of the males and 63% and 67% of the females were living with others, e. g. parents, partner, other relatives, and friends). Five percent and 6% of males and 4% and 3% of

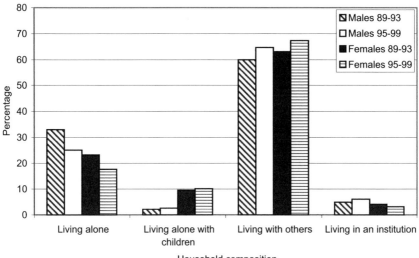

Figure 4. Household composition

females were living in an institution (clinic, sheltered home etc.). In comparison to 1989-1993, in 1995-1999 fewer persons were living in institutions.

It turned out that changes in the normal living situation and household composition had often taken place just prior to the suicide attempt. Thus 9% and 7% of males and 6% and 5% of females had changed their living conditions prior to the suicidal act. The most frequent change was a move from the usual situation to living alone, in an unstable situation, or in an institution. For example, 41% and 42% of the males whose living situation had changed were now living alone, and 29% and 27% had moved to an institution. In females, 27% had changed from living with others to living alone, 26% and 27% had moved to live in an institution.

In the first period, in comparison with males (2.2% and 1.1%), a relatively high percentage of females (23%) who usually lived with a partner and children had changed to living "only with a partner". During the second period these differences disappeared (females 1,7%).

For international comparison, the various national educational categories were recoded into three categories: low, middle and high levels of education. During the first period, an average of 50% of both males and females had only achieved a low level of formal education. In the second period 39% of the males and 37% of the females had achieved a low level of education. (Figure 5). Only 12% and 12% of the males and 13% and 12% of the females had achieved a formal education of the highest level. The data on education for the individual centres did not, in general, match the distributions in the general population, as people of lower educational status were overrepresented among suicide attempters. In general in the second period, fewer persons with a lower level of education and more persons with a middle level of education were observed.

The picture was similar with regard to vocational training. A high average percentage of both male (42% and 36%) and female (52% and 50%) suicide attempters had

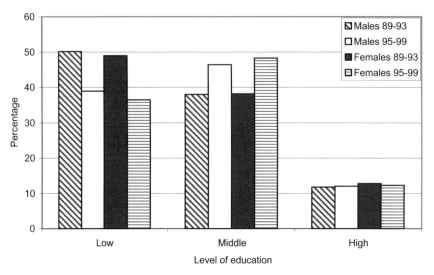

Figure 5. Formal education

received no vocational training. Since persons under 26 years of age have often not finished their vocational training, this variable was also analysed separately for persons older than 25 years. Even then, a very high percentage of males (33% and 27%) and females (44% and 38%) had undertaken no vocational training (see Figure 6).

Of the suicide attempters who were economically active (i. e. those who were able to work), many were unemployed. An average of 24% and 26% of all male and 13% and 14% of all female suicide attempters in the various catchment areas were unemployed, and 33% and 37% of the males and 47% and 52% of the females were economically

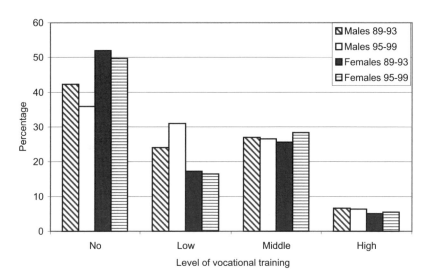

Figure 6. Level of vocational training

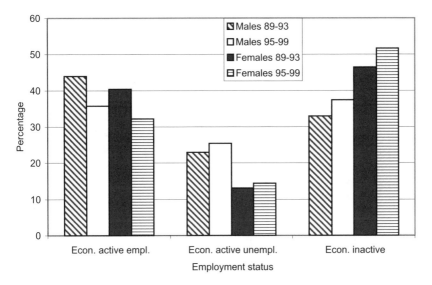

Figure 7. Employment status

inactive (see Figure 7). With regard to economically active persons, the figures obtained indicate that more than one third of males (42%) and about one third of females (31%) were unemployed. Eleven per cent and 10%, respectively, of all male suicide attempters and 23% and 26% of all females had never had a job. Therefore, when comparing both periods, a significant increase in unemployed persons and persons who were economically inactive was seen.

Taking into account the fact that many people up to 25 years of age are economically inactive (e.g. when they are apprentices, students, or have not yet finished a vocational training) this variable was also analyzed separately for persons older than 25 years. Even then an average of 28% and 24% of the economically active males and 22% and 14% of the females were unemployed.

According to the three classes of international categorical coding for social status (level of last/actual job), an average of 60% and 58% of male and 46% and 42% of female suicide attempters in the different centres were classified in the lowest social class. Only 8.9% and 8.4% of the males and 6% and 3% of the females belonged to the highest category (Figure 8).

Psychiatric diagnoses were investigated in five centres (Emilia-Romagna, Padova, Wuerzburg, Innsbruck and Sør-Trøndelag). The diagnoses were made by psychiatrists. Since at the beginning of the study ICD-9 was used, the diagnoses were made according to chapter V of this classification system. Figure 9 shows the results. In the five centres, approximately 33% of attempters were diagnosed as suffering from a psychiatric illness. Wuerzburg was the centre in which the largest percentage of people were diagnosed (71% of all attempters). In Pecs during the second period, 100% of suicide attempers were diagnosed with a psychiatric illness.

In the first period, neuroses and personality disorders were the most frequent diagnosis (males: 26%, females: 32%), followed by substance abuse (19%) and adjustment disorders (19%) for the males. For females, second and third most frequent diagnoses were affective disorders (17%) and neurotic depression and adjustment disorders (16%), respectively. In the second period, the by far most frequent diagnosis was adjustment disorder (males: 43%, females: 47%). For males, it was followed by neurotic and per-

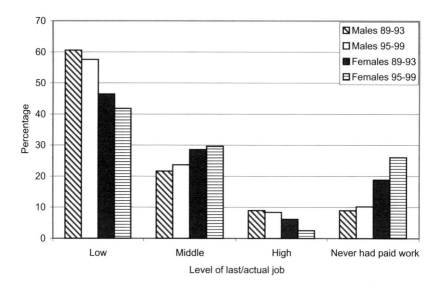

Figure 8. Level of last actual job

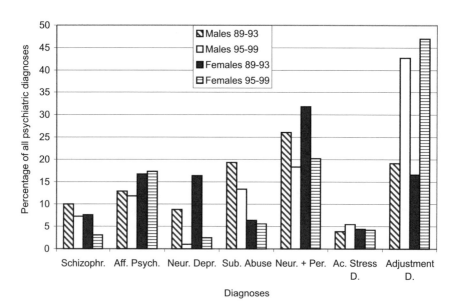

Figure 9. Diagnoses

sonality disorders (18%), substance abuse (13%), and affective disorders (12%). For females, adjustment disorder was followed by personality disorders (15%) and affective disorders (17%).

Comparing the two periods, a significant increase in diagnosed adjustment disorders for males and females could be found. Diagnosed neurotic depression nearly disappeared among females. However, in reference to Lester (1972), adjustment disorder as well as abnormal reaction to stress could possibly represent so-called contaminated diagnoses.

The recommended aftercare following acute medical treatment differed across the centres and between the two periods. In general, in the first period (1989-1993) no further treatment was recommended for an average of 27% of all males. The type of aftercare most often recommended for males was in-patient treatment (39%). Out-patient treatment was recommended in 27% of cases, and non-hospital based treatment in 6% of cases.

For females, no further treatment was recommended after the suicide attempt for a mean percentage of 22%. The most often recommended type of aftercare was in-patient hospital treatment (40%). Out-patient hospital treatment was recommended in 31% of cases, and non-hospital based treatment in 7% of cases.

During the period 1995-1999, 21% of the male suicide attempters were not recommended any further treatment, and in only 47% of all cases was inpatient treatment recommended. The figures for out-patient treatment and non-hospital based treatment were 19% and 12%. In the second period, 20% of females were not recommended any further treatment, compared to 44% of cases who were offered inpatient treatment, and 20% of all cases who were recommended out-patient treatment. Comparing the two periods, aftercare, and specifically inpatient and non-hospital-based treatment were more likely to be recommended to both males and females.

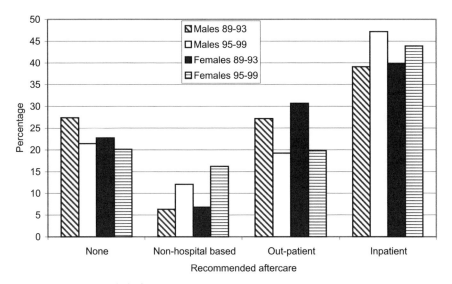

Figure 10. Recommended aftercare

Already in the first observation period a high percentage of previous suicide attempts were found in both males (42%) and females (45%). Of the sample of suicide attempters, 15% of males and 16% of females made one or more further suicide attempts during the study. Sixteen per cent of males and 17% of females repeated the attempt within 12 months of the index event. This percentage increased in the second period for males and females. During the second period, 37% of all male suicide attempters and 40% of all females suicide attempters reported having ever made a previous suicide attempt.

Comparisons between persons who had made only one suicide attempt and those who made two and more suicide attempts (independent of the time period) showed that the mean age did not differ (36.4 and 35.6 years vs. 36.6 and 36.2 years). However, the repeaters were more often divorced or separated (males 22% and 19% vs. 15% and 18%; females 22% and 20% vs. 16% and 19%), and more often unemployed (males 40% and 33% vs. 23% and 24%; females 28% and 17% vs. 17% and 12%). The methods used in the suicide attempts did not significantly differ. However, females who made only one suicide attempt were more likely to use poisoning as a method (86% and 87%) compared to repeaters (83% and 84%). The method cutting was used somewhat more often by the repeaters then the non-repeaters (males 14% and 16% vs. 13% and 16%; females: 10% and 11% vs. 7% and 8%).

The types of psychiatric diagnoses reported among repeaters differed from those reported among persons without a previous history of suicide attempts. More male repeaters were diagnosed as suffering from addiction (23% /16% vs. 14% and 12%), and neuroses and personality disorders (17% and 15% vs. 8% and 17%), and fewer were suffering from adjustment disorders (17% and 42% vs. 34% and 52%), and "acute reactions to stress" (0.7% and 4.9% vs. 9.7% and 6.2%). There were also more diagnoses of schizophrenia in the male repeaters (14% and 7.3% vs. 4.5% and 4.9%).

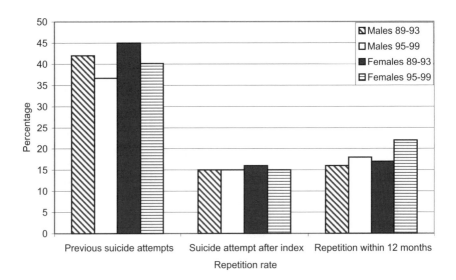

Figure 11. Repetition rates

More female repeaters than first ever suicide attempters were diagnosed as suffering from neuroses and personality disorder (without neurotic depression) (23% and 13% vs. 18% and 15%). The most significant difference concerned the diagnosis of adjustment disorder being reported in 17% and 53% of the repeaters compared to 30% and 52% in first evers.

No significant differences were found between repeaters and non-repeaters regarding recommended aftercare. In-patient treatment was recommended for a slightly higher percentage of repeaters (male repeaters: 46% and 45% vs. 44% and 36% in non-repeaters; females: 46% and 45% vs. 40% and 32%).

Discussion

The study is of course not without its methodological problems (Leenaars, 1994). However, because of the use of common instruments, definitions and case finding criteria, the WHO/EURO Multicentre Study has for the first time provided the means to compare various sociodemographic risk factors over time and to test with a sufficiently large sample the predictive value of various psychological and sociodemographic variables as well as treatment effects.

The new X-classification of methods also offered the opportunity to assess the use of some specific methods. It was found for example, that the suicide attempt method "alcohol" alone is not so rare as previously estimated. The frequency of the method "car accident" is also not negligible. For example, on the basis of the German sample, it was estimated that in one year at least 1500 car accidents were deliberately caused in order to attempt suicide (Schmidtke & Weinacker, 1994). It is also interesting to note that this method seems to be a peculiarity of German-speaking countries and is, according to the data, not seen in the southern part of Europe. On the contrary, there are surprisingly high rates of using herbicides and pesticides in Hungary and in Rennes, France (Michel et al., 2000).

The results also show that perhaps some of the long-standing hypotheses and opinions about suicide attempters should be modified. For example, the first results indicate that for some catchment areas the female:male ratio is not as large as indicated in many previous epidemiological papers on suicidal behaviour (e.g. Böcker, 1973; Diekstra, 1982). In one centre (Helsinki), both the total male event and person rate is even higher than the female rates.

With regard to the sociodemographic variables, the results clearly show that compared with the general population, suicide attempters belong more often to the social categories which indicate social instability and poverty. Thus, this study has also provided additional evidence of covariations of certain sociodemographic and socioeconomic conditions, and the occurrence of attempted suicide (Welz, 1980, 1983; Petronis et al., 1990; Platt & Kreitman, 1985; Platt, 1986; Mösler et al., 1991; Rygnestad & Hauge, 1991).

In general, these variables did not change significantly between the two periods, but there are some exceptions. In the second period, adjustment disorder was diagnosed significantly more often. Also the level of education changed slightly in the direction of more people in the middle category. However, the categories with a lower level of education and vocational training are still overrepresented.

For international comparisons, further analyses are needed regarding the base rates of the different variables in the general population, and a cross-cultural framework to account for the data is also needed (cf. Leenaars, 1994). The results also show that for future research the differentiation of the usual living condition and household composition and the living condition just prior to the suicidal act will be useful. It was found that a significant percentage of suicide attempters in this study had changed their living condition shortly before the actual attempt.

If the rates of repetition of suicide attempts are computed, the results give the impression that the rate of repetition is increasing over time, especially for men. The problem of repetition was already stated in the first publications (e.g. Schmidtke et al., 1996). Among males and females, high percentages of previous suicide attempts were found, and a repetition rate of 15% in the year following the attempt. The short-term repetition of suicidal behaviour is high in several centres. This could lead to the hypothesis that suicide attempters can be relatively easily separated into two groups: one group with only one or two attempts and one with three or more attempts. In comparison to findings from the 1980s, it also seems that the rates of repetition of suicide attempts within 12 months of an attempt are increasing (Schmidtke et al., 1988).

It also seems that the recommendations of aftercare changed over time. In the second period, more aftercare, especially inpatient treatment and non-hospital-based treatment, was recommended. How far this reflects a better network of outpatient treatment in the second period or an improvement of knowledge about suicide attempters has to be tested in further analysis. At least for some centres the number of psychiatrist and psychotherapist increased significantly between the periods (e.g. Wuerzburg).

References

Bille-Brahe U, Bjerke T, Crepet P, DeLeo D, Haring C, Hawton K, Kerkhof A, Lönnquist J, Michel K, Philippe A, Pommereau X, Querejeta I, Salander Renberg E, Schmidtke A, Temesváry B, Wasserman D & Sampaio-Faria JG (1993). *WHO/EURO Multicentre study on parasuicide. Facts and figures.* Copenhagen: WHO.

Böcker F (1973). *Suizide und Suizidversuche in der Großstadt, dargestellt am Beispiel der Stadt Köln.* Stuttgart: Thieme.

Diekstra RFW (1982). Epidemiology of attempted suicide in the EEC. In: Wilmotte J & Mendlewicz J. (Eds.) *New trends in suicide prevention.* Basel: Karger, 1-16.

Kerkhof AJFM, Platt S, Bille-Brahe U, Schmidtke A (1992). *Parasuicide in Europe: A WHO/ Euro multicentre study – Preliminary findings for 1989.* Paper presented at the 25th Annual Conference of the AAS, Chicago.

Leenaars A (1994). Conference report: Attempted suicide in Europe. *Crisis*, 15, 90.

Michel K, Ballinari P, Bille-Brahe U, Bjerke T, Crepet P, DeLeo D, Haring C, Hawton K, Kerkhof A, Lönnquist J, Querejeta E, Salander-Renberg E, Schmidtke A, Temesvary B, Wasserman D (2000). Methods used for parasuicide: Results of the WHO/EURO Multicentre Study on Parasuicide. *Social Psychiatry and Psychiatric Epidemiology,* 35, 156-163.

Mösler TA, Weidenhammer W, Lungershausen E (1991). Vergleich soziodemographischer Daten von selbstaggressiven mit fremdaggressiven Personen im Nürnberger Stadtgebiet. *Nervenheilkunde*, 10, 193-197.

Petronis KR, Samuels JF, Moscicki, EK & Anthony, JC (1990). An epidemiologic investigation of potential risk factors for suicide attempts. *Social Psychiatry and Psychiatric Epidemiology*, 25, 1993-1999.

Platt S (1986).Parasuicide and unemployment *British Journal of Psychiatry*, 149, 401-405.

Platt S, Bille-Brahe U, Kerkhof A, Schmidtke A et al. (1992). Parasuicide in Europe: The WHO/EURO multicentre study on parasuicide. I. Introduction and preliminary analysis for 1989. *Acta Psychiatrica Scandinavica*, 85: 97-104.

Platt S & Kreitman N (1985). Is unemployment a cause of parasuicide? *British Medical Journal*, 290, 161.

Rygnestad T & Hauge L (1991). Epidemiological, social and psychiatric aspects in self-poisoned patients. A prospective comparative study from Trondheim, Norway between 1978 and 1987. *Social Psychiatry and Psychiatric Epidemiology*, 26, 53-62.

Schmidtke A (1989). *WHO/EURO Multicentre study of parasuicide. Copenhagen: WHO, ICP/ PSF 024/18* (WHO paper for the Consultation Meeting on Strategies for Reducing Suicidal Behaviour in the European Region). Szeged.

Schmidtke A, Bille-Brahe U, Kerkhof A, DeLeo D, Platt S, Sampaio-Faria J, Henderson J & Pototzky W (1993). The WHO/EURO Multicentre Project on Parasuicide – State of the art. *Italian Journal of Suicidology 3*, 83-95.

Schmidtke A, Häfner H, Möller HJ, Wedler H, Böhme K (1988). Häufigkeiten und Trends von Suizidversuchen in der Bundesrepublik Deutschland: eine methodische Studie. *Öffentliches Gesundheitswesen 50*, 272-277.

Schmidtke A & Weinacker B (1994). Suizidalität in der Bundesrepublik und den einzelnen Bundesländern: Situation und Trends. *Suizidprophylaxe 21*, 4-16.

Schmidtke A, Kerkhof A, Bille-Brahe U, DeLeo D, Bjerke T, Crepet P, Haring C, Hawton K, Lönnqvist J, Michel K, Pommereau X, Salander Renberg E, Querejeta I, Temesvary B, Wasserman D, Fricke S, Weinacker B & Sampaio-Faria JG (1996). Suicide attempts in Europe: Results of the WHO/EURO Multicentre Study on Parasuicide. *Acta Psychiatrica Scandinavica, 93*, 327-338.

Schmidtke A (1997). Suicide: Individual, cultural and international perspectives: Germany/ Europe. *Suicide and Life-Threatening Behavior*, 27, 127-136.

Uno M, Ando E & Ishikawa K (1987). Ein Beitrag zum Problem des Studentensuizids. *Fortschritte der Neurologie und Psychiatrie 55*, 273-278.

Welz R (1980). Suicidal areas: Cluster analysis profiles of urban environments. *Acta Psychiatrica Scandinavica 62*, Suppl. 285.

Welz R (1983). *Drogen, Alkohol und Suizid*. Stuttgart: Enke.

WHO (1986). Summary Report, Working Group on Preventive Practices in Suicide and Attempted Suicide. York, England. 22 – 26 September 1986. (ICP/PSF 017 (s).

Part II

Results in the Individual Countries

Northern Europe

Chapter 6

Suicidal Behaviour in Finland

A. Ostamo & J. Lönnqvist

Description of the catchment area

The Finnish area under study comprises the City of Helsinki, that is, the urban part of the Finnish capital, with half a million inhabitants, situated in the southern Finland on the Baltic Sea coast. The capital differs in social structure, housing conditions and demography from the rural areas or smaller towns, and the catchment area is therefore not representative of Finland as a whole, the lifestyles in Helsinki are distinctly more modern than in the other Finnish areas.

Sample and method of data collection

Suicide mortality figures are obtained from Statistics Finland. According to the Finnish law, a medicolegal investigation of the cause and manner of death is to be carried out when death has been unnatural, or suspected to be so. Medicolegal autopsies are carried out by well-trained forensic pathologists. The overall autopsy rate in Finland is relatively high: 31% in 1995. The corresponding figures for Denmark, Sweden and Norway in the mid-1980s were similar: 36%, 30% and 20%, respectively (Hesso, 1987). Thus, the registration of the cause and manner of death in Finland is in general considered to be reliable.

The treatment of suicide attempts in Helsinki begins by all attempts being referred to the emergency rooms of three hospitals under Helsinki University Central Hospital and two municipal general hospitals. General practitioners, psychiatric hospitals and other health care facilities refer all suicide attempts to these hospitals. The data gathering process was planned to include all residents of Helsinki aged 15 years or older who during the research periods were admitted to health care because of a suicide attempt. Up-to-date census information made it possible to exclude from the data those living outside the catchment area, and the rates therefore apply exclusively to the population of the capital.

The data were gathered for the whole calendar year of 1989, for seven months in 1990 (1.1.-31.7.) and for two-month periods (15.4.-14.6.) in the years 1991-1993. The specially trained nursing staff of every unit collected the data in 1989-1990 by interviewing the patients in structured interviews. When an interview was not possible, data were taken from case files. The research group members, who checked the daily regis-

ters, ascertained the reliability of the data. Every suspected suicide attempt was identified and the reason for admission confirmed. Any missing cases were added to the
data. From 1991 onwards the medical staff registered the attempted suicide cases, and
in addition the research group checked the daily lists and added any missing cases. The
careful data gathering process ensured that the coverage of all suicide attempts treated
in health care during each study period was 100%.

As the calculation of annual attempted suicide rates was based on individuals, only
the first attempt of a person in each sample period was included in the data. An estimate of the annual rates for 1991-1993 was made from the two-month samples for each
year. In order to avoid bias caused by data-collecting in spring and early summer (Jessen
et al., 1999), an estimation factor of 5.4 for men and 5.1 for women was used to calculate the number of persons per year in 1991-1993. Due to the sample based data monitoring, complete data on repeated attempts were not available and therefore the extrapolation of repetition was not possible. Population statistics for 31 December in
each year were used to denominate sex and age. Event-based admission figures were
used for analysis of the methods of the attempts and the use of alcohol only.

A follow-up study covering a period of on the average 5.3 years was based on the
data from 2782 suicide attempt patients treated in the emergency rooms in 1989-1996
(Ostamo & Lönnqvist, 2001). The mortality of the study cohort was updated from
Statistics Finland.

Results

Suicide

Since the 1820s, the overall suicide rate for Helsinki has exceeded the rate for the rest
of the country. In particular, the female rate has been markedly higher in Helsinki than
it is elsewhere in the country, whereas there has been less difference between the capital city and the rest of the country in the rates for men. Compared to the country as a
whole, during the 1990s the male rate in Helsinki was about one and a half times higher,
while the female rate was more than twice as high (Lönnqvist & Salovainio, 1990). The
difference between urban and rural suicide rates has diminished steadily since the 20th
century. In Helsinki, three percent of all deaths are due to suicide (Statistics Finland,
1999). There are no age-specific suicide data available for Helsinki.

Suicide mortality in Finland increased throughout the 1980s and peaked towards the
end of the economic boom in 1990 (Aromaa et al., 1999). Since the peak figure of 1,512
in 1990, the number of suicides has dropped. In 1997, suicide was the cause of death for
4.3% of male and 1.1% of the female population. For men, death by suicide is three times
more common than death by traffic accidents, and for women twice as common. In comparison with international data, suicide mortality in Finland is particular high among
men; compared with the rest of Western Europe, however, suicide mortality among
women is also high. The frequency of suicide among young Finnish adults is higher
than in anywhere else in Europe, and in 1997, suicide accounted for 36% of all deaths
among men aged 15-34. The corresponding figure for women was 28%.

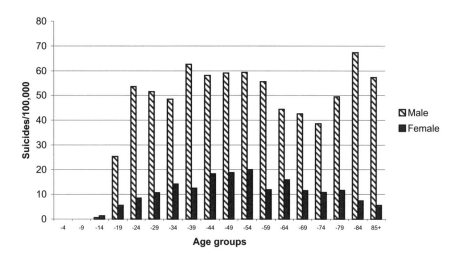

Figure 1. Rates of suicide by sex and age, Finland 1997

The frequency of suicide has always been unevenly distributed within various regions and population groups, the mortality being highest in eastern and northern Finland (Aromaa et. al., 1999), and for decades, the figures for southern and western Finland have been below average. Typically, more men commit suicide in rural areas and more women in more densely populated areas, especially in southern Finland. For men, suicide mortality among lower socio-economic groups is twice as high as among the higher status groups; for women, the differences as to status are far less noticeable. Major risk factors other than previous self-destructive behaviour include mental health problems, alcohol problems, many negative life events, lack of social support and serious somatic illnesses.

Attempted suicide

In all, 3,027 attempted suicide events were registered during the study periods in 1989-1993. Event rates decreased during the five years of research (from 355 in 1989 to 274 in 1993), mainly because of a marked decrease in the male event rates (from 426 to 301). Female event rates decreased from 300 to 253 per 100,000 population. Person rates increased from 1989 to 1990 and then decreased for both genders.

Male rates remained higher than female rates during 1989-1993. The sex ratio (f/m) increased from 0.72 in 1989 to 0.79 in 1993. The rate increased among men aged 20 years or older and decreased for men older than 45 years of age; the peak of the age-specific male rates was in the age group of 30-39 years.

The female rate too, increased towards a peak among the 30-39-year-olds and then decreased evenly with age. Table 2 shows the mean rates for the five years under study (1989-1993), calculated on annual person rates by 5-year age groups. Although the rate for men decreases quite sharply among those 40 years and older, the sex ratio remains in general below 1.0.

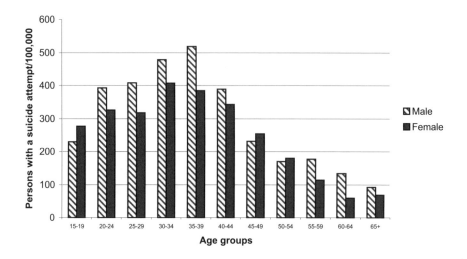

Figure 2. Rates of attempted suicide (persons) by sex and age in Helsinki, 1989-1993

Epidemiological findings

General results

With respect to marital status, in Helsinki divorced men are at highest risk of attempting suicide. The risk for divorced men is five times higher than for married men, who are under-represented among male attempted suicide. Divorced women too, are at a significantly higher risk than married, single or widowed women. Widowers are at a 2-3 times higher risk of attempting suicide than widows, while married women have higher rates of attempted suicide than married men.

The highest rates of attempted suicide in 1989-1994 were found among the unemployed (Ostamo et al., 2001). However, during the recession, the rates of attempted suicide among the unemployed fell markedly for both men and women. During the years 1989-1994, the risk of attempted suicide for unemployed men was on the average 12 times higher than those employed, while the corresponding difference for women was about 7 fold, with the male risk being on the average 1.8 times higher than the female. The relative risk for men peaked in 1991, but declined thereafter, whereas that for women peaked two years later in 1993 (Ostamo et al., 2001).

Among men, self-poisoning was used in 81.6% of all cases of suicide attempts, while women used poisoning even more often (90.9%). Cutting and piercing were the second most often used methods by both men and women, but men used cutting or other methods twice as often as the women.

In 1989, 85.5% of all cases of attempted suicide the level of alcohol in the blood was tested by a breath analyzer, and the results showed that 80.4% of the men and 66.0% of the women had consumed alcohol prior to, or in connection with their suicide attempt.

The lethality or the degree of somatic seriousness of the attempts was assessed in

558 cases. Lethality was categorized as mild in 43.3%, moderate in 42.3%, severe in 11.3%, and very severe in 3.0% of the cases. Male attempts were assessed severe or very severe more often (16.2%) than female attempts (12.8%).

Close to one half (49.1%) of male and two thirds (62.0%) of female suicide attempters were referred for further treatment. At least one out of four men (26.1%) and one out of five women (17.9%) left the hospital immediately after the first aid treatment. Attempters, who had consumed alcohol in connection with the suicide attempt, were referred for psychiatric consultation more seldom than others. In 22.6% of all attempted suicide cases, treatment after the first aid in the emergency room was unknown.

The majority of the assessed suicide attempters was referred for some psychiatric after-care. Every tenth was referred for voluntary psychiatric hospital care (11.2%) and only a small number (6.2%) had to be referred involuntarily. Psychiatric hospitalization was needed more often for male patients (23.5%) than for female patients (17.4%).

The results from the follow-up study on attempted suicide in Helsinki showed that the mortality from both natural and unnatural causes was high among suicide attempters (Ostamo & Lönnqvist, 2001). By the end of the five year follow-up period, 3% of the men and 9.3% of women had died; that is 413 (14.8%) of the 2,782 suicide attempters were dead. Two thirds of the deceased were men, the deceased were in general older than the survivors, and they were or had been significantly more often married.

The deceased persons had used intoxication significantly more often as the method of their index attempt than those alive at the end of follow-up. They had consumed alcohol more seldom in connection with the index attempt than others, and had significantly more often repeated attempts during the follow-up period.

Peculiarities of the catchment area

Contrary to other European areas under study, the male attempted suicide rates in Helsinki are higher than female rates (Schmidtke et al., 1996). The predomininance of males applies to all age groups. Also, self-poisoning as a method for attempting suicide has been found to be used more often in Helsinki than in other European areas under study, especially among men (Michel et al., 2000).

Conclusion

Results from a previous study indicate that in Finland, rates of attempted suicide to some extent correlate with rates of completed suicides (Ostamo et al., 1991). In the western part of Finland, where the rates of suicide traditionally are low, rates of attempted suicide are low, and in northern parts, where the rates of suicide traditionally are high, the rates of attempted suicide are high too.

The data available do not to allow for drawing conclusions on rates of attempted suicide all over Finland, but the results of the studies indicate that the rate of attempted suicide locally varies with the rate of completed suicide, but that in general, rates of attempted suicide are at least ten times higher than the rates of completed suicide. The high rates of attempted suicide in cities and big towns (Ostamo et al., 1991) indicate that in addition to the classical social factors also some special factors might provoke suicidal behaviour. These could be self-destructive life-styles, more possibilities to communicate by using suicidal behaviour, and more contacts to people who are using suicidal behaviour as a way to cope.

The severe economic recession during the 1990s, which led to very high unemployment rates in Helsinki, did not correlate significantly with the frequency of attempted suicide. In particular, the high rates among men, already observed in the first year of the study, remained in comparison with European standards on a very high level throughout the whole study period 1989-1993. Alcohol consumption was involved in the majority of suicide attempts, especially among men, and the decrease in male rates may partly be due to diminished alcohol consumption. According to the sales statistics, the consumption of alcoholic beverages in Helsinki decreased in 1991-1994 (SOTKA DataBase, 1999).

References

Aromaa A, Koskinen S & Huttunen J (Eds.). (1999). *Health in Finland*. Helsinki: National Public Health Institute and Ministry of Social Affairs and Health.

Harries EC & Barraclough B (1998). Excess mortality of mental disorders. *British Journal of Psychiatry*, 173, 11-53.

Hesso R (1987). Scandinavian routines and practices in the registration of suicide. *Acta Psychiatrica Scandinavica*, 76 (Suppl. 336), 17-21.

Jessen G, Andersen K, Arensman E et al. (1999). Temporal fluctuations and seasonality in attempted suicide in Europe. *Archives of Suicide Research*, 5, 57-69.

Lönnqvist J, Salovainio A (1990). *Suicide in Finland 1976-1985*. Suicide mortality by province and communes in 1976-80 and 1981-85. Helsinki, Health Services Research by the National Board of Health in Finland.

Michel K, Ballinari P, Bille-Brahe U et al. (2000). Methods used for attempted suicide: results of the WHO/EURO Multicentre Study on Attempted suicide. *Social Psychiatry and Psychiatric Epidemiology*, 35, 156-163.

Ostamo A, Lahelma E & Lönnqvist J (2001). Transitions of employment status among suicide attempters during a severe economic recession. *Social Science & Medicine*, 52, 1741-1750.

Ostamo A & Lönnqvist J (2001). Excess mortality of suicide attempters. *Social Psychiatry and Psychiatric Epidemiology*, 36, 29-35.

Ostamo A, Lönnqvist J, Heinonen S et al. (1991). Epidemiology of attempted suicides in Finland. *Psychiatria Fennica*, 22, 171-179.

Schmidtke A, Bille-Brahe U, DeLeo D et al. (1996). Attempted suicide in Europe: rates, trends and sociodemographic characteristics of suicide attempters during the period 1989-1992. Results of the WHO/EURO Multicentre Study on Attempted suicide. *Acta Psychiatrica Scandinavica*, 93, 327-338.

SOTKA DataBase. (1999). Helsinki: STAKES, The National Research and Development Centre for Welfare and Health.

Statistical Yearbook of the City of Helsinki, 1989, 1990, 1991, 1992, 1993, 1994, 1995, 1996, 1997. The City Of Helsinki: Information Management Centre.

Statistics Finland. (1999). *Causes of Death 1997.* Helsinki: Statistics Finland.

Suominen K, Henriksson M, Suokas J et al. (1996). Mental disorders and comorbidity in attempted suicide. *Acta Psychiatrica Scandinavica*, 94, 234-240.

Suominen KH, Isometsä ET, Henriksson MM et al. (1998). Inadequate treatment for major depression both before and after attempted suicide. *American Journal of Psychiatry*, 155, 1778-1780.

Vaattovaara M (1998). Residential differentiation within the metropolitan area of Helsinki, Finland Environment and spatiality. Helsinki: City of Helsinki Urban Facts.

Weissman M.M, Bland RC, Canino GJ et al. (1999). Prevalence of suicide ideation and suicide attempts in nine countries. *Psychological Medicine*, 29, 9-17.

World Health Organization. (1999). *WHO/EURO Multicentre Study on Attempted suicide. Fact and Figures*. Second edition. Copenhagen: World Health Organization.

Chapter 7

Suicidal Behaviour in Norway

H. Hjelmeland

Description of the catchment area

The county of Sør-Trøndelag is located in the central part of Norway. The area of Sør-Trøndelag is 18,831 km², which is approximately 6% of the total area of Norway. There are 260,855 inhabitants (1999) in the county, which is approximately 6% of the national population.

The population of Sør-Trøndelag is fairly representative for the total population of Norway for variables like population density, age distribution, economic profile of branches of industry, and level of education.

Sample and method of data collection

Information on completed suicide has been obtained from the Central Bureau of Statistics of Norway (CBS, 1988, 1990, 1991, 1992, 1993, 1994, 1995, 1996, 1997).

The system for monitoring non-fatal suicidal acts was established in October 1988, consisting of all community health centres, general practitioners in private practice, and all the psychiatric and somatic hospitals.

All patients admitted to one of the county's health care facilities following a non-fatal suicidal act were to be registered. The complete monitoring system was maintained until the end of 1993. From 1994 onwards, the monitoring was limited to the two main somatic hospitals in the county. This was mainly due to the fact that the general policy for the various health services in the county was to refer all non-fatal suicidal act patients to the somatic hospitals anyway. From 1994 onwards, the non-fatal suicidal act rates have been calculated with an estimation factor of 1,022, based on the average percentage of monitoring forms received from other units than the two hospitals during the first years of the study.

The monitoring forms have been completed after interviews carried out by health care personnel. Where interviews have been prohibited, such as when patients had left the hospital before being interviewed, some basic information has been sought in the patient files. Throughout the monitoring period, the data collection has been administered and coordinated by a psychiatric nurse at the outpatient clinic.

During the first years of the project, the monitoring forms consisted of 46 items of which the first 25 (mainly sociodemographic) were those that were common to the whole WHO-EURO study, with 21 additional items (mainly psychological-behavioural-clinical) selected for our local study. The number of variables has been somewhat reduced during the last years of the study. Due to the outpatient clinic's close connection to the University hospital of Trondheim, where most of the non-fatal suicidal act patients are admitted, the monitoring system is estimated to have been reliable throughout the registration period.

Results

Suicide

The suicide rates for both Sør-Trøndelag and Norway for the period 1988-1997 are presented in Table 1.

Table 1. Suicide rates per 100,000 in Norway and Sør-Trøndelag 1988-1997

	1988	1989	1990	1991	1992	1993	1994	1995	1996	1997
Norway										
Males	24.5	23.0	23.2	23.7	21.2	21.1	17.7	19.1	18.0	17.8
Females	9.3	8.4	8.0	8.2	7.7	6.5	6.9	6.2	5.8	6.6
Total	16.8	15.6	15.5	15.8	14.4	13.7	12.2	12.6	11.9	12.4
Sør-Trøndelag										
Males	23.7	27.6	23.4	26.6	17.6	16.0	15.8	13.4	19.7	20.4
Females	3.2	10.3	8.7	8.7	7.0	3.9	7.7	3.9	8.5	9.2
Total	13.3	18.8	16.0	17.5	12.3	9.9	11.7	8.9	14.0	14.7

After a continuous increase since the late 1960s, the suicide rate in Norway reached a peak in 1988, when 788 persons committed suicide (16.8/100,000). After 1988, the rate flattened out at first, before starting to decline and has since decreased by 26%. In 1997 (last available year), 533 persons committed suicide in Norway (12.4/100,000), 387 men and 146 women. The male:female ratio for suicide in Norway is 3:1.

The suicide rates in age groups for 1997 are presented in Figure 1. As shown in this figure, the suicide rate does not increase continuously with age for neither males nor females. For males, the highest rates are, indeed, found in the oldest age groups (75+). However, relatively high rates are also found among the 20-24-year-olds, the 40-44-year-olds and among the 55-64-year-olds. For females, the highest suicide rate is found among the 50-54-year-olds.

The number of suicides in the county of Sør-Trøndelag has varied from one year to another since 1988 until 1997 (for example 47 in 1989, 22 in 1995 and 38 in 1997), with no clear decreasing trend throughout the country as a whole. The suicide rates of Sør-Trøndelag during some of the years have been both somewhat higher, and somewhat lower than the national rates. However, the mean suicide rate for Sør-Trøndelag

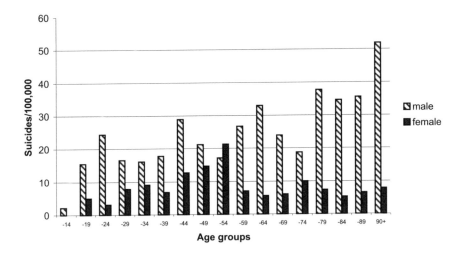

Figure 1. Suicide rates per 100,000 in Norway, 1997

(13.7/100,000) for the whole period (1988-1997), is fairly similar to the mean national suicide rate (14.1/100,000) in the same period.

In Norway, the most common suicide methods for men are hanging (36%), shooting (33%) and poisoning (16%). For women, the most common suicide methods are poisoning (42%), hanging (30%) and drowning (13%) (CBS, 1996).

Non-fatal suicidal acts

The total number of non-fatal suicidal acts registered in Sør-Trøndelag in the period from October 1st 1988 until December 31st 1998 was 3416, involving 2379 different

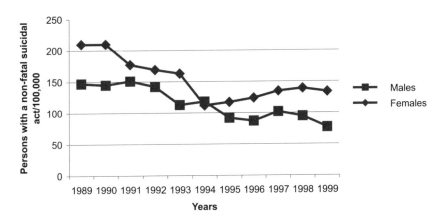

Figure 2. Person-based rates of non-fatal suicidal acts per 100,000 in Sør-Trøndelag, 1989-1999

persons, 1358 (57%) females and 1021 (43%) males. The mean age was 35.9 for both females (SD=15.2, range 15-89) and males (SD=14.0, range 15-85).

The annual person based non-fatal suicidal acts rates for females and males through the whole period (1989-1999) are presented in Figure 2. The female rate decreased during the first half of the monitoring period, but started to increase during the last half. The male rate remained relatively stable during the first four years, then started decreasing somewhat, and seems to have levelled out at a lower level during the last years of the registration period compared to the first.

The annual non-fatal suicidal act rates in age groups for both females and males are presented in Table 2, while the rates in age groups for 1999 are presented in Figure 3. A change in the age distribution has occurred for females during the monitoring period. In the beginning of the period, the rates were highest among the 20-49-year-old females. However, due to a larger increase among the youngest females during the last years, the rates are now highest in this group (15-19-year-olds).

Table 2. Person based rates of non-fatal suicide acts per 100,000 by age and gender, Sør-Trøndelag, 1989-1999

	1989	1990	1991	1992	1993	1994*	1995*	1996*	1997*	1998*	1999*
Females											
15-19	229	257	230	283	190	163	156	255	287	272	315
20-29	313	320	183	205	204	173	164	161	175	196	189
30-39	299	280	346	276	242	123	144	177	186	227	170
40-49	264	289	201	166	216	147	157	163	157	116	174
50-59	190	153	180	160	140	103	116	70	103	77	67
60-69	61	62	80	66	59	45	18	28	48	88	69
70+	66	54	12	40	51	23	40	29	28	11	17
Total	210	210	177	169	163	112	117	124	135	135	134
Males											
15-19	100	114	85	143	127	100	64	80	80	47	79
20-29	241	245	227	202	144	174	162	100	149	127	97
30-39	194	188	229	202	165	173	119	139	168	148	106
40-49	214	178	167	152	133	129	78	78	84	106	133
50-59	110	65	82	135	70	94	106	92	101	48	33
60-69	25	52	89	9	28	39	10	41	21	64	11
70+	0	36	36	53	52	18	17	26	17	43	17
Total	147	145	151	142	113	118	92	87	102	95	77

*The rates are calculated with an estimation factor of 1.022

For the youngest females, the rate fluctuated from around 250/100,000 in the beginning, before starting to decline to approximately 150/100,000. However, from 1995 onwards there has been an almost continuous increase, and the rate for young females wasdocumented as 315/100,000 in 1999. There has also been an increasing tendency in some of the other age groups, but not to the same degree as for the young. For the whole period, the rates are lower in 1999 than they were in 1989 for all age groups except for the youngest where it is higher, and among women in their 60s, where the rate has remained relatively stable throughout the period. The difference between the age group with the highest and the lowest rate has increased from 1989 to 1999 for females.

For males, the rates have been highest among the 20-49-year-olds during the whole period, although the total rates have decreased from between 200-250/100,000 in 1989 to approximately 100/100,000 in 1999. The rates in the other age groups have fluctuated from year to year, but on the whole remained relatively stable. The difference in rates between the male age groups has decreased from 1989 to 1999.

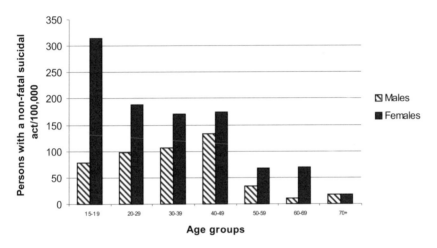

Figure 3. Person based rates of non-fatal suicide acts per 100,000 by age and gender, Sør-Trøndelag 1999

Repetition was calculated both retrospectively and prospectively. Forty-five per cent of the total sample were reported to have one or more previous non-fatal suicidal act(s) at the time they where registered (47% of the females and 43% of the males, χ^2 (3) = 3.36, n.s.). The annual prospective repetition rate is defined as the proportion of the patients registered for their first non-fatal suicidal act within one calendar year, who repeated the non-fatal suicidal acts within 12 months (moving window; Table 3).

Table 3. Annual prospective repetition rates in per cent

	1989	1990	1991	1992	1993	1994	1995	1996	1997
Females	18.0	25.3	21.4	14.1	21.1	24.1	19.4	22.4	30.6
Males	20.7	25.1	14.8	14.6	20.9	20.9	20.9	22.0	20.0
Total	19.1	25.2	18.5	14.4	21.0	22.5	22.5	22.2	26.6

The repetition rates have fluctuated around 20% for both females and males with no increasing or decreasing trend.

The methods used for the non-fatal suicidal acts are presented in Table 4. The most important methods were classified into soft (all self-poisonings, X60-69) and hard (all other, X70-82) methods. Of the females, 89.3% employed a soft method compared to 80.9% of the males (χ^2 (1) = 28.18, p<.0001, Cramer's V = 0.12). The most common hard method was cutting for both females and males.

Table 4. Methods of parasuicide

Methods	Women (N=1359)		Men (N=1021)	
	N	%	N	%
Drugs (X60-64)	1195	87.9	748	73.3
Alcohol (X65)	371	31.0	365	35.7
Gas, vapours (X67)	2	0.1	3	0.3
Solvents, pesticides and other agricultural chemicals (X66, X68-69)	6	0.4	20	2.0
Hanging (X70)	7	0.5	14	1.4
Drowning (X71)	12	0.9	7	0.7
Guns and explosives (X72-75)	1	0.1	12	1.2
Fire, steam etc. (X76-77)	1	0.1	4	0.4
Sharp and blunt objects (X78-79)	94	6.9	109	10.7
Jumping from high place (X80)	7	0.5	14	1.4
Lying in front of moving object (X81)	2	0.1	1	0.1
Crashing motor vehicle (X82)	1	0.1	1	0.1
Other (X83-84)	4	0.3	7	0.7

Note. Up to four methods per person

Epidemiological findings

General results

The social characteristics of the non-fatal suicidal act patients are presented in Table 5. The results are presented for females and males separately, and statistical analyses to identify potential sex differences have been performed.

As to marital status, a previous report from the same study (first five years) has shown that the non-fatal suicidal act patients were married less often and more often separated, divorced or widowed compared to the general population (e.g., Hjelmeland & Bjerke, 1996).

Marital status per se is probably not as informative as a risk factor for suicidal behaviour any more. Family patterns in Norway have changed rapidly during the last decades, and family structures other than the traditional nuclear family with married parents and 1.7 children, have become more frequent (Brandt & Moxnes, 1996; Moxnes, 1990). Moreover, it has previously been reported that 33% of the unmarried, 35% of

Table 5. Sociodemographic characteristics of the patients

Sociodemographic variables	Women N	Women %	Men N	Men %	χ^2	Cramer's V
Marital status (n=1749)					41.22*	0.15
Never married	359	34.0	318	45.8		
Married or cohabiting	349	33.1	207	29.8		
Separated	54	5.1	42	6.1		
Divorced	216	20.5	111	16.0		
Widowed	77	7.3	16	2.3		
Household comp. (n=1786)					98.01*	0.23
Alone	269	25.1	252	35.2		
Alone w/children	146	13.6	17	2.4		
With partner (+ children)	454	42.4	245	34.3		
Other	202	18.9	201	28.1		
Level of education (n=1631)					1.42	
Lowest level	451	45.8	287	44.4		
Middle level	322	32.7	205	31.7		
Highest level	211	21.4	155	24.0		
Economic situation (n=1681)					51.29*	0.17
Employed	350	35.1	255	37.3		
Unemployed	125	12.5	167	24.5		
Economically inactive	523	52.4	251	38.2		
Country of birth (n=2055)					0.58	
Norway	1143	95.5	826	96.3		
Other	54	4.5	32	3.7		
Change of address last year (n=1674)					1.45	
No change	721	71.9	485	72.1		
Within county	213	21.3	136	20.2		
Within country	53	5.3	37	5.5		
Abroad	15	1.5	15	2.2		

*p<.0001

the separated and 59% of the divorced female patients were living with a partner, with the corresponding percentages for males being 19%, 32% and 32%, respectively (Hjelmeland & Bjerke, 1996). Thus, looking at the actual household composition will probably yield more valuable information.

Table 5 shows that the majority of the female patients lived with a partner with or without children, while approximately equal proportions of the males lived alone or with a partner. A relatively large proportion of the males also lived in 'other' household compositions, mainly with their parents or with friends or relatives. There was a statistically significant sex difference in household composition.

The majority of both male and female patients had only the lowest level of education. As to economic situation, males were more often than females, unemployed, while females were more often economically inactive (for example, housewives, students, retired, disability pensioners). More than 95% of the patients registered were born in Norway, and more than 70% had not changed their address during the last year prior to the non-fatal suicidal act.

A sex difference was found in three of the six variables analyzed, namely in marital status, household composition and economic situation. However, although these differences were statistically significant, the corresponding effect sizes were rather low, indicating that the large sample size resulting in a very high statistical power, caused small effects to become statistically significant. Thus, although statistically reliable, the sex differences found should not be over-interpreted.

Peculiarities of the catchment area

As mentioned previously, the centre in Sør-Trøndelag has also collected information on some variables in addition to those in common for all the centres participating in the study. The results of these variables are presented in Table 6.

Approximately 70% of both the female and male patients had been in contact with some health care service during the last month prior to the non-fatal suicidal act. The majority of them had been in contact with their general practitioner (all inhabitants in Trondheim have been assigned their own regular general practitioner from 1993 onwards). This result might indicate that the level of competence in identifying risk for suicidal behaviour in their patients is too low among general practitioners (and other professionals). Thus, the sub-objective of the National plan for suicide prevention (National board of health, 1996) stating that raising the level of competence in suicidology among health care personnel is important, seems highly warranted.

About half the patients claimed that the intention of the non-fatal suicidal act had been to die. Other common intentions were temporary escape (more often for females than for males) and to influence some significant other(s). A relatively large proportion of the males had other intentions, did not remember or would not say anything about their intention with the non-fatal suicidal act.

Approximately 40% of the males and 30% of the females had made serious suicide attempts in the medical sense of the word serious. The suicidal act was considered serious when on admission the patients were in deep coma with no pain reaction (self-poisoning) or where the condition was considered to be life-threatening (self-injury).

The majority of the patients reported that family problems or their own psychiatric problems had been their main concern preceding the non-fatal suicidal act, females more often than males. Males more often than females reported financial problems or problems with substance abuse.

Male patients were more often than female patients abusing alcohol and/or illegal drugs, while females more often than males abused legal drugs.

A considerable proportion of the patients reported exposure to physical and/or sexual abuse in childhood or later in life, this being twice and three times as common in

Table 6. Clinical and psychological characteristics of patients with non-fatal suicide acts.

	Women		Men		χ^2	Cramer's V
	N	%	N	%		
Contact with health care (n=1231)					6.45	
Psychiatric	156	21.2	82	16.6		
General practitioner	252	34.2	163	32.9		
Other	104	14.1	88	17.8		
Medical seriousness (n=1706)					17.97**	0.10
Low	711	70.7	425	60.7		
High	295	29.3	275	39.3		
Intention (n=1714)					34.67**	0.14
To die	533	51.8	343	50.1		
Temporary escape	186	18.1	84	12.3		
Influence others	128	12.4	63	9.2		
Other	182	17.7	195	28.5		
Main problem (n=1697)					92.86**	0.23
Family	385	37.9	182	26.7		
Financial	44	4.3	55	8.1		
Psychiatric	355	34.9	190	27.9		
Substance abuse	71	7.0	141	20.7		
Other	161	15.8	113	16.6		
Alcohol abuse (n=1592)					174.94**	0.33
Abuse	144	15.3	222	34.3		
Alcoholic (at present)	29	3.1	89	13.7		
Alcoholic (reformed)	15	1.6	17	2.6		
Drug abuse (n=1483)					7.03**	0.14
Legal drugs	466	51.7	270	46.4		
Illegal drugs	55	6.1	82	14.1		
Physical abuse (n=1236)	287	37.4	87	18.6	47.71**	0.20
Sexual abuse (n=873)	128	23.8	29	8.7	31.04**	0.19
Models						
Parasuicide (n=1209)	226	30.6	145	30.9	0.00	
Suicide (n=1192)	140	19.0	116	25.6	6.83*	0.08
Criminal record (n=1164)	47	6.7	171	37.2	168.01**	0.38
Imprisonment (n=1163)	22	3.1	125	27.1	142.11**	0.35

*p<.01, **p<.0001

females compared with males, respectively. However, it is important to note that a relatively large proportion of the patients have not been asked, or have not been willing to answer, these two questions. The main reason for not asking these questions to all was that the interviewers often found it difficult or inappropriate to ask such personal and emotional questions during a relatively short first-time interview.

As to models of suicidal behaviour, almost one third of the patients knew someone who had committed non-fatal suicidal acts and about one fifth of the females and one quarter of the males knew someone who had committed suicide (most often close friends or relatives other than the close family). A relatively large proportion of the male patients had a criminal record and had been imprisoned.

Statistically significant sex differences were found for all these variables except contact with health care. However, the effect sizes were, again, low, and one must be careful not to put too much weight on them. The strongest sex differences were found in alcohol abuse, criminal record and imprisonment, but even for these variables, the effect sizes were only of medium strength, according to Cohen (1988).

Conclusion

The suicide rate in Norway has decreased by 26% from 1988 to 1997. The total rates of non-fatal suicidal acts in Sør-Trøndelag are considerably lower today than they were in the beginning of the study. For males, the rates have decreased from around 150/100,000 in 1989 to 77/100,000 in 1999. For females, the rates have decreased from over 200/100,000 in 1989 to around 140/100,000 in 1999. However, for females the rates have started to increase again during the last half of the 1990s. This increase has been particularly strong and alarming for the young (15-19-year-olds), where the rates now are higher than when the monitoring started (over 300/100,000). Preventive efforts for the young are urgently needed, and this is, fortunately, incorporated in the three-year follow-up project 2000-2002 (National board of health, 2000) of the National plan for suicide prevention.

The social, clinical, behavioural and psychological characteristics of the non-fatal suicidal act patients in Sør-Trøndelag are similar to those found in previous research conducted in both Norway and in other parts of the Western world. Statistically significant sex differences were found for most of the variables. However, the effect sizes of these differences were small-medium, indicating that the large sample size resulting in a very high statistical power caused small effects to become statistically significant. Thus, although statistically reliable, the sex differences found should not be over-interpreted.

Acknowledgements

The author wants to thank Tore Bjerke, Petter T. Jørgensen and Tore C. Stiles for initiating the Norwegian part of the study, and health care personnel in Sør-Trøndelag for collecting the data. In particular, I am grateful to the staff of the Psychiatric outpatient clinic Øya who has filled out most of the monitoring forms, especially to Lisbeth O. Skjærvold who has been responsible for co-ordinating the data collection throughout the monitoring period.

References

Bille-Brahe U (1999). *WHO/EURO Multicentre Study on Attempted suicide*. Facts and figures. 2. edition. World Health Organization, Regional Office for Europe, Copenhagen.

Brandt B & Moxnes K (1996). *Familie for tiden, stabilitet og forandring.* Trondheim: Tano Aschehoug.

Central Bureau of Statistics of Norway. (1988, 1989, 1990, 1991, 1992, 1993, 1994, 1995, 1996, 1997). Dødsårsaker.

Cohen J (1988). *Statistical power analyses for the behavioural sciences.* Hillsdale, New Jersey: Erlbaum.

Hjelmeland H & Bjerke T (1996). Attempted suicide in the county of Sør-Trøndelag, Norway. General epidemiology and psychological factors. *Social Psychiatry and Psychiatric Epidemiology*, 31: 272-283.

Moxnes K (1990). Kjernesprengning i familien? Familieforandringer ved samlivsbrudd og dannelsen av nye samliv. Oslo: Universitetsforlaget.

National Board of Health. (1996). *The National Plan for suicide Prevention 1994-1998* (1999), Oslo.

National Board of Health. (2000). *Tiltak mot selvmord 2000-2002,* (unpublished) Oslo.

Chapter 8

Suicidal Behaviour in Sweden

E. Salander Renberg, G.-X. Jiang, L. Olsson, J. Estari & D. Wasserman

Descriptions of the catchment areas

In Sweden, two catchment areas are under study, namely the Stockholm catchment area and the Umeå catchment area.

Description of the Stockholm catchment area

The catchment area under study is in the south-western part of Stockholm, the capital of Sweden and located at North 59.03° and East 18.2°. The catchment area includes two municipalities of Huddinge and Botkyrka as well as three parishes (Hägersten, Brännkyrka and Skärholmen in Stockholm municipality). The whole catchment area is 360 km² and forms a distinct medical care district.

Description of the Umeå catchment area

The Umeå centre, located in Västerbotten county in the north of Sweden, is the northernmost of the centres participating in the WHO/EURO Multicentre Study on Suicidal Behaviour. The study area comprises the county of Västerbotten, with a total population of about 257,000 inhabitants (1999), of which about 222,000 are 15 years and older. With its huge area of about 55,500 km², the county corresponds to 13.5% of the total area of Sweden, but to only 3% of the total population. The population density is consequently very low, 5 per km².

Sample and method of data collection

Data collection in the Stockholm area

As early as in 1988, a pilot study for monitoring patients who had attempted suicide in the catchment area was carried out during a three-month period from October to December (Wasserman et al., 1994). Results of the pilot study indicated that at least 90-95% of patients who sought medical care after attempting suicide in the catchment area had attended Huddinge University Hospital. Consequently, the monitoring of patients who had attempted suicide has been conducted at this hospital. All hospitalized patients in Sweden have systematically been registered at the national Hospital Inpatient Registry since 1980s or earlier. Therefore, the information obtained through monitoring the population in this catchment area could be complemented by, and adjusted with materials from the Hospital Inpatient Registry. The information was collected for each patient who attempted suicide including general demographic, social and medical characteristics and detailed materials regarding the self-harm event, like previous suicide history, motives, methods, etc.

The coverage of the study population in the catchment area during the study period was assessed with an estimation factor, which was calculated by the number of individuals who attempted suicide that were obtained yearly from the Hospital Inpatient Registry divided by the number of individuals who attempted suicide and were registered in the study for the same period. The annual estimation factor during the study period was from 1.05 to 1.15 indicating that the coverage of the study population was quite good.

Data collection in the Umeå area

For the period 1989 to 1995 all medically treated attempted suicides, aged 15 or more, were monitored according to the common protocol for the WHO/EURO multicentre study. The cases were registered at the clinic at one of the three general hospitals and at the child psychiatric unit in Umeå, where the patient was actually treated. In a few cases, the attempter was treated at a primary health care centre, but due to lack of resources it was not considered possible to cover these cases fully, as 25 primary health care centers are located in this geographically large area. From contact with district doctors (general practitioners), it was suggested that only very were occasionally suicide attempt cases treated at primary health care centers. Most patients were transferred to one of the hospitals.

The patients were approached by a specially trained interviewer as soon as possible after the attempted suicide event, in most cases one or two days later. During nights and weekends the doctor on duty at the psychiatric clinics made the registrations. When the interviews were not possible to perform, mainly due to practical obstacles and refusals, basic information was gathered from case-records. To make sure that no cases were missing there were a number of checks, for example at the emergency unit at the hospitals, and at every hospital a coordinator was appointed to ensure the quality of data. Therefore the estimated coverage of the monitoring of medically treated attempted suicides was considered to be very close to 100%.

For practical and economical reasons the monitoring during the period 1996-1998 is based on reports from the psychiatric clinics in the county. The information was gathered with the purpose of following trends and includes basic information on annual gender and age-specific numbers of attempted suicide. For these cases no socio-economic information was gathered.

Results I

Suicide in Sweden and in the two catchment areas

Suicide rates have continuously been declining in Sweden since the beginning of the eighties (Official Statistics Sweden, 1997). In Figure 1 the annual suicide rate (ICD-9: E950-959 and ICD-10: X60-X84) per 100,000 inhabitants, aged 15 years and over, in Sweden, Stockholm and Västerbotten, is presented for the period 1989-1997.

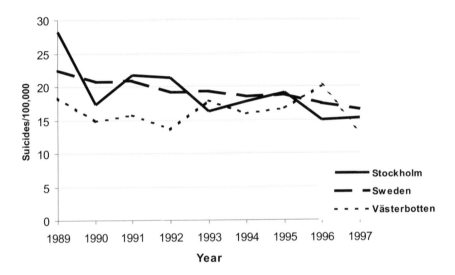

Figure 1. Annual suicide (certain) rate per 100,000 for people (males and females) aged 15 years and over during 1989-1997 in Sweden

The national suicide rates showed a steady decline, while rates in the two Swedish catchment areas fluctuated more, mainly due to smaller numbers. Despite this instability, different regional patterns could be distinguished. The Stockholm rates more closely resembled the national rates and revealed an overall decline, while rates in the north of Sweden initially were lower than national rates, followed by an increasing tendency, except for the last year, 1997. The male/female ratio of suicide rates for the study period was in Sweden 2.4, in the Stockholm area 1.4, and in Västerbotten 4.2, depicting an urban pattern in Stockholm with relatively lower male rates and higher female rates compared to national rates, and a rural pattern in northern Sweden with relatively higher male rates and lower female rates.

The age-specific suicide rates per 100,000 in Sweden in 1997, are displayed in Figure 2.

The suicide rates increased with age for males in general with exceptions for a few age groups. Particularly higher rates of suicide were found among the eldest males

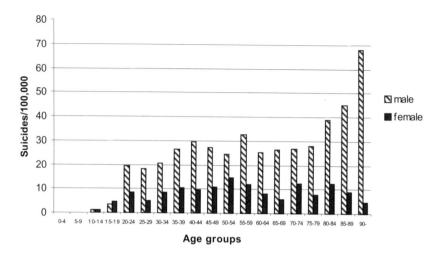

Figure 2. Age-specific suicide rates per 100,000 in Sweden in 1997

(aged 85 years and over). For females, the highest suicide rate was found in the age group 50-54 years. The distribution of age-specific suicide rates in the catchment areas were quite similar to that in the country.

Results II

Attempted suicide in the Stockholm area

During the study period of 1989-1998, 2,557 individuals with an index suicide attempt were registered from the catchment area. The total number of attempted suicide events (Table 1) was registered as 3,651 (males: 1,312; and females: 2,339), and the numbers of the index suicide attempts presented a similar annual distribution (data not shown).

In total, 979 (43%) males and 1,578 (62%) females were included in the register. There were 559 (22%) people in the age-group of 15-24 years, 669 (26%) and 535 (21%) in the age-groups of 25-34 and 35-44 years respectively, as well as 263 (10%) people aged 65 years and over.

The average age-specific incidence of index suicide attempts in the catchment area during the period of 1989-1998 showed a clear reduction with age (Figure 3). The age distribution of rates in 1998 (data not shown) was almost the same, although the rates were relatively lower. The annual number of individuals with an index suicide attempt per age group during the study period is shown in Table 2.

Table 1. Annual number of attempted suicide events in south-west Stockholm (Huddinge University Hospital)

Year	Male Number	%	Female Number	%	Total Number
1989	184	34.0	357	66.0	541
1990	178	41.8	248	58.2	426
1991	123	37.4	206	62.6	329
1992	157	41.8	219	58.2	376
1993	154	35.6	278	64.4	432
1994	125	37.1	212	62.9	337
1995	108	38.2	175	61.8	283
1996	94	29.7	222	70.3	316
1997	92	32.6	190	67.4	282
1998	97	29.5	232	70.5	329
1989-98	1,312	35.9	2,339	64.1	3.651

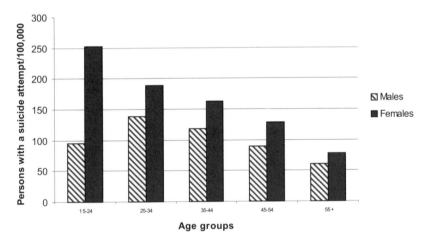

Figure 3. Age specific rates per 100,000 person-years of the index attempted suicide in south-west Stockholm (Huddinge University Hospital) during 1989-1998

Among males, the individuals in the age group of 25-34 years accounted for the highest proportion of attempted suicide, except for a few years when the proportion was slightly lower than that for the age-group of 35-44 years. For females, the individuals in the younger age groups consistently accounted for the highest proportions of attempted suicide.

The annual rates of attempted suicide during the study period depicted a decreasing trend, which was particularly evident for the first two years, but not so clear in the years following 1996.

Table 2. Annual number of individuals with the index attempted suicide in south-west Stockholm (Huddinge University Hospital) during 1989-1998

		\multicolumn{13}{c}{Age group}											
		15-24		25-34		35-44		45-54		55-64		65-		Total
Year	Sex	No	%	No	%	No	%	No	%	No	%	No	%	No
1989	Male	27	16.4	40	24.2	43	26.1	30	18.2	12	7.3	13	7.9	165
	Female	62	20.0	90	29.0	67	21.6	44	14.2	15	4.8	32	10.3	310
	All	89	18.7	130	27.4	110	23.2	74	15.6	27	5.7	45	9.5	475
1990	Male	25	16.8	54	36.2	28	18.8	20	13.4	6	4.0	16	10.7	149
	Female	43	22.6	48	25.3	39	20.5	19	10.0	17	8.9	24	12.6	190
	All	68	20.1	102	30.1	67	19.8	39	11.5	23	6.8	40	11.8	339
1991	Male	13	15.3	23	27.1	20	23.5	14	16.5	4	4.7	11	12.9	85
	Female	42	29.2	22	15.3	30	20.8	25	17.4	13	9.0	12	8.3	144
	All	55	24.0	45	19.7	50	21.8	39	17.0	17	7.4	23	10.0	229
1992	Male	22	20.6	27	25.2	23	21.5	15	14.0	12	11.2	8	7.5	107
	Female	31	21.5	39	27.1	32	22.2	15	10.4	7	4.9	20	13.9	144
	All	53	21.1	66	26.3	55	21.9	30	12.0	19	7.6	28	11.2	251
1993	Male	14	12.8	32	29.4	33	30.3	16	14.7	3	2.8	11	10.1	109
	Female	55	31.3	35	19.9	31	17.6	26	14.8	8	4.5	21	11.9	176
	All	69	24.2	67	23.5	64	22.5	42	14.7	11	3.9	32	11.2	285
1994	Male	9	10.2	27	30.7	20	22.7	16	18.2	6	6.8	10	11.4	88
	Female	37	26.8	29	21.0	36	26.1	17	12.3	6	4.3	13	9.4	138
	All	46	20.4	56	24.8	56	24.8	33	14.6	12	5.3	23	10.2	226
1995	Male	12	14.5	27	32.5	20	24.1	13	15.7	7	8.4	4	4.8	83
	Female	24	23.3	25	24.3	16	15.5	17	16.5	9	8.7	12	11.7	103
	All	36	19.4	52	28.0	36	19.4	30	16.1	16	8.6	16	8.6	186
1996	Male	9	14.1	17	26.6	15	23.4	10	15.6	5	7.8	8	12.5	64
	Female	41	29.7	38	27.5	21	15.2	20	14.5	3	2.2	15	10.9	138
	All	50	24.8	55	27.2	36	17.8	30	14.9	8	4.0	23	11.4	202
1997	Male	11	16.4	15	22.4	13	19.4	16	23.9	3	4.5	9	13.4	67
	Female	38	36.5	26	25.0	15	14.4	14	13.5	3	2.9	8	7.7	104
	All	49	28.7	41	24.0	28	16.4	30	17.5	6	3.5	17	9.9	171
1998	Male	11	17.7	19	30.6	13	21.0	11	17.7	4	6.5	4	6.5	62
	Female	33	25.2	36	27.5	20	15.3	25	19.1	5	3.8	12	9.2	131
	All	44	22.8	55	28.5	33	17.1	36	18.7	9	4.7	16	8.3	193
1989-98	Male	153	15.6	281	28.7	228	23.3	161	16.4	62	6.3	94	9.6	979
	Female	406	25.7	388	24.6	307	19.5	222	14.1	86	5.4	169	10.7	1,578
	All	559	21.9	669	26.2	535	20.9	383	15.0	148	5.8	263	10.3	2,557

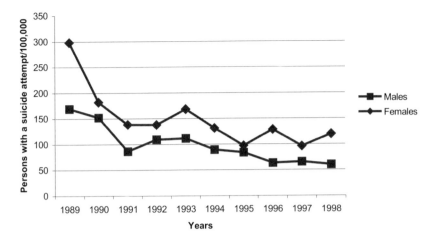

Figure 4. Rates of suicide attempts by age and gender

The rate of index suicide attempts were always higher for females than for males, and the variation of the annual rates was larger for females.

Epidemiological findings at the Stockholm Centre

General results

Among 2,202 individuals with available information, 1,259 (57%) people had never attempted suicide before the index attempt, 152 (7%) people had attempted suicide within the previous 12 months before the index attempt, and 752 (34%) people had shown such behaviour more than 12 months before. A further 39 (2%) people reported an unknown or unsure date of a previous suicide attempt.

The proportion of people reporting a previous suicide attempt did not show big variations during the study period, and the annual proportion of individuals with previous suicide attempts was slightly higher in females (44% during the whole period) than in males (40% during the whole period), with exceptions of a few years.

Although there are variations through these years, the percentage of individuals who had never married was around 50%, similar for males and females. This finding might be related to the higher proportion of young people in the whole sample.

The proportion of individuals without cohabitants was slightly higher than 40% for almost every year, which was similar for both males and females. Only a few individuals had cohabitants of the same sex.

Among individuals with an index suicide attempt less than 20% of both males and females had achieved the highest educational level.

Table 3. Annual number of individuals with previous attempted suicide in south-west Stockholm (Huddinge University Hospital) during 1989-1998*

		Previous attempted suicide								
		Never		Yes (within last 12 months)		Yes (more than 12 months ago)		Yes (date un-sure/unknown)		Total
Year	Sex	No	%	No	%	No	%	No	%	No
1989	Male	45	55.6	9	11.1	26	32.1	1	1.2	81
	Female	90	46.4	24	12.4	71	36.6	9	4.6	194
	All	135	49.1	33	12.0	97	35.3	10	3.6	275
1990	Male	59	63.4	4	4.3	28	30.1	2	2.2	93
	Female	80	54.4	11	7.5	46	31.3	10	6.8	147
	All	139	57.9	15	6.3	74	30.8	12	5.0	240
1991	Male	42	53.2	7	8.9	26	32.9	4	5.1	79
	Female	69	49.6	10	7.2	56	40.3	4	2.9	139
	All	111	50.9	17	7.8	82	37.6	8	3.7	218
1992	Male	59	57.3	8	7.8	35	34.0	1	1.0	103
	Female	84	62.7	11	8.2	39	29.1	0	0	134
	All	143	60.3	19	8.0	74	31.2	1	0.4	237
1993	Male	57	55.3	7	6.8	36	35.0	3	2.9	103
	Female	101	60.5	12	7.2	54	32.3	0	0	167
	All	158	58.5	19	7.0	90	33.3	3	1.1	270
1994	Male	50	61.0	4	4.9	28	34.1	0	0	82
	Female	69	52.7	5	3.8	56	42.7	1	0.8	131
	All	119	55.9	9	4.2	84	39.4	1	0.5	213
1995	Male	51	62.2	10	12.2	20	24.4	1	1.2	82
	Female	52	51.0	5	4.9	45	44.1	0	0	102
	All	103	56.0	15	8.2	65	35.3	1	0.5	184
1996	Male	42	65.6	2	3.1	19	29.7	1	1.6	64
	Female	86	62.8	9	6.6	41	29.9	1	0.7	137
	All	128	63.7	11	5.5	60	29.9	2	1.0	201
1997	Male	46	68.7	3	4.5	17	25.4	1	1.5	67
	Female	64	61.5	6	5.8	34	32.7	0	0	104
	All	110	64.3	9	5.3	51	29.8	1	0.6	171
1998	Male	38	61.3	3	4.8	21	33.9	0	0	62
	Female	75	57.3	2	1.5	54	41.2	0	0	131
	All	113	58.5	5	2.6	75	38.9	0	0	193
1989-98	Male	489	59.9	57	7.0	256	31.4	14	1.7	816
	Female	770	55.6	95	6.9	496	35.8	25	1.8	1,386
	All	1,259	57.2	152	6.9	752	34.2	39	1.8	2,202

* 355 individuals with "unknown" information not included.

During the later part of the study period, contrary to the former part, the proportion of people with the lowest education level was less than that of people with a middle education level. This may be related to a decreasing trend in the proportion of people in the whole population with a low level of education.

Among individuals with an index suicide attempt, the majority (around 80%) were employed, with similar proportions for males and females.

There seems to be a slightly decreasing trend in proportion of employed persons in the sample, as well as a slightly increasing trend in the proportion of students and those who had never had a job in the labour market.

According to the WHO International Classification of Diseases, 10th revision (ICD-10), methods of attempted suicide were roughly classified into two categories: methods X60-X69 as soft methods (mainly self-poisoning with medicaments, drugs or other substances), and methods X70-X84 as hard (mainly attempted suicide by hanging, jumping or cutting by sharp objects).

Soft methods were used much more frequently than hard methods for attempting suicide, with a higher proportion observed among females. There seemed to exist a slightly increasing trend in the use of soft methods during the study period.

The most commonly reported motive for the index suicide attempt was having a problem with a partner (25%). If the patients who reported separation, threatened separation and/or having a problem with a partner as a cause of the index suicide attempt were considered together, the proportion was 41%. Twenty-eight percent of patients reported their own psychiatric illnesses, and 13% of patients reported somatic conditions, as the cause of the index suicide attempt. Around one fifth (20%) of all attempted suicide events were attributed to problems with work, education, housing, or economy. In general, the annual proportion of such problems was slightly higher in males than in females.

Peculiarities of Stockholm catchment area

The catchment area in the Stockholm centre for the study of attempted suicide is a developed urban district and the population is an industrialized and educated community with a modern life style. With the quick development of new technology and new economy, mental health problems in the society are increasing. In the meantime, personal relationships and communications are becoming more and more important for the mental health of the human being. One of the important focuses of the Swedish National Centre for Suicide Research and Prevention of Mental Ill-Health is the research and prevention of suicidal behaviours among young people. In response to this, several courses for education in the high schools for prevention of suicidal behaviour in young people have been in operation for a few years.

Conclusions from the Stockholm Study

The monitoring of patients of attempted suicide in a well defined general population in south-west Stockholm has been continuously conducted over the recent decade. The overall rates of suicide and attempted suicide have decreased in the catchment area during 1989-1998. Different aspects of the suicide attempt were described according to information from the patients who were registered in the study, which will contribute to an improved understanding of the prevention of suicidal behaviours.

Results III

Attempted suicide in the catchment area of the centre in Umeå

For the period 1989 to 1995, a total of 1980 attempted suicide events were monitored, representing a total of 1,483 annually registered persons. For the period 1996-1998, another 563 persons were registered, giving a total number of 2,046 persons.

The annual number of person-based suicide attempters in the county of Västerbotten varied from 165 to 253, with an average annual person-based suicide attempt rate per 100,000 inhabitants of 99, reflecting an average female rate of 129 and an average male rate of 69. For males a marked decrease in attempted suicide rates was observed (of about 57%), from the highest rate in 1990 (104 per 100,000) to the lowest in 1998 (45 per 100,000). Female rates showed another pattern of initially quite stable rates around 150 per 100,000, followed by a clear decline of about 33% from 1992 to 1995. This was followed by a rise during recent years reaching the same level as for 1989 to 1992. Consequently the female/male person-based attempted suicide ratio varied over the period, from 1.58 in 1995 to 2.9 in 1998.

Suicide statistics for Sweden, presented in a previous section of this chapteras well as in this section, are presented in a comparison between local suicide and attempted suicide rates. Latest figures on suicide are available from 1998. As depicted in Figure 5,

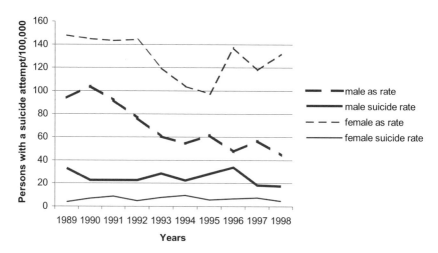

Figure 5. Annual attempted suicide (as) and completed suicide rate per 100,000 persons aged 15 years and over in Vasterbotten county (Umea centre) during 1989-1998

suicide rates for females were quite stable with only minor fluctuations, while male rates were more fluctuating and reached a peak in 1996 (33.8 per 100,000). As already presented, the attempted suicide rates initially declined for both genders, and then increased among females. As a consequence of these changes, the attempted suicide/ suicide rate ratio for females varied between 37.5 (in 1989) to 10.9 (in 1994), and for males between 4.6 (in 1990) to 1.4 (in 1996).

Repetition rates were calculated for attempted suicides monitored between 1989-1995. The event/person ratio over the seven-year period was 1.7 (for females 1.9, for males 1.3), implying that 41% of the attempts were repeated suicide attempts. The annual event/person rate was on average 1.3, and, consequently, nearly one in four (23%) attempted suicides over a year were repeated suicide attempts.

Epidemiological findings at the Umeå centre

General results

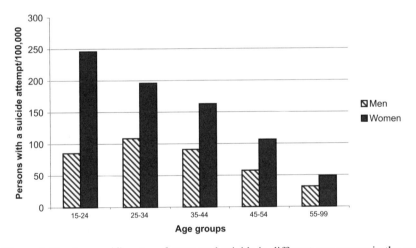

Figure 6. Gender specific rates of attempted suicide in different age groups in the county of Västerbotten, average 1989-1998

Over the period 1989 to 1998, the highest rates for females were found within the age group 15-24 years, and for males within the age group 25-34 years. The annual person based mean age for females was 35 years (SD ±15), for males 38 years (SD ±15). For females the mean age decreased by 5 years over the period (from 38 to 33), partly due to a decrease in attempted suicide rates among older women, but mainly because of a clear increase among the youngest females (Figure 7). The mean age among males increased over the period by 3 years. This change was mainly due to a decline in attempted suicide rates in the age group 25-34 years.

The most common attempted suicide method was via intoxication by drugs (X60-64), for both women and men. Cuttings with sharp objects (X78), were used in 22.9% of female attempted suicides, and in 18.2% of male attempted suicides. In Table 4, attempted suicide methods are combined into two main categories, soft (X60-69) and hard (X70-84).

For men the proportional use of hard methods decreased from 37.1% as highest in 1990 to 23.4% as lowest in 1995. For women there was an opposite change (except for 1990), with a steady increase in the use of hard methods of about 10%.

A shift in type of drugs used for intoxication was identified, where the use of analgesics, antipyretics and antirheumatics (i.e. drugs which can be available without a doctor's prescription) increased in total from 10% to 21%. More males than females used alcohol in connection with the suicide attempt, for most years about double the proportion, and with a minor tendency towards an increase in this gap. After acute

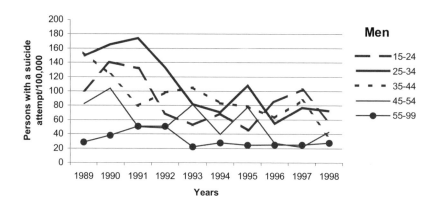

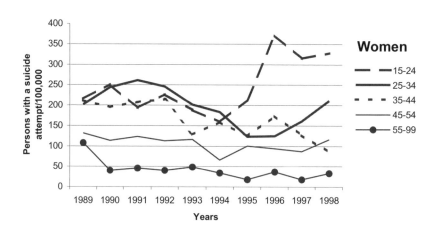

Figure 7. Age-specific rates of attempted suicide by gender in the northern Swedish catchment area (Västerbotten), 1989-1998

medical treatment, females were more often recommended aftercare, and were more often admitted to a hospital ward.

Table 4. Methods for suicide attempts in the county of Västerbotten 1989-1995

Year	Gender	Method of attempted suicide				
		Soft (X60-69)		Hard (X70-84)		Total
		No	%	No	%	No
1989	Male	74	78.1	29	28.2	103
	Female	144	77.8	41	22.2	185
1990	Male	82	63.1	48	36.9	130
	Female	140	62.8	83	37.2	223
1991	Male	69	65.1	37	34.9	106
	Female	133	71.1	54	28.9	187
1992	Male	62	68.1	29	31.9	91
	Female	150	71.4	60	28.6	210
1993	Male	48	73.8	17	26.2	65
	Female	134	68.7	61	31.3	195
1994	Male	53	70.7	22	29.3	75
	Female	105	66.5	53	33.5	158
1995	Male	57	78.1	16	21.9	73
	Female	119	66.5	60	33.5	179
1989-95	Male	445	69.2	198	30.8	643
	Female	925	69.2	412	30.8	1,337
	All	1,370	69.2	610	30.8	1,980

The most pronounced differences between males and females were observed concerning household composition and economic activity, wereby more females were living alone with children and more males were unemployed.

Peculiarities of the Umeå catchment area

Rates of fatal repetition among suicide attempters monitored 1989-1995 was calculated. These findings have also been presented elsewhere (Salander Renberg, 1999). Out of the 1,194 persons attempting suicide, 1.8% (N=22), committed suicide within 12 months after index attempt. Among attempters registered 1989-1993, 3% (N=32), committed suicide within 36 months. For those who eventually committed suicide within 36 months, the mean age at index attempt was 40 years (SD13.5, median=36), compared to 37 years (SD15.8, median=35) for those who did not complete suicide. Further characteristics are shown in Table 5.

There was a relatively smaller proportion of females in the suicide group, more persons living alone, more 'middle educated', more unemployed, fewer from urban regions, more use of violent suicide attempt methods, more non-fatal repetition, and

Table 5. Comparisons between the group of non-suiciders (N=936) and suiciders within 36 months after index attempt (N=32), based on suicide attempts during 1989-1993 in the county of Västerbotten

	Non-suiciders %	Suicide within 36 months %
Women	60.8	40.6
Living alone	35.0	43.8
Years of education 9	58.5	44.8
10-13	32.9	51.7
14+	8.6	3.4
Economic active, employed	45.4	53.1
Urban region	47.5	43.8
Violent method[a] for index parasuicide	26.7	37.5
Previous parasuicides	46.9	42.3
Exclusively index parasuicide	43.9	34.6
Non-fatal repetition within 36 months after index parasuicide	25.9	34.4
Intake of alcohol in connection with index parasuicide	47.5	15.4
Admittance to psychiatric care after index parasuicide	56.3	71.9

[a] All methods except intoxication by drugs, chemicals and gases. From Salander Renberg 1999.

more often admittance to psychiatric in-patient treatment. However, the most pronounced difference between the two groups concerned the intake of alcohol in connection with the index suicide attempt. Persons who subsequently committed suicide had more seldom consumed alcohol in connection with the attempt. Furthermore, of those who had consumed alcohol in connection with the index suicide attempt, only 1% committed suicide within a following 3 year period (as compared to 3.3% in the total group). Another striking difference was that among those who completed suicide, violent suicide attempt methods were never combined with the intake of alcohol, compared to 40% of the non-suicide group.

Among suicide attempts monitored during 1989-1995, a total number of 55 persons comlpeted suicide during 1989 to 1996 inclusive, which constituted about 14.5% of all suicides in the catchment area during the corresponding period. For women, 23 of 79 suicides (29%) were found in the attempted suicide group, and for men 32 of 297 suicides (11%) (Salander Renberg, 1999).

Conclusions from the study in Umeå

Male attempted suicide rates showed a clear decline of approximately 50% over the ten year period. On the contrary, after an initial decline, female rates showed an increase in rates of a similar level as those reported during the beginning of the 90s, leading to an increase in the female/male ratios. This finding differs from those from other studies, which document decreasing ratios (Hjelmeland, 1996).

Comparisons between gender-specific attempted suicide and suicide rates clearly underline the consistently differing patterns among females and males, as well as the fact that there were no indications of an equalization between male and female ratios, rather, increasing differences.

Concerning non-fatal repetition, the results show a high proportion of repeated suicide attempts, implying that much more effort is needed in the field of prevention to develop efficient methods for aftercare interventions.

The increase in suicide attempt rates especially among younger women, calls for attention, particularly when considering the fact that in Sweden the total suicide rates have continuously declined since the beginning of the 80s, with the exception of females aged 11 to 24 years (Hultén, 2000), where the rates have been stable and unchanged. The same pattern is found among males 11-19 years of age.

The finding that females may be increasingly using harder suicide attempt methods corresponds with findings that females are using more and more violent suicide methods as well (Hultén & Wasserman, 1992; DeLeo et al., 1995).

The fact that of individuals who presented with an index suicide attempt, those who completed suicide compared to those who did not, reported less alcohol intake in connection with the index attempted suicide, gives the clinical implication that special attention should be paid to attempts with no alcohol involved. These persons might have a lower threshold for deliberate self-harm, and that their acts may be more planned and severe, since alcohol often works to trigger the onset of suicidal thoughts or to break down the inhibitions before the act (Böhme, 1994).

Finally, these findings indicate that even if all known suicide attempt cases admitted to hospital were treated, it would only be possible to prevent suicide mortality to a limited extent, especially among males. Furthermore, even if all persons that ever had made a suicide attempt were identified and successfully treated (also those not medically treated), at least half of all future suicides would probably still occur, since about 50% have made previous attempts (Barraclough et al. 1994). Consequently, to prevent suicide, interventions have to approach earlier phases of the suicidal process as well.

Acknowledgements

The study was supported by grants from the Swedish Council for Planning and Coordinating of Research, the Swedish Council for Social Research, the psychiatric clinics in Umeå, Skellefteå, and Lycksele, and Stockholm County Council, Sweden.

References

Barraclough B, Bunch J, Nelson B, Sainsbury P (1994). A hundred cases of suicide: clinical aspects. *British Journal of Psychiatry*, 125: 355-373.

Bohme K (1994). Drug and alcohol induction of suicidal behaviour. In M. J. Kelleher (Ed.), *Divergent perspectives on suicidal behaviour* (pp. 128-139). Fifth European Symposium on Suicide, Cork: D & A O'Leary Ltd.

DeLeo D, Carollo M, Mastinu A (1995). Epidemiology of suicide in the elderly population in Italy 1958-1988. *Archives of Suicide Research.* 1: 3-18.

Hjelmeland H (1996). Attempted suicide in the county of Sør-Trøndelag, Norway. General epidemiology and psychological factors. *Social Psychiatry and Psychiatric Epidemiology,* 31(5): 272-283.

Hultén A (2000). *Suicidal Behaviour in Children and Adolescents in Sweden and Some European Countries.* Dissertation, Stockholm 2000. ISBN: 91-628-4254-4.

Hultén A & Wasserman D (1992). Suicide among young people in Sweden. *Scandinavian Journal of Social Medicine,* 20(2), 65-72.

Official Statistics Sweden, Causes of Death, 1997.

Salander Renberg E (1999). Parasuicide in a northern Swedish county 1989-1995 and its relation to suicide. *Archives of Suicide Research,* 5: 97-112.

Wasserman D, Larsson N, Estari J, Adamsson C, Spellerberg S (1994). Parasuicide in Stockholm, Sweden, 1989-1991. Chapter 11. In: Kerkhof AJFM, Schmidtke A, Bille-Brahe U, De Leo D, Lönnqvist J (Eds.) *Attempted Suicide in Europe, Findings from the Multicentre Study on Parasuicide by the WHO Region Office for Europe.* The Netherlands: DWSO Press, Leiden University. pp 175-187.

Chapter 9

Suicidal Behaviour in Denmark

U. Bille-Brahe & K. Andersen

Description of the catchment area

The Danish area under study comprises the Funen County with a population of close to 470,000 inhabitants, of which approximately 390,000 are 15 years and older. The catchment area covers both urban and rural areas (Bille-Brahe (ed), 1999). About one third of the population is living in Odense, which is the main city of the county.

Funen County is considered to mirror Denmark as a whole. As to space and the size of population, the area comprises about 10 per cent of the country, and studies on sociodemographic parameters and socio-economic conditions regarding health, etc, have shown that the inhabitants of the county constitute a representative sample of the Danish population, and that epidemiological studies carried out in the catchment area under study by the Centre for Suicidological Research in Odense yield reasonable estimates for the country as a whole.

Sample and method of data collection

Data on suicide are obtained from the Cause-of-Death Register, compiled by the Danish Statistical Bureau. The rates presented are calculated on national data, while data on the county of Funen has been used for calculating the ratio suicide attempts/suicides.

The monitoring of attempted suicide in the county of Funen started 01.04.89, and since then all suicide attempters treated at the hospitals in the county are registered. Information is collected by the centre staff according to a routine agreed upon by the staff at the respective units or services at the hospitals and the centre, who also will try and gather any missing information on sociodemographic data from hospital case files, etc. The monitoring of the attempts is checked by cross-references to the Patient Register for Funen County. During the first years of monitoring, an additional number of suicide attempts was registered during this control, but now less than 1 per cent of the final figures comes from the control procedure. Also, at the centre, all forms are controlled for double-registrations before the data are entered into the centre's official Register of Attempted Suicide.

Results

Suicide

The Danish rate of suicide used to be among the highest in the Western world. However, after the marked increase during the 1960s and 1970s that peaked arround 1980,
rates have dropped significantly, and are today closer to the average for Europe.

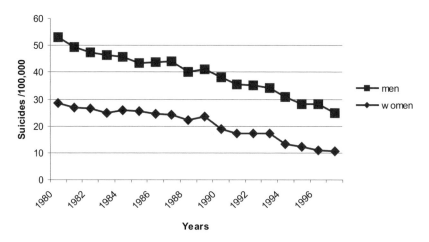

Figure 1. Rates of suicide per 100,000 (15 years +) by sex, 1980-1997.

As in most other countries, the risk of suicide is higher for men than for women. At
the beginning of 1920s, the sex ratio (m/f) was 3:1, but from 1922 to 1980, the female
rate increased by 154 per cent, while the male rate increased by 'only' 53 per cent, the
sex ratio then being down at 1.86. Since 1980, a decrease by 32 per cent has taken place
for both genders, and by 1996, the sex ratio had increased to 2.5.

Rates for young people have been rather stable, except for the increasing rates for
young females during World War II. For elderly people too, rates have been relatively
stable, although there has been a slightly increasing trend among elderly women.

During the 1970s and 1980s, rates for 45-49-year-old men increased with the result
that although the risk for men is still increasing by age, the high risk group now also
comprises somewhat younger age groups. Female rates, however, continuously peak
among the middle-aged, and in later years a further increase has been taking place in
this group.

In Denmark, self-poisoning is the most frequently chosen suicide method, especially among women; second comes hanging, especially among men, while suicide by
shooting is rather rare.

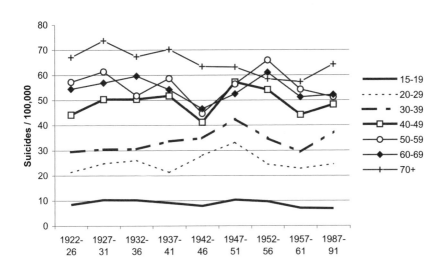

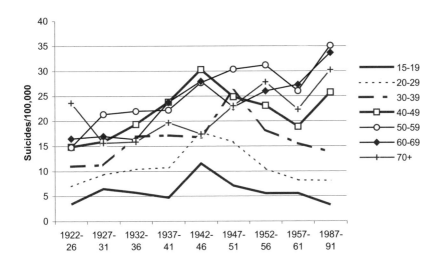

Figure 2. Age-specific rates of suicide by sex, 1922-1997

Attempted suicide

Table 1 shows the frequencies of attempted suicide during ten years of monitoring.

Table 1. Attempted suicide in the County of Funen, events and persons, 1989-1998

	Events		Persons		Ratio
Year	N	Rate*	N	Rate*	Events/Persons
1989[1]	1026	269	802	211	1.27
1990	911	239	719	188	1.27
1991	783	203	626	163	1.25
1992	817	212	645	167	1.27
1993	880	227	716	185	1.22
1994	819	211	641	165	1.27
1995[2]	716	188	575	151	1.25
1996[2]	650	171	533	140	1.22
1997[2]	637	167	534	140	1.19
1998[2]	699	183	556	146	1.25

* per 100,000 inhabitants at the age of 15 year or over
[1] extrapolated on the base of 9 months of registration
[2] estimation factor 1.02

In the area under study, 7,938 suicide attempts were committed by 6,347 persons during the period 1989-1998. The ratio events/persons varied over the years between 1.27 and 1.19, the average being 1.25. In 1998, rates of attempted suicide (events) and rates of suicide attempters (persons) were 32 and 31 percent, respectively, lower than in 1989. During the 10 years, 579 of the suicide attempters died – of these 153 (26%) from suicide.

Figure 3 shows that the decrease in the frequencies of attempted suicide has taken place for both sexes and in all age groups – with the exception of the 15-19-year-old girls, who during the 1990s have tripled their rate of non-fatal suicidal acts. This extraordinary finding (which, by the way, has been confirmed by emergency units all over the country) has caused great concern, and attempts to find an explanation are now going on (Bille-Brahe, 2001).

At the beginning of the registration period, the sex ratio (male/female) was 0.81, but in the following years, the ratio varied between 0.91 (in 1992) and 0.78 (in 1994) to 0.62 in 1998, the low ratio at the end of the period reflecting the increasing rates of attempted suicide among the young girls.

As a group, the male attempters became older through the period; the mean and the median age increased from 36 to 44 years and from 35 to 39 years, respectively. In contrast, the female attempters became somewhat younger; the mean age decreased from 41 to 39 years, while the median age remained almost the same.

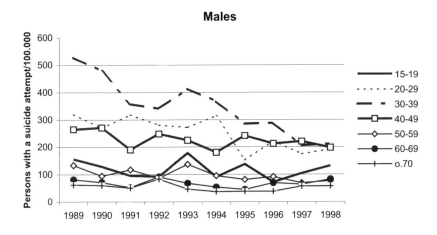

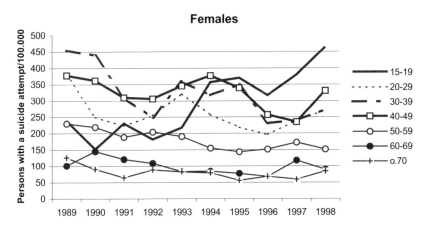

Figure 3. Age-specific rates of attempted suicide by sex, 1989-1998

Table 2. Mean age and median age among suicide attempters by sex and year

Year	Mean		Median	
	m	f	m	f
1989	36.0	40.8	35.1	38.3
1990	37.9	42.5	36.7	41.5
1991	37.3	41.4	35.6	40.5
1992	39.2	42.2	37.1	40.6
1993	36.9	40.4	35.0	38.9
1994	36.7	40.3	34.5	39.4
1995	37.6	38.9	36.7	37.7
1996	39.2	40.2	37.4	39.7
1997	38.9	39.8	36.1	38.9
1998	40.4	39.3	38.6	38.1

The decrease in the mean frequencies of non-fatal suicidal acts reflects a similar decrease in the frequency of fatal suicidal acts, but the ratio attempted suicide/suicide varies markedly with age and sex.

Table 3. The ratio suicide attempts/suicide by sex and age

	1989-1991		1992-1994		1995-1997	
Age	m	f	m	f	m	f
15-19	19:1	91:0	29:1	57:1	9:1	71:1
20-29	15:1	26:1	15:1	71:1	6:1	70:1
30-39	13:1	32:1	10:1	37:1	9:1	19:1
40-49	4:1	20:1	5:1	17:1	8:1	14:1
50-59	3:1	6:1	2:1	8:1	2:1	10:1
60-69	1:1	3:1	2:1	6:1	1:1	6:1
70+	1:1	3:1	1:1	2:1	1:1	2:1

The figures in table 3 show clearly that the ratio is markedly higher among women than among men, and that it is decreasing by age. During the period, the ratio has increased especially for young women, again reflecting the marked increase in the frequency of suicide attempts in these female groups.

As in most countries, also in Denmark self-poisoning is the method most commonly used – on the average about three fourths of the attempters had tried to poison themselves. Most common were overdoses of medicine, usually benzodiazepine or analgesics. Especially the young girls would take overdoses of agents containing paracetamol. Cutting was the second most frequent method, and some men had tried to hang or suffocate themselves. Using alcohol as the sole agent for poisoning is getting very rare, but drinking at the time of the suicide attempt is getting more common. Studies indicate that at least 50 per cent of the attempters have been drinking just before or in connection with the attempt (e.g. Søgaard Nielsen et al., 1993). As the choice of method has been rather stable over the years under study, table 4 shows the average distribution in per cent.

Table 4. Choice of method, average 1989-1998 in per cent

	Men		Women	
	N	%	N	%
Poisoning	2394	70,0	3414	80,1
Cutting	772	22,6	652	15,3
Hanging	97	2,8	47	1,1
Drowning	27	0,8	43	1,0
Other	128	3,7	107	2,5

The practice of referral has changed somewhat over the years. When we started monitoring, close to half the patients went home after being somatically treated at the emergency unit/service; in later years only about one third has gone home without any further treatment. One reason is that an 'Observation Unit' has been established at the Department of Psychiatry at Odense University Hospital (OUH), where a suicidal patient can stay for 48 hours without being registered as a psychiatric patient. Also, in 1992, a Centre for Prevention of Suicidal Behaviour was established in the municipality of Odense, offering aftercare to the non-psychiatric suicidal patients who had been in contact with OUH in connection with their attempt.

Epidemiological findings

General results

As the monitoring of attempted suicide in Denmark has been based on the case report files regularly completed by the hospital staff at the emergency units, detailed information on social characteristics will usually be missing. This has especially been the case since the case report form was changed in 1995, as the new form no longer includes information on civil status, employment, etc. In some cases, where the attempter was admitted to a hospital bed for further treatment, more information has been available, but there will still be too many missing values for proper analyses. Comparing the information we do have with the information reported in a previous report (Bille-Brahe et al., 1994), the results indicate that the characteristics of Danish suicide attempters to some extent remain the same; i.e. they were often living alone, being previously married or not-married, their level of education and vocal training in general being low and so was their level of economic activity, on the average five times as many as in the main population were on disability pension. In some respects, however, the differences between suicide attempters and the so-called normal population are getting smaller, in other respects they have increased. For example, civil status among suicide attempters is now closer to the distribution in the population at large, as living alone and/or being divorced is getting more and more common in the Danish society. Contrary, the differences as to economical activity are increasing; while the rate of unemployment in general have been decreasing, suicide attempters are relatively more often *long term* unemployed or on disability/early retirement pension.

In general, it can be said that a considerable part of the attempters still have to be characterized as social casualties having a very low social status – but at the same time, suicide attempters, especially among the young, now also include more and more persons from higher status groups.

Prediction

From Figure 3, it was seen that the steady decrease in the frequency of attempted suicide that took place in all age groups – but for the 15-19 young girls – more or less ended in the middle of the decade and for the last years there seem to be an tendency towards an increase in most age groups, especially among the women. It is, however, too early to say whether these increases are incidental or will turn out to be a new trend.

Peculiarities of the catchment area

Monitoring attempted suicide in the County of Funen offer special opportunities to study the frequency of repeated attempts. Table 1 showed the ratio events/persons for each year. The ratio events/persons does not, however, yield a good estimate of the frequency of recidivism: a sudden peak in the ratio may be due to a few persons showing what one could call chronic suicidal behaviour, the next peak being due to these persons dropping out of the material. For example, in our material, one woman made 13 attempts during one year; her 14th attempt, carried out in the following year, proved to be a fatal one.

The problem of repeated suicide attempts is a serious one, and suicide attempts are seen as a heavy risk factor when the future risk of suicidal behaviour is assessed. There are, however, several problems when trying to estimate the frequency of recidivism; one of them concerns the validity of information on previous attempts given at the index attempt (Bille-Brahe et al., 1995). Even in our study, where the possibilities to get this information were good, information was lacking in too many cases. Also, in some cases, the attempter would deny any previous attempt, even though both case files and our register showed that this person had been admitted to hospital after a suicide attempt once or sometimes even several times before the index attempt. A valid estimation of the frequency of recidivism can therefore only be calculated for suicide attempters where *confirmed* information at the time of the index attempt regarding previous attempts is available.

As the length of the follow-up period has to be the same for all persons under study, our material permits a maximum follow-up period of eight years for those who were registered between 01.04.89 (when the monitoring started) and 31.04.90. Of the 773 suicide attempters registered during this first year of monitoring, valid information on previous suicidal behaviour was available for 392 persons only. Seventy-five persons died during the 8-year follow-up period, of these 30 by suicide. The final number of suicide attempters included in the 8-year follow-up study therefore amounts to 317 persons.

Table 5. An eight year follow-up study of suicide attempters.

	After index attempt		
	Index-attempt	1 or more repeated att.	Total
No previous attempt	97 (31%)	42 (13%)	139 (44%)
Previous attempt	76 (24%)	102 (32%)	178 (56%)
Total	173 (55%)	144 (45%)	317 (100%)

Of the 317 persons, about *one third (31%) had attempted suicide only once* (the index attempt); 24 per cent had only attempted suicide before the index attempt, 13 per cent only after, and 32 per cent both before and after the index attempt.

Conclusions

Since the frequency of suicidal behaviour in Denmark reached its peak around 1980, both rates of completed suicide and of non-fatal suicide attempts have been decreasing markedly. During the 10-year-period of monitoring, rates of suicide attempts (events) have decreased from 269 per 100,000 in 1989 to 183 per 100,000 in 1998, which is 32%. Most noteworthy is that the decrease has taken place for both sexes and in all age groups – with the exception of the 15-19-year-old girls, who have tripled their rate of non-fatal suicidal acts during the 1990s. Another noteworthy finding concerns the frequency of recidivism, indicating that only one third of the suicide attempters are non-repeaters, thus underlining the problem of repeated attempts.

References

Bille-Brahe U, Jessen G, Nielsen E, Schiødt H. & Søgaard Nielsen A. (1994). Attempted suicide in a Danish Region, 1889-1992. In: Kerkhof A.J.F.M, Schmidtke A, Bille-Brahe U, DeLeo D, Lönnqvist J. (eds). *Attempted Suicide in Europe. Findings from the Multicentre Study on Attempted suicide by the WHO Regional Office for Europe,* Leiden: DSWO Press.

Bille-Brahe U, Jessen G, Jensen B (1995). Monitoring repeated suicidal behaviour: Methodological problems. In: Mishara B (ed.) *The Impact of Suicide.* New York: Springer. pp. 156-166.

Bille-Brahe U (2001). Suicidal Process and Society. In: van Heeringen K (ed.), *Understanding Suicidal Behaviour*, pp. 182-211 Chichester: Wiley.

Nielsen AS, Stenager E, Bille-Brahe U (1993). Attempted suicide, suicidal intent, and alcohol. *Crisis*;14/1: 32-38.

WHO Regional Office for Europe. Bille-Brahe U (Ed.). (1999). *Facts & Figures.* Copenhagen: WHO.

Central Europe

Chapter 10

Suicidal Behaviour in Ireland

P. Corcoran, U. Burke, S. Byrne, D. Chambers, C. Daly, A. M. Hennessy, H. S. Keeley,
M. Kelleher, M. J. Kelleher, C. McAuliffe, J. McCarthy, M. McCarthy, M. Lawlor,
S. Neilson, M. O'Sullivan, I. J. Perry & E. Williamson

Description of the catchment area

There are two Irish centres in the WHO/Euro Multicentre Study, both of which are administered by the National Suicide Research Foundation. The Cork centre covers Cork city and the counties of Cork and Kerry, while the Limerick centre covers Limerick city and the counties of Limerick, Clare and North Tipperary.

The Cork centre is in the south-west of Ireland and constitutes 18% of the country in terms of area. With a population of 546,640, it makes up approximately 15% of the Irish population. Just over half of these people live in urban settings, mostly in the city of Cork and its suburbs and satellite towns. The Limerick centre lies just to the north of Cork and constitutes 11% of the country's area. Nine per cent of the population of Ireland live in the area (population 317,069). Unlike Cork, the majority of the population in the Limerick catchment area live in rural settings. For the purposes of this chapter, the two centres will be considered as one catchment area. This area makes up almost 30% of the country geographically and contains almost one quarter of the Irish population (863,709), half of whom live in urban settings.

Sample and method of data collection

Statistics on suicide in Ireland are compiled by the Central Statistics Office (CSO). The information given to the CSO is confidential and may only be used for statistical purposes.

For this study, data relating to all Irish suicides occurring between the years 1976 and 1997 have been obtained. Where rates are calculated relating to suicide they have been age-adjusted to the European Standard Population (Waterhouse et al., 1976). Due to the relatively small population base in Ireland, current trends have been illustrated through the analysis of suicide data from the five most recent years available, i.e. 1993 through 1997.

Monitoring of attempted suicide as defined by the Working Group of the WHO/ Euro Multicentre Study (Platt et al., 1992), began on 1 January, 1995 for the Cork centre and on 1 July, 1995 for the Limerick centre, and continued in each centre through to 31 December, 1997. To counter the fact that data collection commenced six months later in the Limerick centre than in Cork, data from the first six months in Limerick was weighted by a multiple of two. Therefore, the study period for the two centres can be considered to be the three calendar years, 1995, 1996 and 1997. In any case, where relevant, average annual person-based rates age-adjusted to the European Standard Population (Waterhouse et al., 1976) are calculated.

Since 1 January, 1998, the Irish centres have continued to collect data on attempted suicide using a minimum data set. When the results of a survey of GPs in the Cork region indicated that in excess of 90% of suicide attempts encountered by GPs were referred to either a general accident and emergency department or psychiatric hospital (Fitzsimons et al., 1997), it was decided that the monitoring of attempted suicide would be solely based on hospital-treated cases. General hospitals with accident and emergency room facilities, psychiatric hospitals and prisons were included in the monitoring study.

At each of the two centres, dedicated data collectors were appointed. They would pay regular visits to the general hospitals checking through all entries in the casualty book (which logs every attendance at the general hospital's accident and emergency department) and identifying possible cases of attempted suicide. All monitoring forms were brought to the National Suicide Research Foundation where they were entered manually into prepared data files using the Statistical Package for Social Sciences (SPSS). Data analysis was carried out using SPSS. Population data was derived from the national census conducted in 1996.

Results

Suicide

Ireland has experienced a sharp and steady rise in male suicide over the past two decades (Figure 1). While the actual number of male suicides has quadrupled over the past twenty years, the age-adjusted rate has exhibited a 200% increase between 1977 and 1997 (from approximately 7 to 22 per 100,000).

Across this time period, the female rate has remained virtually unchanged at approximately 4.5 per 100,000. As a consequence, the male/female ratio has more than doubled so that now an Irish man is more than four times as likely to die by suicide than his female counterpart. While not shown here, the most striking rise in male suicide has occurred for those aged 15 to 24 years. Irish women in this age group have also shown a rise in suicide in recent years, albeit from a very low base rate. However, in terms of the deaths registered in Ireland in 1998 and 1999, suicide was the leading cause of death in 15-24 year-olds exceeding road traffic accident deaths for the first time.

Figure 2 illustrates the average annual age-specific suicide rates per 100,000 for Irish men and women based on suicide data from 1993 through 1997, a period in which there were 1,588 male and 385 female suicides. Immediately, a sharp contrast can be seen between the genders.

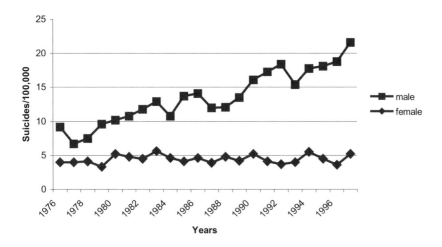

Figure 1. Suicide in Ireland, 1976-1997

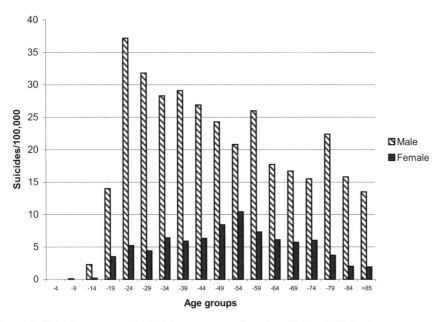

Figure 2. Suicide rates per 100,000 in age groups (based on 1993 –1997 data)

For all ages, the male suicide rate far exceeds the female rate. This contrast is most pronounced in the younger age groups where the risk of suicide is seven times higher for men than it is for women. When previous work by the National Suicide Research Foundation, based on suicide data for the years 1988-1992 had shown a sex ratio (m/f) among the young of 7:1, it was found to be the highest sex ratio of any country reporting suicide figures to the World Health Organisation (Kelleher, 1998).

Traditionally, as is still the case in many European countries, the highest rate of male suicide in Ireland was among the elderly. Now men aged 20-24 years constitute the high risk group. With increasing age, the rate of male suicide falls gradually with the exceptions of slight peaks for the 55-59 and 75-79 year age groups. The suicide rate for women is relatively low across all age groups. The pattern shows a steady rise in rate with increasing age, peaking for the 50-54 year age group before falling gradually across the older groups.

The methods employed differ significantly by gender ($\chi^2 = 91.5$, df = 4, p < 0.001). Specifically, women are most likely to choose drowning (38%) and poisoning (28%) whereas hanging is the commonest method used by men. For both genders, choice of method is significantly associated with age (Male $\chi^2 = 111.7$, df = 8, p < 0.001; Female $\chi^2 = 63.1$, df = 8, p < 0.001). With men and women, hanging is less common with increasing age while the reverse is true with regard to drowning. It is also noteworthy that the use of guns has recently become the second commonest method of suicide for young men.

Table 1. Method of suicide in Ireland by age and gender, 1993-1997

		Under 30 years		30-54 years		Over 55 years		All ages	
		n	%	n	%	n	%	n	%
Male	Hanging	299	(51)	272	(39)	112	(37)	683	(43)
	Drowning	91	(15)	170	(24)	105	(35)	266	(23)
	Poisoning	66	(11)	168	(24)	48	(16)	282	(18)
	Guns	99	(17)	47	(7)	25	(8)	171	(11)
	Other	33	(6)	42	(6)	11	(4)	86	(5)
Female	Hanging	43	(44)	36	(19)	13	(13)	92	(24)
	Drowning	15	(15)	69	(37)	62	(63)	146	(38)
	Poisoning	28	(29)	62	(33)	19	(19)	109	(28)
	Guns	6	(6)	6	(3)	1	(1)	13	(3)
	Other	5	(5)	16	(8)	4	(4)	25	(6)

The suicide rates of single and widowed men are approximately three times higher than the rate for ever-married men which supports the previous finding that marriage is protective of men. Single women are currently three times more likely to die by suicide than ever-married and widowed women.

Attempted suicide

A total of 4,669 episodes of hospital-treated attempted suicide were registered as part of the monitoring study over the period 1995-1997, an average of 1,556 episodes per year. Just under half of the attempts were by men (2,207, 47%) while 2,462 (53%) were by women. In total, there were 3,500 persons involved, 1,613 (46%) men and 1,887 (54%) women. The average annual person-based age-specific suicide attempt rates per 100,000 for men and women of the Irish catchment area are given in Figure 3.

The pattern is similar for both genders in that the rate is at its highest for those aged 15-24 years, although this is much more pronounced for the females, and the rate decreases with age. With the exception of the young group where the female rate is far in excess of the male, the men and women exhibit similar rates of attempted suicide. The male and female European age-standardised rate (aged over 15 years) is 166 and 194 per 100,000, respectively. The equivalent crude rate for men and women is 180 and 206 per 100,000, respectively.

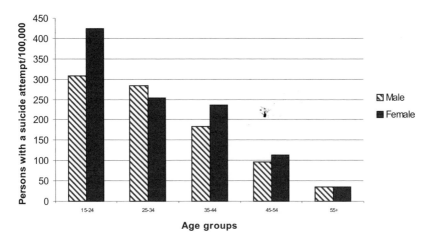

Figure 3. Attempted suicide rates in age groups

Based on calendar year, the mean annual number of persons treated following a suicide attempt was 1,273. With an average of 1,556 episodes per year, this yields an annual person/event ratio of 1:1.22. The annual male and female person/event ratios were 1:1.24 and 1:1.20, respectively, which indicates a higher level of repetition for men. Over the three years of the study period, 20% of the men were treated for a repeat suicide attempt. This is significantly higher than the 16% level of repetition in the women ($\chi^2 = 9.2$, df = 1, p = 0.002).

For 85% of the episodes registered during the study period, information as to whether the individual had made a previous suicide attempt, whether medically treated or not, was recorded. Based on persons monitored during a calendar year, 45% of the men and 42% of the women had made at least one previous attempt at suicide. This reduced to 20% of the men and 17% of the women when only attempts within the previous 12 months were considered.

Repetition within 12 months of an act was examined for those treated following a suicide attempt during 1995 and 1996, i.e. those for whom the study period extended for at least 12 months after their act. Twenty-seven per cent of the male episodes and 25% of the female episodes were followed by a repeat act within 12 months. When only the index acts during each of the years 1995 and 1996 were analyzed it was found that 19% of the men and 17% of the women had repeated within 12 months. The higher levels of repetition indicated by the episode-based analysis are due to the presence of a small minority of multiple repeaters.

To investigate the relationship between previous and future suicide attempts, all episodes registered during 1995 and 1996 were crosstabulated based on whether there had been a previous attempt and whether a further attempt was made in the following 12 months. The results are summarised for male and female episodes in Table 2.

Table 2. Percentage of male and female suicide attempts followed by a repeat attempt within 12 months, stratified by previous history of attempted suicide

	Male	Female
No previous suicide attempt	12%	7%
Previous attempt within past 12 months	51%	54%
Previous attempt more than 12 months ago	34%	27%
Previous attempt, date unknown	16%	16%

For both genders, there is a highly significant association between past and future suicide attempts (Male $\chi^2 = 185.2$, df = 3, p < 0.001; Female $\chi^2 = 314.2$, df = 3, p < 0.001). For male and female suicide attempters, where there is no history of previous attempts, the chance of repeating the attempt within the following 12 months is 12% and 7%, respectively. In contrast, a repeated attempt will occur in approximately half of all cases where there has been an attempt within the previous 12 months. One third and one quarter of male and female acts, respectively, result in repetition if the most recent attempt occurred more than a year ago. This indicates that the proximity of the previous suicide attempt affects the likelihood of repetition.

The methods of attempted suicide are quite different to those of suicide. A high proportion of suicide attempts involved a combination of methods. Overdose of medication was by far the most common method, used in two-thirds of male episodes and over 80% of female suicide attempts. Alcohol, albeit in combination with another method, was involved in one in three male episodes and one-quarter of female episodes. The only other common method is cutting which accounted for one in four male episodes compared to one in seven for females. Some of the more lethal methods are included in the other category, for example, hanging, drowning and jumping from a height.

Epidemiological findings

General results

Of all the cases of attempted suicide treated by the hospitals, less than two per cent were by people who were resident outside of the catchment area at the time. Information relating to nationality is not collected routinely within the accident and emergency departments of Irish general hospitals. However, it was noted that less than two per cent of the individuals in the monitoring study were of a nationality other than Irish, although this is likely to be an underestimate. As expected the vast majority of non-nationals treated following a suicide attempt were British.

While the monitoring study recognises people who are legally cohabiting as a separate category, the Irish census does not provide any relevant population data. This group made up three per cent of those monitored in the Irish centres. In the calculation of rates, they were counted within the single category which would have been the case for the majority. There is wide variation in the rates of attempted suicide when examined by marital status. For both genders, the lowest rate is for married people whereas those who are separated are at highest risk. In fact, the male and female rates for separated people are more than four times higher than for the general population.

The availability of population data dictated that only crude rates of attempted suicide could be calculated by household composition. Furthermore, rates could not be calculated for some of the types of household composition recorded in the monitoring study. These included: 'living with parents', 'living with friends/other relatives' and 'living in an institution'. As one would expect from their young age profile, the suicide attempters were most commonly living with parents (43%). Data were missing for 7% of individuals. Compared with the crude rates of 180 and 206 per 100,000 for the general population of men and women, respectively, men living alone and women living alone with children appear at increased risk of attempted suicide. Those living with partner, whether with children or not, have the lowest risk of attempted suicide. This is particularly so for the men as their rates are half that of the general population.

The relevant population data on education are only available for those who have ceased their education and therefore students were excluded from the analysis. Data were missing for 39% of individuals. This high proportion of missing data is due to the fact that level of education is not commonly recorded in hospital records. Our data indicate that the higher the level of education attained, the lower the risk of attempted suicide. Individuals whose education reached a medium or high level exhibit lower than average rates; in particular, highly educated men seem to be protected. The rate of attempted suicide among people with a low level of education is more than four times that of the general population. Women within this group appear to be at especially high risk.

Among the economically active there is a sharp contrast in rates between those in work and out of work. The rate among the employed, particularly among employed males, is low, approximately half that of the general population. The unemployed, on the other hand, have rates that indicate that their risk of attempted suicide is more than seven times higher than among the employed. Unemployed women are particularly at high risk with average annual rates of approximately one per cent. The economically inactive category represents a heterogenous group including students, retired people, people working in the home and those unable to work due to illness or disability. The rate among the males is over 60% higher than that of the general population and three times higher than the employed whereas women in the economically inactive group do not show an increased rate of attempted suicide. The composition of the male and female populations in this group would be different in that a significant proportion of the women would be housewives. This may be a low risk group which would go someway to explaining the differential rates.

Conclusion

This chapter has illustrated that Ireland has experienced a sharp and steady rise in male suicide over the past two decades. This has resulted in a stark contrast between the genders in relation to suicide. In recent years, the risk of suicide in Irish men has been more than four times higher than their female counterparts. Among the young where the rise in male suicide has been most striking, the sex ratio (m/f) is 7:1. In general, the hypotheses that have been suggested to explain these trends in Irish suicide have related to the rapid social change that the country has experienced (Kelleher, 1998). Religious practice has declined, there has been significant urbanisation with an economic boom and a resultant move away from what was the mainstay of the Irish economy, farming. Many of the changes relate to the family. These include falling marriage rates and increased numbers of births outside of marriage. Particularly related to the young would be the increased availability of illicit drugs and misuse of alcohol. While more research work is required in order to test the various hypotheses, it is heartening that many initiatives are now being undertaken to address suicide prevention.

The rates of attempted suicide for the Irish centres are not exceptional when compared to those of the other centres in the WHO/Euro Multicentre Study. The finding that Irish men and women have almost equal rates of attempted suicide is unusual given that previously, all centres, with the exception of Helsinki, found the female rate to be far higher. High levels of repetition have been shown by the Irish data. This has provided some of the motivation for a large-scale intervention study which is currently being piloted in the two Irish centres. The intervention study aims to test the efficacy of interpersonal problem solving therapy in reducing rates of repeated attempted suicide. If found to be successful, it is planned to introduce the therapy as an additional health service for suicide attempters.

The characteristics of suicide attempters in Ireland indicate that they are socially deprived. In particular, being separated, living alone (for men), living alone with children (for women), having a low level of education and being unemployed have all been shown to be associated with increased rates of attempted suicide. While further work is required to more fully understand the association between social deprivation and attempted suicide, these findings may be indicating that broader approaches aimed at tackling social inequality and deprivation may have a positive effect in reducing levels of attempted suicide.

Acknowledgements

The work of the National Suicide Research Foundation has been made possible through the support of the Irish Government's Department of Health and Children, the Southern and Mid-Western Health Boards and a Unit Grant from the Irish Health Research Board. We would also like to acknowledge the many hospital, health board and prison personnel who have facilitated and supported the parasuicide monitoring study. We would further like to thank the Vital Statistics Department of the Irish Central Statistics Office for the provision of the suicide data and their on-going assistance.

References

Fitzsimons MM, Kelleher MJ, Keeley HS, Corcoran P, Byrne S, Williamson E, Burke U (1997). Attempted suicide in general practice: A pilot study. *Irish Medical Journal*, 90(5): 190-192.

Kelleher MJ (1998). Trends in youth suicide in Ireland. *British Journal of Psychiatry*, 173: 196-197.

Platt S, Bille-Brahe U, Kerkhof A, Schmidtke A, Bjerke T, Crepet P, DeLeo D, Haring C, Lönnqvist J, Michel K, Philippe A, Pommereau X, Querejeta I, Salander Renberg E, Temesvary B, Wasserman D, Sampaio Faria J (1992). Attempted suicide in Europe: The WHO/Euro Multicentre Study of Attempted suicide. I. Introduction and preliminary analysis for 1989. *Acta Psychiatrica Scandinavica*, 85: 97-104.

Waterhouse et al. (eds.) (1976). *Cancer incidence in five continents.* Lyon: IARC.

Chapter 11

Suicidal Behaviour in Belgium

C. van Heeringen, T. Meerschaert & N. Braeckman

Description of the catchment area

Gent city is the capital of the province East-Flanders, situated in the north-east of Belgium. The Gent catchment area comprises Gent City (111,402 inhabitants) and 14 suburbs (112,407 inhabitants), and covers about 156 km². The average population density is 1,435 inhabitants per km². In 1998, 48.5% of the residents were males, and 51.5% females. Seven percent of the population in the catchment area are of an ethnic minority group, approximately half of them being Turks.

Sample and method of data collection

There are no nation- or region wide data on attempted suicide in Belgium or Flanders, respectively. Since 1987, attempted suicides have been monitored at the Emergency Department of the Gent University Hospital. Since 1996, data from the ongoing monitoring study are included in the WHO/Euro Multicentre Study of Suicidal Behaviour.

Information on attempted suicide in the Gent catchment area is based on data collected in six general hospitals, three psychiatric clinics, a crisis intervention centre and the prison. Additionally, 51 general practitioners (from a total of 288 general practitioners in the catchment area) monitored suicide attempts seen in their practice. All general and psychiatric hospitals in the area agreed to participate in the study.

By means of estimation factors the actual number of attempted suicide episodes is approximated. For the general practitioners, the estimation factor was defined by dividing the total number of general practitioners by the number of general practitioners participating in the monitoring study. The estimation factor for the general hospitals is calculated by dividing the exact number of suicide attempts (defined by means of a monthly quality control in the general hospitals by checking the admission books for attempted suicides) by the number of attempts for which a registration form was filled in.

Results

Suicide

Comparative epidemiological studies on the occurrence of suicide have shown relatively high rates in Belgium (Cantor, 2000). In 1997, for instance, suicide rates for Flanders (the Dutch-speaking part of Belgium) were 26.4 per 100,000 for males and 9.6 per 100,000 for females (Min. Vl. Gemeenschap, 2000).

Suicidal behaviour represents an important mental health problem in Flanders, as suicide rates for males and females are high when compared to other European countries. In 1997, suicide was the major external cause of death for Flemish males, while suicide was the second external cause of death among females.

An analysis of the evolution of suicide rates over time shows that, after a small decrease of male suicide rates during the end of the eighties and the early nineties, the rates have been increasing since 1993. The female suicide rates decreased during the eighties and stablised during the nineties.

Attempted suicide

As shown in Table 1, the event-based number of monitored suicide attempts decreased between 1996 and 1998 from 764 to 584 per 100,000. Person-based annual attempted suicide rates decreased during the same period from 356 to 256 per 100,000.

Table 1. Number of suicide attempts (events), number of attempters (persons), ratio and rate per 100,000 inhabitants (aged 15+)

	Males			Females			Total		
	1996	1997	1998	1996	1997	1998	1996	1997	1998
Events	373	334	218	391	360	366	764	694	584
Persons	322	289	198	352	306	302	674	595	500
Ratio	1.16	1.15	1.10	1.11	1.18	1.21	1.13	1.16	1.17
Rate per 100,000 inhabitants	355	320	219	356	311	308	356	315	265

The decrease in rates was found among males and females, though more pronounced among males. While rates among males and females were approximately similar in 1996, female rates were substantially higher than male rates in 1998. Notable is the gender-specific difference in the change in the event to person ratios during the study period, the ratio decreasing among males and increasing among females.

All suicide attempts referred to the Gent University Hospital have been monitored since 1987. By extrapolating the number of referred attempts to the total number of suicide attempts in the Gent catchment area, they can be compared to the number of suicide attempts obtained by the WHO/Euro Multicentre Study.

As shown in Figure 1, attempted suicide rates increased during the early 1990s following a decrease during the end of the 1980s. Since 1995, rates have decreased for both sexes, except for in 1998, where the female rate increased compared to 1997.

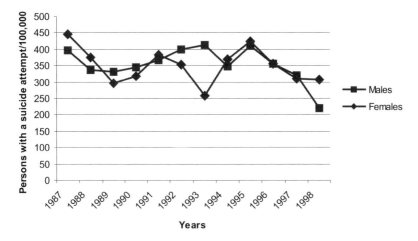

Figure 1. Person-based attempted suicide rates per 100,000 inhabitants (age +15 years) for the Gent catchment area

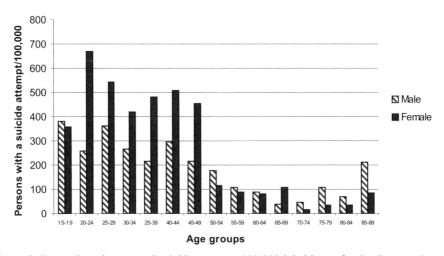

Figure 2. Person-based attempted suicide rates per 100,000 inhabitants for the Gent catchment area by age and gender for 1998

A strong effect of gender on the occurrence of attempted suicide becomes apparent from the monitoring data, as in 1998, 39% of attempted suicide patients were men and 61% women. The mean age of suicide attempters was 36.2 years in 1998. The mean age among men (M=37.0; SD=15.17) was non-significantly higher than that among women (M=35.7; SD=13.09; t=0.964; df=482; p=0.336).

The highest suicide attempt rates were found among young people, that is 671 per 100,000 for women in the age category 20-24 and 379 per 100,000 for men aged between 15 and 19 (Figure 2). Under the age of 50 years, the female rates for attempted suicide were higher than the rates for men, whereas from the age of 50 years and on, male rates were higher (except for the age group 65-69).

Epidemiological findings

General results

A majority of the suicide attempters who were referred in 1998, had never been married (41.2%), while 30.9% were married or legally cohabiting, 24% were divorced and 3.9% were widowed. The majority of the attempters (64.8%) did not live together with a partner at the time of the suicide attempt. No significant difference was found between men and women ($\chi^2 = 0.708$; df = 2 ; p = 0.702).

Only a minority of the suicide attempters (17.2%) had finished higher education, and 82.7% had finished elementary or secondary school. Again, no significant difference was found between males and females ($\chi^2 = 2.245$; df = 2 ; p = 0.325).

In 1998, approximately half of the attempters (49.8%) were economically inactive (student, housewife, disabled or retired), while 29.6% were employed and 20.5% were unemployed. There was no significant difference between males and females regarding socio-economic status ($\chi^2 = 4.875$; df = 2; p = 0.087). In 1998, 96.7% of the referred suicide attempters were of Belgian nationality.

The most commonly used method (86.7%) for suicide attempts was self-poisoning by medication, alcohol, pesticides and/or vapours. More than one method was used by 38.4% of the suicide attempters.

A majority of attempted suicide patients (69.6%) were referred for hospitalisation, while 15.6% were referred to an ambulatory treatment setting, and 14.8% were not referred. There was no significant difference in referral patterns between male and female suicide attempters ($\chi^2 = 4.087$; df = 3; p = 0.252).

In 63.8% of the cases, the index attempt was the first suicide attempt, while 17.9%

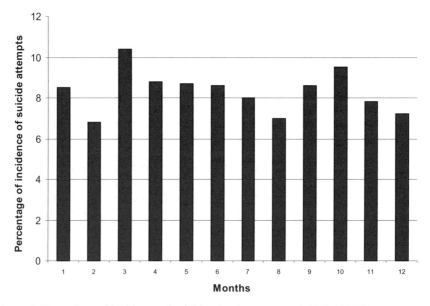

Figure 3. Percentage of incidence of suicide attemtps per month (1996-1998)

reported a history of one previous suicide attempt. In 18.3% of the patients the current suicide attempt was preceded by two or more attempts.

Figure 3 shows the proportional distribution of the mean number of referred suicide attempts per month during the study period 1996-1998. Two peaks can be discerned, i.e. one in March and one in October. During the months of February, August and December, numbers of referred suicide attempts were comparatively lower.

Conclusion

Several conclusions may be drawn from the results of the epidemiological study of the occurrence of attempted suicide in the Gent region in the period between 1 January 1996 and 31 December 1998. Firstly, annual person-based rates of attempted suicide decreased gradually during the study period from 365 in 1996 to 265 per 100,000 in-habitants in 1998. However, when compared to other European centres attempted sui-cide rates remain high in Gent (van Heeringen et al., 1999). Secondly, gender appears to have an effect on the change in rates, evidenced by a decrease in male rates com-pared to female. The notable decrease in rates among females, which started in 1995, has apparently become less striking. Thirdly, there is a clear association with sociodemographic variables, such as age, marital status, living situation, educational level, and socio-economic status. Fourthly, a majority of suicide attempters were re-ferred for inpatient care following their attempt, while a smaller proportion were re-ferred to outpatient care. Approximately 16% were not referred to treatment, mainly because patients decided to leave the hospital before an appointment could be made with a doctor.

References

Min. Vl. Gemeenschap. (2000). Vlaamse regionale indicatoren 99. Brussel: Ministerie van de Vlaamse Gemeenschap.

Cantor CH (2000). Suicide in the Western World. In K Hawton and C van Heeringen (Eds.) *The international handbook of suicide and attempted suicide,* pp. 9-28. Chichester: Wiley.

Van Heeringen C, Meerschaert Th, Berckmoes A (1999). Attempted suicide in Gent : results from the Who/Euro Multicentre Study on Attempted suicide in 1996. *Archives of Public Health*, 57: 171-184.

Chapter 12

Suicidal Behaviour in Austria

D. Dunkel, E. Antretter, R. Seibl & C. Haring

Description of the catchment area

The Austrian catchment area is located in the centre of the Tyrol. The catchment area consists of the two administrative districts Innsbruck/City and Innsbruck/County. Approximately 250,000 inhabitants live in the catchment area (242,586 inhabitants; last population census 2001); the population of the catchment area comprises more than one third of the total Tyrolean population. The population density equals 1,126 (Innsbruck/City) and 71 (Innsbruck/County) inhabitants per square kilometre (last census 1991). Compared to other Austrian cities with more than 100,000 inhabitants, the population density is lower for Innsbruck/City.

Sample and method of data collection

National suicide data were obtained by the National Bureau of Statistics. For the catchment area, records of completed suicides were obtained from the local police office responsible for the districts of Innsbruck/City and Innsbruck/County.

Episodes of attempted suicide were sampled from the Psychiatric State Hospital Hall and the Psychiatric University Hospital Innsbruck. All medical records from 1989 to 1998 were systematically scrutinised. For the year 1994 it was not possible to obtain all relevant information due to changes in the co-operating staff responsible for carrying out the monitoring study. Hence, reported rates of attempted suicide for 1994 are too low. We assume approximate "true" rates for 1994 are roughly 20% higher (based on comparison with the material from the other years) than those reported in this article. However, reporting the estimated "true" rate would not have changed the overall pattern in attempted suicide rates for the period of observation (i.e. a decline of rates from 1993 to 1994). Except for the year 1994, the coverage of all attempted suicide events admitted to both clinics comes close to 100%.

Results

Suicide

The suicide rates adjusted for gender and age groups are presented in figure 1. For adolescents and young adults (aged 15 to 24 years) the mean male suicide rate was 18.0 per 100,000 (median = 17.6), whereas the female suicide rate showed a mean of 5.1 per 100,000 (median = 5.0). Tests on linear trends with time (Spearman rank correlation with exact permutation tests) were found to be non-significant (male suicide rate: r = 0.45, female suicide rate: r = -0.08).

In adults (aged 25 to 54 years) the mean suicide rates were 33.3 (median = 32.3) for males, and 13.5 (median = 12.7) for females. Trend tests revealed non-significant linear associations between suicide rates and time in this age group (male suicide rate: r = 0.27; female suicide rate: r = 0.36).

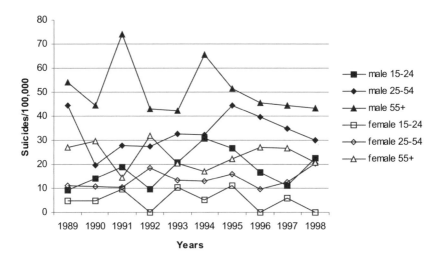

Figure 1. Rates of suicide per 100,000 by age and gender, 1989-1998

For adults aged 55 years or more, the highest mean suicide rates compared to the two other age groups were found for both males (m = 50.8, median = 45.1) and females (m = 23.6, median = 24.3). Tests on linear trends with time did not indicate a trend (males suicide rate: r = -0.21; female suicide rate: r = -0.18).

Attempted suicide

All event-based attempted suicide rates were tested on first order serial correlation with a permutation procedure to determine whether attempted suicide rates were severely influenced by repeated self-harm episodes of the same persons. All tests yielded non-significant results (Type-I error was set to $p < .05$).

Mean event-based rates of attempted suicide in adolescents and young adults (aged 15 to 24 years) of m = 152.5 (median = 157.3) for males, and of m = 177.6 (median = 146.1) for females were found for the Austrian catchment area. Trend tests yielded a significant result for an increasing male rate of attempted suicide in this age group (males: r = 0.61, p < .05, one-sided; females: r = -0.30).

In adults (aged 25 to 54 years) a mean attempted suicide rate for males of 152.4 (median = 149.9) was found, whereas the mean female attempted suicide rate was slightly higher (m = 168.7, median = 155.8). Permutation tests indicated random variations of the association of rates and time (male attempted suicide rate: r = 0.50; female attempted suicide rate: r = -0.03).

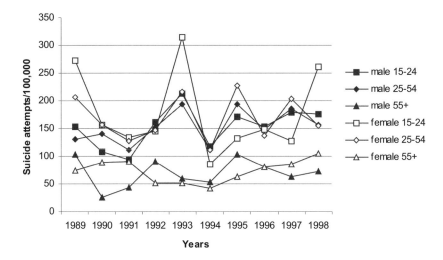

Figure 2. Rates of attempted suicide per 100,000 by age and gender, 1989-1998

For adults aged 55 or more, mean attempted suicide rates for both males and females were of a similar magnitude (males: m = 69.4, median = 67.6; females: m = 73.4, median = 77.8). For both genders linear associations of rates with time were found to be non-significant in this age group (male rate: r = 0.12; female rate: r = 0.15).

Epidemiological findings

General results

Correlation analysis (Spearman rank correlation with exact permutation tests, two-sided) of the association between attempted suicide rates and suicide rates (gender and age specific comparisons) did not yield any statistically significant result. Highest correlations were found for both males and females in the age group from 25 to 54 years.

(15-24-years-old males: r = 0.08, p > .05; females: r = -.25, p > 0.5; 25-54-years-old males: r = .36, p > .05; females: r = .30, p > .05; 55 years and more – males: r = -.07, p > .05;females: r = .02, p > .05).

All recorded 3,013 attempted suicide events within the observation period from 1989 to 1998 were systematically compared with the local suicide register for the same period. Results showed that 43 cases in the monitoring study committed suicide before the end of 1998. This equals a suicide rate of 2.0% of all cases (n = 2,151 cases; ratio episodes to cases = 1.4).

Due to limitations of space the following presentation of comparative results concerning suicide completers and non-completers will be restricted to the minimum. It is important to mention that for some comparisons, results are based on the total number of episodes for both suicides and non-suicides (i.e. when variables are presented that allowed for multiple category memberships of a person like diagnosis or methods). Person-based percentages will be reported for variables that could have changed over time but allowed for only one exclusive category membership of a person at a specific point in time (i. e. economic activity and marital status). Psychiatric diagnoses and methods used for attempted suicide will be reported for the percentage of episodes that the attribute was present due to the fact that a single episode could comprise more than one diagnosis or method.

Group differences (groups based on the number of cases) on interval scaled variables were tested with the non-parametric Mann-Whitney U-Test because assumptions concerning the applicability of a parametric analysis of variance (or t-test) were clearly violated on theoretical and/or empirical grounds (normal distribution, equal group sizes, homogeneity of variances). If not indicated otherwise, the following data refer to the index event.

The male and female proportions in both groups of suicidal persons were found to be nearly the same (non-suicide group: males = 46.5% (n = 981), females = 53.5% (n = 1127); suicide group: males = 48.8% (n = 21), females = 51.2% (n = 22)). Thus, 2.1% of males and 1.9% of females had committed suicide in our sample.

With regard to the educational background a tendency towards higher educational degrees was observed for the group of completed suicides (non-suicide group: highest educational level = 6.5%; suicide group: highest educational level = 20.9%).

Results concerning marital status depict a familiar picture: a higher proportion of divorced or widowed persons were observed among completed suicides (non-suicide group: divorced/widowed = 13.0%; suicide group = 23.3%). Hence, both variables also reflect the higher mean age of those who committed suicide (age figures refer to the last observation available; non-suicide group: m = 38.9, median = 35; suicide group: m = 46.3, median = 43). Only for female suicides could a significantly higher mean age be confirmed (female non-suicide group: m = 39.7, median = 36.0; suicide group: m = 48.3, median = 46.5, p < .01-male non-suicide group: m = 37.9, median = 34; male suicide group: m = 44.2, median = 40.0, p > .05). Furthermore, a considerably higher proportion of married persons were observed in the group of completed suicides (non-suicide group: 25.4%; suicide group: 37.2%). Similar results were obtained for the present living situation. The proportion of persons living alone was more than twice as high in the suicide group than in the group of "survivors" (non-suicide group: living alone = 18.0%; suicide group: living alone = 39.5%). In accordance with the results found for marital status, in the suicide group the proportion of persons living with a partner was found to be considerably higher than in the non-suicide group (non-suicide group: 28.8%; suicide group: 44.2%). Results also indicated that living in an institution might protect against completing suicide (non-suicide group: living in institution = 10.2%; suicide group: living in institution = 0.0%).

Economic activity appears to be related to suicide in a way that persons who committed suicide were older and, thus, were more often retired than those who did not commit suicide (non-suicide group: economically inactive = 27.3%; suicide group: economically inactive = 39.5%). It should also be pointed out that the previously discussed differences between both groups should be interpreted in the light of considerable missing value rates on all mentioned sociodemographic variables (average 25%).

Gender specific analyses of non-completers and suicide completers on sociodemographic variables were performed in order to give a more precise description. Contingency table analysis was performed, applying Fisher's exact test due to expected frequencies lower than 5. Considering possible distortions of results induced by missing data, we first compared the results of analyses including missing data with the results based on the complete data (missing data excluded). The findings did not support contrary conclusions if missing data were not considered in the analyses. Therefore, we will present the results based on the complete data set.

For male suicide completers, a tendency to possess higher educational degrees was observed ($p < .05$, $n_1 = 648$ [non-completers], $n_2 = 18$ [suicide completers]). For females no significant difference concerning educational level was found ($n_1 = 726$, $n_2 = 18$). Contrary to what was expected, male suicide completers were more often married and less often divorced or widowed, however, the distribution did not deviate from that expected under random conditions ($n_1 = 732$, $n_2 = 21$). Contrary to males, female suicide completers were significantly more often divorced or widowed than female non-completers ($p < .05$, $n_1 = 875$, $n_2 = 22$). A slightly different picture was revealed for the present living situation. Male suicide completers significantly more often lived alone or lived with a partner than the male non-completers ($p < .001$, $n_1 = 693$, $n_2 = 20$). None of the male suicide completers lived in an institution at the time of suicide. Similarly, female suicide completers were more frequently living alone than the female non-completers ($p < .05$, $n_1 = 839$, $n_2 = 22$). Also, none of the female suicide completers lived in an institution. Economic activity did not differentiate between male suicide completers and non-completers ($n_1 = 794$, $n_2 = 21$), whereas female suicide completers were less often economically active and more often economically inactive than expected ($p < .001$, $n_1 = 1126$, $n_2 = 22$).

Another finding that deserves special attention relates to the fact that on average, suicides were committed only two years after the index suicide attempt. Furthermore, the median age of suicide completers was 42 years when they joined the study, whereas the median age increased only to 43 years at the date of the suicide. This result indicates that at least 50% of suicides were committed within one year after the last recorded suicide attempt. This result remained stable after controlling for gender. For both women and men, the mean rank observational period for suicide completers was significantly lower than for non-completers (female non-suicide group: $m = 1752$ [days], median = 1751; suicide group: $m = 907$, median = 426, $p < .001$-male non-suicide group: $m = 1684$, median = 1612; male suicide group: $m = 557$, median = 278, $p < .001$).

Another risk factor for completed suicide refers to the number of previous attempted suicide acts. Suicide completers in our sample showed higher mean rates of previous deliberate self-harm acts (before 1989) compared to non-completers (non-suicide group: m = 0.29, median = 0.0; suicide group: m = 0.72, median = 0.0, p > .05). However, the significant difference between the non-suicide group and the suicide group is exclusively attributable to previous suicide attempts among women (female non-suicide group: m = 0.29, median = 0.0; female suicide group: m = 1.23, median = 0.0, p < .01 – male non-suicide group: m = 0.30, median = 0.0; male suicide group: m = 0.19, median = 0.0, p > .05).

The same was true for the repetition rates within the observation period between 1989 and 1998. On the average, suicide completers had more often repeated self-harm acts than non-completers (non-suicide group: m = 0.40, median = 0.0; suicide group: m = 0.63, median = 0.0, p < .05). Gender specific analysis showed that the difference in repetition rates was due to the number of female repetitions in the suicide group (female non-suicide group: m = 0.40, median = 0.0; female suicide group: m = 0.86, median = 0.0, p < .01-male non-suicide group: m = 0.39, median = 0.0; male suicide group: m = 0.38, median = 0.0, p > .05). Consequently, the group of suicide completers showed a higher mean of total attempted suicide events than the group of non-completers (non-suicide group: m = 1.69, median = 1.0; suicide group: m = 2.35, median = 1.0, p < .05), although the difference is completely accounted for by female attempted suicide events in the group of completed suicides (female non-suicide group: m = 1.70, median = 1.0; female suicide group: m = 3.10, median = 3.0, p < .001-male non-suicide group: m = 1.69, median = 1.0; male suicide group: m = 1.57, median = 1.0, p > .05). However, due to the extremely different sample sizes and the highly skewed distribution of the attempted suicide variable (especially the "floor-effect" of high proportions of non-repeaters) in both groups, means and medians might not be the appropriate parameters for which to describe the central tendency in both groups. Thus, the results should be interpreted with caution.

Psychiatric diagnosis according to the International Classification of Diseases, 10th revision turned out to be a distinguishing variable for at least five psychiatric disorders. Suicide completers exhibited considerably higher proportions of schizophrenia (3.8% [non-completers] vs. 12.9% [suicide]; ICD-10/F20) and other psychotic disorders (2.2% vs. 12.9%; ICD-10/F21-29), whereas for non-completers considerably higher proportions of alcohol abuse and dependence (20.7% vs. 4.3%; ICD-10/F10), depressive episodes (18.4% vs. 11.4%; ICD-10/F32), and maladaptive reactions to stress/adjustment disorders (36.7% vs. 22.9%; ICD-10/F43) were found. In the male suicide group, predominantly higher proportions of schizophrenia (3.2% [non-completers] vs. 6.0% [suicide]), and other psychotic disorders (2.2% vs. 8.0%) were found, whereas male non-completers more often had diagnoses of alcohol abuse/dependence (28.9% vs. 4.0%), polytoxic substance abuse/dependence (16.2% vs. 6.0%), depressive episodes (15.8% vs. 8.0%), and maladaptive stress reactions/adjustment disorders (37.2% vs. 18.0%). Female suicide completers more often had a diagnosis of schizophrenia (4.2% vs. 9.5%), and other psychotic disorders (2.2% vs. 7.9%) were found. Female non-completers revealed higher proportions of alcohol abuse/dependence (13.5% vs. 1.6%), depressive episodes (20.6% vs. 6.3%), and maladaptive stress reactions/adjustment disorders (36.2% vs. 11.1%).

The choice of the method used for suicide attempts and for completed suicide roughly reflects the distinction between "violent" and "non-violent" methods. Non-completers more often preferred the intake of toxic substances (52.9% [non-completers] vs. 38.9% [suicide]) and cutting (21.2% vs. 8.0%), whereas completers more often drowned themselves (2.9% vs. 7.1%), used firearms (0.8% vs. 3.5%), jumped from a high place (5.5% vs. 13.3%), or harmed themselves by exposure to a moving object (2.1% vs. 10.6%). Gender-specific analysis revealed that male suicide completers were characterised by high proportions of gun use (1.2% [non-completers] vs. 8.0% [suicide]), jumping from a high place (5.4% vs. 14.0%), and by exposure to a moving object (3.1% vs. 12.0%). Female suicide completers more often than non-completers strangled (2.0% vs. 6.3%) or drowned themselves (2.9% vs. 12.7%), or jumped from a high place (5.5% vs. 12.7%). Similar to their male counterparts, female suicide completers more often exposed themselves to a moving object (1.3% vs. 9.5%). Hence, male and female suicide completers only differed with regard to the use of firearms, a method more frequently chosen by males than by females (McIntosh, 1992).

Prediction

Contrary to the findings reported for the shorter period from 1989 to 1992 (Schmidtke et al., 1994), a general decrease of attempted suicide rates in the Tyrolean catchment area could not be confirmed for the period from 1989 to 1998. Instead, a moderate, positive and significant association of male attempted suicide rates with time in the youngest age group (15-24 years) was found. Whether this trend is to be regarded as stable however, will depend on evaluation within the next ten years. Changes in attempted suicide rates appear to be influenced by considerable yearly fluctuations. However, patterns of change in our catchment area might be better conceptualised by non-linear models. For adolescents and young adults, almost a five year peak has been observed, beginning with peak rates (relative to the rates for the other years in the catchment area) in 1989, followed by a decline of rates until 1991, and followed then by an increase until 1993. After 1993 a similar overall pattern could be observed, although increases and decreases were more alternating. Nevertheless, for males another peak was reached in 1997 and 1998, whereas for females another peak year was observed only for 1998. Preliminary considerations suggest that it might be worthwhile to investigate cyclical models of the development of attempted suicide rates for the youngest age group.

For attempted suicide rates among adults aged 25 to 54 years an alternating pattern of two year "ups" and "downs" since 1993 was predominantly found. If this pattern remains stable in future years, at least a yearly prediction of increases and decreases appears to be a realistic projection.

A cyclical model of changes in attempted suicide rates might be also appropriate for the group aged 55 years and more. The length of intervals between peak years was roughly the same for males (1989/1995) and females (1991/1998). However, a longer observation period is necessary to confirm this pattern.

In general, it appears that predictions of attempted suicide rates are not possible if linear models of change are applied. Hence, non-linear models, such as local regression models, might be more promising.

Conclusion

The low female to male ratio of attempted suicide rates in the Tyrolean catchment area deserves some consideration. In all age groups, higher male than female rates were found for at least three years. Especially in the youngest age group, a higher attempted suicide rate among males was observed over four consecutive years (1994-1997). Similar higher male attempted suicide rates were only found for Helsinki between 1989-1992 (Schmidtke et al., 1994). Several reasons appear to provide a plausible explanation for this finding. First, the result might reflect random variation due to the relatively small absolute numbers of attempted suicide events in each age group of the catchment area. Hence, a longer observation period is necessary to clarify this issue. Second, there might be a systematic selection bias preferring male admittances to both clinical institutions. For example, it can be speculated that for several reasons, male admittances are more often labelled as due to attempted suicide. However, any reference in the relevant literature that would support such an assumption was not found. Instead, considering the discussion on the gender difference between male and female attempted suicide rates, methodological, institutional and cultural factors, especially cultural expectations concerning male and female behaviour, can be identified as elements that might be responsible for the systematic underreporting of male suicide attempts (Canetto & Sakinofsky, 1998). Third, the fact that males commit more lethal acts of attempted suicide may be reflected in the seriousness of attempts and consequent admissions to hospital. Analysis of the association between gender and lethality of suicide attempt in our sample (based on the total number of events) revealed that males tend to use more lethal methods than females, such as strangulation, firearms, and exposure to moving object/accident, however, the occurrence of more lethal methods appears to be too seldom to significantly influence the rates. In addition, it cannot be decided with regard to toxic substance intake and cutting which of the associated attempted suicide events should be judged as more lethal than the other. Fourth, due to the fact that the male attempted suicide rate in the group aged 15 to 24 years was found to significantly increase within the ten year period, research should focus upon possible sex-role changes and shifting sociocultural conditions which impact upon adolescents' and young adults' socialisation.

The association between attempted suicide and suicide rates in the Tyrolean catchment area has been found to be non-significant in all gender-adjusted age groups. Thus, our results, based on ten years of observation, do not support preliminary results of an association of male rates as reported by Hawton et al. (1998). However, the results of the mentioned authors were calculated with the pooled dataset of all participating centres.

References

Canetto SS & Sakinofsky I (1998). The Gender Paradox in Suicide. *Suicide and LifeThreatening Behavior*, 28(1): 1-23.

Hawton K, Arensman E, Wasserman D, Hulten A, Bille-Brahe U, Bjerke T, Crepet P, Deisenhammer E, Kerkhof A, DeLeo D, Michel K, Ostamo A, Philippe A, Querejeta I, Salander Renberg AE, Schmidtke E, & Temesvary B (1998). Relation between attempted suicide and suicide rates among young people in Europe. *Journal of Epidemiology & Community Health*, 52(3): 191-194.

McIntosh JL (1992). Methods of Suicide. In: RW Maris, AL Berman, JT Maltsberger & RI Yufit (Eds.). *Assessment and Prediction of Suicide.* New York, London: The Guilford Press, 381-397.

Schmidtke A, Bille-Brahe U, DeLeo D, Kerkhof A, Bjerke T, Crepet P, Deisenhammer E, Hawton K, Lönnqvist, J, Michel K, Pommereau X, Querejeta I, Philippe A, Salander Renberg E, Temesvary B, Wasserman D, Samaio-Faria JG, & Weinacker B (1994). Rates and Trends of Attempted Suicide in Europe, 1989-1992. In: AJFM Kerkhof, A Schmidtke, U Bille-Brahe, D DeLeo & J Lönnqvist (Eds.). *Attempted Suicide in Europe. Findings from the Multicentre Study on Parasuicide by the WHO Regional Office for Europe.* Leiden: DSWO Press, 209-229.

Chapter 13

Suicidal Behaviour in England and Wales

K. Hawton, L. Harriss, S. Simkin, E. Bale & A. Bond

Description of the catchment area

Oxford City is in the county of Oxfordshire, which lies roughly in the centre of England at the boundary between Southern England and the Midlands. The county has a total population of approximately 500,000. Oxford City has approximately 120,000 inhabitants, including a large number of students, particularly at Oxford University and the recently established Oxford Brookes University. The city is situated nearly 60 miles north-west of central London.

The trends in attempted suicide in Oxford and characteristics of the patients involved are known to be reasonably representative of those elsewhere in the United Kingdom (e.g. Platt et al., 1988), in spite of the City having two Universities and several other educational establishments. The method of data collection in the general hospital is long-standing and comprehensive.

Sample and method of data collection

The data on suicides in England and Wales for 1989-1999 were supplied by the Office for National Statistics. Data on attempted suicide are based on all episodes of attempted suicide in persons aged 15 years and over presenting to the general hospital from the Oxford City population. The general hospital receives all hospital-referred cases from the city and much of the surrounding area. However, because some patients from the surrounding area go elsewhere and the data collected for the WHO/Euro study are primarily based on rates, the analyses here are restricted to the Oxford City population.

The majority of attempted suicide patients (80-85%) who present to the general hospital are identified because they are referred to the psychiatric service in the Department of Psychological Medicine in the hospital. The remainder are identified through scrutiny of Accident and Emergency (A&E) Department records. During 1989 and 1990 this was achieved by examining log books and since then has been through screening the A&E Department computerised recording system. Patients referred to the psychiatric service receive a detailed psychosocial assessment (Hawton and Catalan, 1987) by specially trained clinical staff (nurses or psychiatrists). Each assessment is discussed in detail with a senior psychiatrist. A range of patient characteristics and clinical items are recorded by the assessors on data sheets which are then coded and the data entered into a computerised data file. A limited amount of information is also obtained from

A&E Department records for patients referred to the hospital but not to the psychiatric service. Each patient is allocated a unique numerical code and each episode has a unique serial number. The identifying information (name, date of birth, address and postcode) of patients is separated from the main data file at the point of data entry in order to ensure that individuals cannot be identified within the database.

It should be noted that for persons who were included in this database because they were resident in Oxford City at the time of a deliberate self harm episode but who subsequently made a repeat attempt while living elsewhere in Oxford District, these subsequent episodes are also included in the database.

The denominators used to calculate rates are based on mid-year population estimates. These are provided by the Office for National Statistics, based on extrapolation and interpolation from Census data. The Census occurs ten-yearly (the last one was in 1991). Migration rates are also taken into account when estimating the annual population figures.

The period examined was 1989-1999. The statistical analyses included χ^2 for examining differences in proportions and χ^2 for trend where the trends under analysis appeared to be linear. The analyses were conducted using EpiInfo.

Results

Suicides in England and Wales

During the study period (1989-1999) the suicide rate in England and Wales in males aged 65+ years declined substantially and there was a smaller decrease in suicides in age group 45-64 years. After a period of substantially increasing rates, data for the period under review showed that the rates in males had levelled off, but with some marked fluctuations.

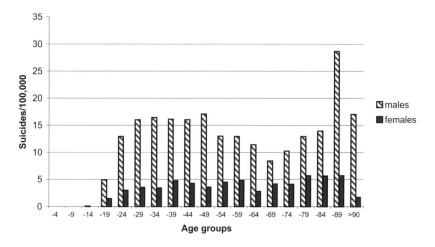

Figure 1. Suicide rates in England and Wales in age groups, 1999

In females, suicide rates in those aged 65+ years and 45-64 years declined markedly, especially during the first part of the study period. Those in 25-44-year-olds also declined somewhat, while those in 15-24-year-olds remained largely stable. As a result of these changes, female suicide rates in 1999 (see Figure 1) showed only a slight increase with age. In males there was a more bimodal distribution, with high rates in 19-49-year-olds, and further high rates in the oldest age groups.

Attempted Suicide

The number of persons presenting to the general hospital following suicide attempts, and the overall number of episodes, are shown for each year during the study period, and for the two sexes and overall, in Table 1. (It should be noted that the data for 1999 are provisional). During the eleven-year study period there were 5,843 episodes involving 4,217 individuals. In females, there were 3,271 episodes by 2,394 individuals; in males there were 2,572 episodes involving 1,823 individuals.

Table 1. Number of suicide attempters (persons) and attempts (episodes), Oxford City, 1989-1999

	1989	1990	1991	1992	1993	1994	1995	1996	1997	1998	1999	Total
Males												
Persons	133	133	139	123	143	171	199	200	208	198	176	1,823
Episodes	164	174	159	155	194	248	303	260	349	296	270	2,572
Females												
Persons	189	181	189	190	171	208	246	235	265	260	260	2,394
Episodes	242	223	217	234	212	285	349	318	398	385	408	3,271
Both sexes												
Persons	322	314	328	313	314	379	445	435	473	458	436	4,217
Episodes	406	397	376	389	406	533	652	578	747	681	678	5,843

The person-based rates of attempted suicide during the study period are shown in table 2 and figure 2. There was some variation in rates over the study period, but there did not appear to be a linear trend; rather, rates increased until 1997, and began to decline during 1998 and 1999. However, the rates towards the end of the study period were considerably higher than those at the beginning of it. The trend for episodes showed a similar pattern. The overall mean annual rate for persons was 338 per 100,000, and for episodes was 467 per 100,000

Table 2. Suicide attempt rates per 100,000 population (persons and episodes), Oxford City, aged 15+ years

	1989	1990	1991	1992	1993	1994	1995	1996	1997	1998	1999	Mean
Persons	295	287	300	285	286	344	398	382	404	384	356	338
Episodes	373	363	343	355	369	483	582	507	638	571	554	467

Comparison of the rates in Oxford with those published for other centres participating in the WHO/Euro Study of Suicidal Behaviour (Platt et al., 1992; Schmidtke et al., 1996) indicate that the Oxford rates have consistently been amongst the highest in Europe.

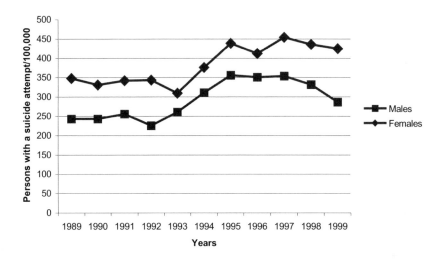

Figure 2. Annual persons-based attempted suicide rates (per 100,000), Oxford 1989-99

The person-based rates of attempted suicide for the individual years 1989-1999 showed a steady increase in males until the mid-1990s, and a reduction in 1998 and 1999 (Table 3 and Figure 2). The rates in females were relatively steady between 1989 and 1993 but increased substantially in both 1994 and 1995. They then remained at a similar elevated rate until the end of the study period. The mean rate (per 100,000) during the study period for females aged 15 years+ was 383 and for males was 293. The female-to-male rate-ratio decreased markedly between 1989 and the middle of the study period but increased again during the last three years of this period. Thus the gender ratio was 1.43 in 1989, 1.21 in 1994 and 1.48 in 1999. The mean annual gender ratio was 1.31. These figures are all much lower than those which were recorded in the 1970s and early 1980s: the ratio was 2.1 in 1976 and 1.9 in 1984.

Table 3. Suicide attempt rates (persons) per 100,000 population, Oxford City, aged 15+ years by gender

	1989	1990	1991	1992	1993	1994	1995	1996	1997	1998	1999	Mean
Males	243	243	256	226	261	311	356	351	354	332	287	293
Females	348	331	342	344	310	376	439	412	454	436	425	383

The mean annual rates for the eleven year study period were highest in females in age group 15-24 years (658/100,000) and in males in age group 25-34 years (430/

100,000). Dividing the age groups into narrower bands showed that the highest rates in females were in age group 15-19 years (875/100,000) and in males age 25-29 years (483/100,000). During the study period a further 108 individuals aged under 15 years presented following attempted suicide. The youngest male was aged 10 years and the youngest female 9 years. The number of under 15-year-old females increased towards the end of the study period. The oldest male who presented was aged 94 years and the oldest female 95 years.

The highest mean annual rates in males were among the divorced (754/100,000) and single (380/100,000) (Table 4). The same pattern was found for females, with the divorced also having the highest rate (699/100,000) and people of single marital status the next highest (497/100,000).

Table 4. Mean annual attempted suicide rates (persons), Oxford City, aged 16+ years by marital status and gender

	Single	Married	Widowed	Divorced
Males	380	113	151	754
Females	497	183	127	699

'Separated' individuals are not included in these figures

There were no clear trends over the study period in relation to rates within marital status categories. The 'single' category comprised the highest proportion of individuals presenting. For males this varied over the study period from 60.3% to 75.3%, and for females between 57.8% and 70.7%.

A comparison of marital status and living situation (Table 5) indicates that large proportions of the widowed and divorced individuals were living alone, whereas nearly two-thirds of the single individuals and nearly all of those who were married were living with a partner. Overall, nearly three-quarters of the patients were living with a partner.

Table 5. Suicide attempts by marital status and living situation (alone or with partner), 1989-1999 combined (persons)

Cohabiting status	Single		Married		Widowed		Divorced		Total	
	%	N	%	N	%	N	%	N	%	N
Lives alone	39.4	223	2.2	14	91.5	54	52.4	118	27.2	409
Lives with partner	60.6	343	97.8	637	8.5	5	47.6	107	72.8	1,092
Total		566		651		59		225		1,501

Missing values:13

As in previous years we have studied, substantial proportions of the patients were unemployed (Table 6). More males than females were unemployed (and seeking work). The proportion of males who were economically active (i.e. employed or unemployed and seeking work) but unemployed decreased during the first half of the study period, and increased towards the end of the period. There was no marked change over time in the proportion of unemployed economically active females.

The relative risk of attempted suicide in unemployed persons compared with those who were employed was 10.5 for males and 11.2 for females.

Table 6. Suicide attempts (persons) by employment status and gender, Oxford City, 1989-1999 combined

Employment status	Males			Females		
	%	N	Rate/100,000	%	N	Rate/100,000
Employed	32.0	548	186	30.8	674	263
Unemployed	42.8	734	1,943	22.1	483	2,959
Economically inactive	25.2	431	311	47.1	1,028	424
Total		1,713			2,185	

Missing values:161

In the United Kingdom, a traditional measure of socio-economic status is termed 'social class'. It is determined solely according to occupation. There are five basic levels of social class: I, II, III, IV and V, with social class I (professional occupations) being the highest and V (unskilled manual occupations) the lowest. Mean annual rates of attempted suicide according to social class across the study period were as follows: males – I (64), II (109), III (376), IV (413) and V (765); females – I (182), II (148), III (513), IV (541) and V (439). Over the study period the relative risk of attempted suicide in persons in social classes III-V compared with those in classes I and II was 6.0 for males and 3.0 for females.

One measure of repetition is the episodes-to-persons ratio. The mean annual ratio during the study period was 1.39 in males and 1.35 in females. This ratio increased in the latter part of the study period, indicating a rise in the proportion of people repeating (Table 7).

Table 7. Events:persons ratio, Oxford City 1989-1999, by gender

Ratio	1989	1990	1991	1992	1993	1994	1995	1996	1997	1998	1999	Mean
Males	1.23	1.31	1.14	1.26	1.36	1.45	1.52	1.30	1.68	1.49	1.53	1.39
Females	1.28	1.23	1.15	1.23	1.24	1.37	1.42	1.35	1.50	1.48	1.57	1.35

Previous attempts at the time of first presentation by individuals during the study period were recorded for nearly half of both the males and females (Table 8).

Table 8. Previous attempts at time of first episode in study period, persons whose history was known, 1989-1999 combined, by gender

Any previous attempts	Males		Females		Both	
	%	N	%	N	%	N
No	51.8	576	52.5	805	52.2	1,381
Yes	48.2	537	47.5	727	47.8	1,264

The main measure of repetition is the actual proportion of individuals who make a repeat within a year of their first attempt in a calendar year. Repetition rates calculated in this way are shown for 1989 to 1998 in Table 9 (the repetition rate for 1999 will of course not be available until the end of 2000). There was a steady increase in the proportions of individuals of both genders making repeat attempts within a year of a first attempt in any calendar year. These trends were significant for both males (χ^2 for trend = 28.0, p < 0.00001) and females (χ^2 for trend = 25.3, p < 0.00001).

The vast majority of attempts involved self-poisoning (88.0%). Of self-poisoning episodes, 42.3% involved paracetamol, 20.8% minor tranquillisers and hypnotics, 19.7% antidepressants, 11.4% non-opiate analgesics other than paracetamol and 26.3% other prescribed drugs (many overdoses included more than one substance). There was a steady increase in antidepressant overdoses during the study period, from 11.7% in 1989 to 25.2% in 1999 (χ^2 for trend = 53.2, p < 0.00001).

Of the self-injuries, cutting was by far the most common method, with 73.8% of all self-injury episodes involving cuts to the wrists and 12.2% cuts elsewhere on the body.

Alcohol was consumed as part of the attempt by 34.0% of males and 23.2% of females (χ^2 = 63.2, p < 0.00001). The proportion of episodes involving alcohol did not change markedly in males during the study period. However, in females there was a marked increase (χ^2 for trend = 13.8, p < 0.001).

Table 9. Repetition of attempts within one year of first attempt in any calendar year, persons, Oxford City

Year	Males		Females		Both	
	%	N	%	N	%	N
1989	19	14.3	21	11.1	41	12.6
1990	21	15.8	33	18.2	54	16.9
1991	23	16.5	31	16.4	56	16.7
1992	26	21.1	30	15.8	57	17.9
1993	29	20.3	36	21.1	65	20.1
1994	46	26.9	52	25.0	97	25.3
1995	49	24.6	66	26.8	117	26.3
1996	50	25.0	55	23.4	105	24.1
1997	61	29.3	64	24.2	126	26.6
1998	65	32.8	71	27.3	136	29.7

Alcohol was consumed within the six hours before the attempt in 58.4% of episodes involving males and 43.0% of episodes involving females (χ^2 = 113.1, p < 0.00001). Again there was no major change in the proportion of episodes by males where alcohol had been consumed beforehand but in females the proportion increased somewhat during the study period (χ^2 = 6.7, p < 0.01).

The most frequent problems patients were facing at the time of their attempts are shown by gender in Table 10. Problems in relationships with partners were the most frequent for both genders. In females, problems in relationships with other family members were nearly as frequent as problems with partners and were significantly more common than in males. Problems related to alcohol, unemployment, social isolation, housing, finances and drugs were all significantly more common in males than females. Four out of ten males had problems related to the use of alcohol and approximately one in six had problems related to the use of drugs; in many of these patients both problems were present.

A history of violence showed marked gender differences. Thus within the five years before their attempts 25.9% of males and 9.0% of females were known to have been violent towards other people ($\chi^2 = 153.2$, p < 0.00001). In contrast, 24.8% of females had been victims of violence in the previous 5 years compared with 14.2% of males ($\chi^2 = 47.4$, p < 0.00001).

The aftercare offered to patients assessed by the hospital psychiatric service was (on the basis of episodes) as follows: outpatient or community mental health team care 50.8%, inpatient admission 9.8%, referral to other agency (Social Services, Probation Service, Marriage Guidance, voluntary agency) 11.8%, and return to general practitioner care 25.6%. In addition, 2.1% were referred to psychiatric hospitals outside Oxford District.

Table 10. Problems patients were facing at the time of attempts – 1989-1999 combined, top ten categories

Problem	Males		Females		Both sexes		
	N	%	N	%	N	%	
Relationship with partner	774	43.0	1,066	46.0	1,840	44.7	NS
Relationship with family	575	32.0	1,031	44.6	1,606	39.1	$\chi^2 = 67.2$, p<0.00001
Alcohol	727	40.5	546	23.6	1,273	31.0	$\chi^2 = 135.0$, p<0.00001
Employment	649	36.1	600	25.9	1,249	30.4	$\chi^2 = 49.6$, p<0.00001
Social isolation	466	25.9	509	22.0	975	23.7	$\chi^2 = 8.7$, p<0.01
Housing	439	24.4	489	21.1	928	22.6	$\chi^2 = 6.3$, p<0.05
Financial	466	25.9	433	18.7	899	21.9	$\chi^2 = 30.9$, p<0.00001
Relationship with friends	296	16.5	380	16.4	676	16.4	NS
Drugs	303	16.9	214	9.2	517	12.6	$\chi^2 = 53.4$, p<0.00001
Physical health	196	10.9	257	11.1	453	11.0	NS

Conclusion

Attempted suicide was particularly common in young females, especially those aged 15 to 19 years. In males the highest rates were in 25-29-year-olds. Rates of attempted suicide in young males rose markedly during the early part of the study period, following a rise in national rates of suicide in this group (Kelly and Bunting, 1998).

As found in other studies, rates of attempted suicide were highest among the divorced and single, with single individuals comprising the largest proportion of patients. It was striking, however, that nearly three quarters of all patients were living with a partner.

A disturbing finding from this study was the increase in repetition of attempted suicide over the study period. This was marked in both genders and raises important questions about whether this reflects a deterioration in quality of services, which seems unlikely, or changes in the characteristics of the attempted suicide population. This finding is in keeping with the general impression that there has been an increase in the proportion of attempted suicide patients with psychiatric disorders. A recent investigation from Oxford, also within the WHO/Euro Multicentre Study of Suicidal Behaviour, has demonstrated that psychiatric disorders are present in the vast majority of patients (Haw et al., 2001). These trends have important implications for clinical services.

Acknowledgements

The Oxford Monitoring System for Attempted Suicide, and associated research projects, have received financial support during the period of this study from The Department of Health, Oxford Regional Health Authority, and the South East Region NHSE Research and Development Committee. We thank the staff at the Barnes Unit in the Department for Psychological Medicine at the John Radcliffe Hospital in Oxford for their ongoing and considerable assistance with the work necessary to maintain the Monitoring System and Joan Fagg for her dedicated work on this project in previous years.

References

Haw C, Hawton K, Houston K, Townsend E (2001) Psychiatric and personality disorders in deliberate self-harm patients. *British Journal of Psychiatry*, 178: 48-54.

Hawton K, Catalan J (1987) *Attempted suicide: a practical guide to its nature and management.* Oxford: Oxford University Press.

Kelly S, Bunting J. (1998) Trends in suicide in England and Wales, 1982-96. *Population Trends*, 92: 29-41.

Platt S, Bille-Brahe U, Kerkhof A, Schmidtke A, Bjerke T, Crepet P, De Leo D, Haring C, Lönnqvist J, Michel K, Phillippe A, Pommereau X, Querejeta I, Salander Renberg E, Temesvary B, Wasserman D, Sampaio-Faria JG (1992) Attempted suicide in Europe: the WHO-EURO multicentre study on attempted suicide. 1. Introduction and preliminary analysis for 1989. *Acta Psychiatrica Scandinavica*, 85: 97-104.

Platt S, Hawton K, Kreitman N, Fagg J, Foster J (1988) Recent clinical and epidemiological trends in attempted suicide in Edinburgh and Oxford: a tale of two cities. *Psychological Medicine*, 18: 405-418.

Schmidtke A, Bille Brahe U, De Leo D, Kerkhof A, Bjerke T, Crepet P, Haring C, Hawton K, Lönnqvist J, Michel K, Pommereau X, Querejeta I, Phillipe I, Salander Renberg E, Temesvary B, Wasserman D, Fricke S, Weinacker B, Sampaio Faria JG (1996) Attempted suicide in Europe: rates, trends and sociodemographic characteristics of suicide attempters during the period 1989- 992. Results of the WHO-EURO Multicentre Study on Attempted suicide. *Acta Psychiatrica Scandinavica*, 93: 327-338.

Chapter 14

Suicidal Behaviour in France

A. Batt, F. Eudier, A. Philippe & X. Pommereau

Description of the catchment areas

In France, the monitoring study has been carried out by three successive centres, namely Bordeaux (Dr. Pommereau, 1989), Cergy-Pontoise (A. Philippe, 1990-1991) and of late Rennes (A.Batt and F. Eudier). Respectively, these three centres are located in three different regions, namely, Aquitaine, Ile de France and Brittany. These regions differ in many aspects. France is divided by 22 regions grouping several historical departements created by the revolution of 1789. Each departement is divided in smaller entities corresponding to different needs, including cantons and communes (towns and/or villages).

Some of the text and tables below are contained in previously published reports. The catchment area of each centre will be successively described and the results presented for each centre.

The Bordeaux catchment area with a population of 517,326 (15+ years) covers the whole urban area including the city centre and its suburban areas. Bordeaux is the head-office of the regional government as well as of many administrations and the centre of the "employment area". The Regional University Hospital is located in Bordeaux.

The Pontoise catchment area comprises four rural districts and the city of Cergy-Pontoise, a new dormitory town located 20 km north-west of Paris, with 112,272 inhabitants (15+ years). More than half of the population has moved into the area within the last decade previous to the study, and the population is younger than the rest of France.

The catchment area of the Rennes centre covers an "employment area" comprising 26 cantons with 421,971 inhabitants (15+ years) or 1 per cent of the total population of the country. Rennes is the head-office of the regional government as well as of many administrations and is the centre of the "employment area". Also located in Rennes is the Regional University Hospital.

Sample and method of data collection

The National Institute for Health and Medical Research (INSERM) collects suicide data on a national basis from the anonymized section of the death certificates written by general practitioners (GP). Following various controls of litigious cases, figures are published with a one- to two-year delay, at the national, regional, departmental and, on demand, cantonal level. A certain percentage of all deaths are those of "unknown causes", which probably include suicides. There are no national or regional data on the incidence of attempted suicide in France. Data has, however, been collected by specific surveys carried out on well delimited regions and for a restricted period of time (Davidson & Philippe, 1986; Batt et al. 1994)

In Rennes, the latest comprehensive prospective epidemiological survey was carried out in 1990 by the Regional Observatory for Public Health (ORSB) in order to evaluate the incidence of attempted suicide in the region of Brittany (Batt et al. 1994). The catchment area covered the four "départements" (2,795,552 inhabitants). Data were gathered from the 26 general (main or university) hospitals (CHRU) having an Accident and Emergency (A&E) department.

By law, the CHRU is to receive every person after a suicide attempt. However, it is suspected that at least 10 per cent of suicide attempters are not hospitalised, either because they are only treated by their GP or not at all. The proportion seems to be of the same magnitude in Bordeaux and probably in Cergy-Pontoise as well.

At all three centres, the data refer to every person admitted to the emergency ward in the catchment area and include those directed to hospital emergency wards, but who are referred to treatment at home or by their GP, or are transferred directly to the intensive care unit or a surgical ward due to their condition.

At the time of monitoring in the Rennes catchment area, problems are including the lack of referral of many patients to the main or university hospitals and the difficulties in tracing self-destructive behaviours transferred to an intensive care unit or to a surgical ward which might not report the event. As a result, an "estimation factor" was calculated.

Results

Suicide

The crude rates of suicide in France per 100,000 inhabitants increased from 19.6 in 1981 to 22.7 in 1985, whereafter decreasing slowly from 22.6 in 1986 to 20.1 in 1990, and further to 19.0 in 1997. The year of 1993 was an exception, where the crude rate was 21.2 per 100,000.

In order to minimise the influence of the structure of the population on the data, the standardised rates by age and sex were calculated for France, the region of Brittany, and the departement of Ille et Vilaine by the ORSB. Calculations were made on a three year basis centred on a year of census, except for the last period where the estimation of the population was made in the absence of recent census.

In the département of Ille et Vilaine, the male rate of suicide in 1954 was below both the regional and the national average. While the figures increased at the regional and the national level, the male rate in the catchment area remained, even at its maximum in 1982, on a lower level. A similar trend can be observed for female rates until 1975, whereafter the female rate in the département for the next 15 years or more outpaced both the regional and national data. However, an estimate based on a three year average and the 1996 consensus indicates a slight decrease.

Table 1. Evolution of the mortality ratios in Ille et Vilaine. Comparison with Brittany and France

		Catchment area	Brittany	France
Males	1954	33	47	35
	1962	41	48	34
	1968	39	49	33
	1975	42	51	32
	1982	65	68	43
	1990	57	63	39
	1996	54	61	38
Females	1954	9	9	9
	1962	10	11	9
	1968	11	11	10
	1975	15	14	11
	1982	24	20	14
	1990	25	22	13
	1996	18	20	12

The data given for Aquitaine are not as detailed however, the rates calculated by the FNORS (Fédération Nationale des Observatoires Régionaux de Santé) in 1998 are twice as low in that region than in those reported above. For Ile de France (which is a much larger area than the catchment area of Cergy Pontoise), the data are questionable, particularly in light of the fact that in Paris, many deaths are classified as "unknown causes". In a recent assessment of the situation in France, the SMRper 100,000 in Aquitaine was reported to be 91.6 for males and 90.0 for females, and in Brittany 159.9 for males and 151.5 (base France = 100).

Attempted suicide

The chapter presents data from the three centres that have taken part in the WHO/ EURO survey since its beginning in 1989. Although the data are heterogeneous, they give a few hints of the frequencies of attempted suicide in various parts of France.

Table 2. Person-based suicide attempt rates per 100,000, 15+ years, 1989 and 1998 by area.

Males							
	1989	1990	1991	1995	1996	1997	1998
Bordeaux	129	-	-	-	-	-	-
Cergy-Pontoise	248	263	246	-	-	-	-
Rennes	-	-	-	337	337	277	258

Females							
	1989	1990	1991	1995	1996	1997	1998
Bordeaux	248	-	-	-	-	-	-
Cergy-Pontoise	509	570	546	-	-	-	-
Rennes	-	-	-	533	531	558	488

Figures 1a, b and 2a, b show the rates of attempted suicide by age. The diagrams group the data in periods of two consecutive years. Data from Cergy Pontoise and Rennes are presented on different figures as the contexts are very different. It is obvious that in all three centres, curves show a different pattern of suicidal behaviour for males and females.

In Cergy Pontoise, the rate for the 25-29 years old was lower than for the younger and the elder groups. The same is true in Rennes during the years 1995-96, but cannot

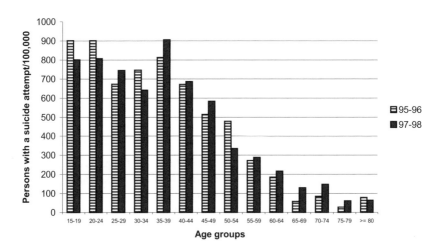

Figure 1a. Age distribution among females in Rennes. 1995-96 and 1997-98

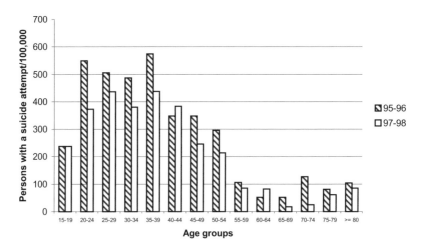

Figure 1b. Age distribution among males in Rennes. 1995-96 and 1997-98

be confirmed for the following period. In Rennes, the highest rates in the period 1995-96 were among the youngest females and for males below the age of 35 years. From the age of 40 years and on, rates decreased regularly among both males and females. In the Rennes catchment area, a total of 5,958 persons (2,287 males and 3,671 females) domiciled in Brittany were referred to an emergency ward after a suicide attempt in 1990. The crude incidence event rates of attempted suicide in Brittany were 200 per 100,000 for males and 330 per 100,000 for females.

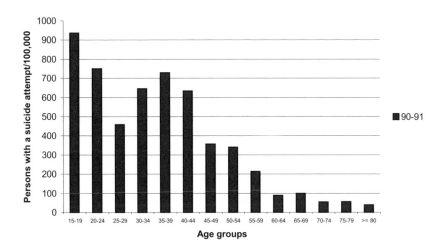

Figure 2a. Age distribution among females in Cergy-Pontoise, 1990-91

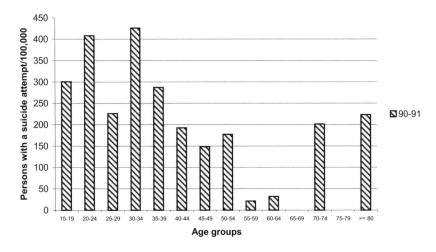

Figure 2b. Age distribution among males in Cergy-Pontoise, 1990-91

Table 3. Number of parasuicide event rates by gender age and "département" (/100,000)

	Côtes d'Armor		Finistère		Ille et Vilaine		Morbihan	
Males	N	R	N	R	N	R	N	R
15-24	93	235	173	270	191	280	91	190
25-34	120	344	304	490	257	420	134	290
35-44	105	265	180	290	182	300	90	190
45-54	35	133	46	110	55	150	42	150
55-64	14	50	24	50	20	50	25	70
65+	14	30	21	40	18	40	13	30
All ages 15+	386	190	759	230	729	240	401	160
Females	N	R	N	R	N	R	N	R
15-24	170	470	276	450	406	590	181	410
25-34	170	514	303	530	352	590	152	350
35-44	157	420	251	430	322	550	161	370
45-54	77	290	119	290	116	300	71	240
55-64	40	110	69	130	52	120	36	120
65+	34	50	38	40	32	50	35	90
All ages 15+	650	300	1,062	320	1,283	380	644	260

Source: The epidemiology of attempted suicide in Brittany in *Attempted suicide in Europe,* DSWO Press. 1994; pp245-252.

Rates by gender, age, and département range between 30 and 590 per 100,000. In all age groups, rates are higher for women than for men. The highest rates are observed among the 25-34-year-olds (except for in one "département", where the rate peaked among the 15-24-year-olds). A cohort of 1,180 patients admitted to the A&E ward has

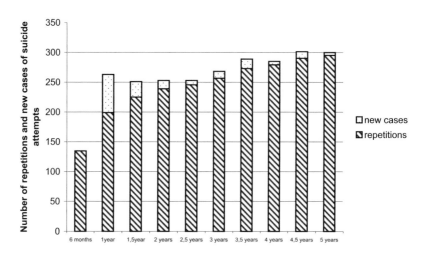

Figure 3. Number of repetitions per 6 month periods and of new cases of suicide attempts

been followed up until the end of 1999. Figure 3 shows the number of repetitions per 6-month periods and the number of new cases.

In a previous publication, we showed that the proportion of early repetitions, carried out within less than 6 months increased from 5 per cent among first-evers to 22 per cent among major repeaters. The time lapse between the referral episode and the first repetition was computed according to a method derived from that used in Kaplan-Meier survival curves. The first-evers, first-repeaters and the major repeaters individualised themselves very clearly. Among the first-evers, a small number of persons repeated within a very short time (less than 30 days) or much later, at the end of the 6-month period. In between, a plateau was observable. Among the major repeaters there was a regular trend of repetition during the 6-month study period and the three phases could hardly been distinguished.

Prediction

The age group 35-39 years seems a very vulnerable one, their rates in 1995-1996 being the highest for both males and females. This is, a most important point to note, as the persons concerned here are young adults in an age of parenthood and at the same time they are in the middle of psychological turmoil. The potential risk of future fragility of the children cannot be ignored.

The decreasing trend between the two periods are encouraging, but the need for further studies is strongly urged.

Peculiarities of the Rennes area

The frequency of attempted suicide in the catchment area under study by the centre in Rennes varies markedly within the area; the standardized rates within the département range from 30 per 100,000 in rural areas to 590 per 100,000 in the towns. This should be seen in relation to the fact that the département is large, and very geographically and economically a complex, comprising huge rural areas with dispersed settlements and a low density population, semi-rural or semi-urban areas, and large cities surrounded by heavily urbanised areas. The varying rates of attempted suicide should therefore be seen in light of specific sociological and socio-economimal conditions as well as accessibility to health facilities. Such factors were taken into consideration when choosing the catchment area for the study in Brittany.

Conclusion

The chapter has presented data obtained from the three French centres that has taken part in the multicentre study, namely the Bordeaux centre in 1989, the centre in Cergy-Pontoise in 1989-1991, and the centre in Rennes since 1995. Although the results are rather heterogeneous, data do give a few hints. The very high rates of attempted suicide previously published for Cergy Pontoise are confirmed and even exceeded in the Rennes catchment area. This is not good news for the region but certainly reinforces the conviction that the region must participate further to the survey. So far, the study has positively confirmed much of the epidemiological data that has been gathered in Brittany during the last 10 years. Undoubtedly, such findings will serve as a useful lever in the development of further research programs.

References

Batt A, Depoivre C, Eudier F, Tron I, Tréhony A (1994). The epidemiology of attempted suicide in Brittany, France 1990. In: AJFM Kerkhof et al.(Eds) *Attempted suicide in Europe.* 15, 245-252. Leiden: DSWO Press.

Batt A, Eudier F, LeVaou P, Breurec JY, Baert A, Curtès JP, Badiche A, Chaperon J (1998). Repetition of attempted suicide: risk factors in general hospital referred patients. *Journal of Mental Health.* 7/3:285-297.

Davidson F & Philippe A (1986). Suicide et tentatives de suicide aujourd'hui: Etude épidémiologique. Paris: INSERM/Doin.

FNORS. Bilans régionaux (1998). *Prévention des suicides et tentatives de suicide 1995-1997.* CNAM/Mutualité Française/Prémutam eds.

Pennognon L & Tréhony A (2001). Working paper, unpublished.

Tréhony A, Batt A, Depoivre C, Tron-Pasquet I (1992). *Les tentatives de suicide en Bretagne.* Rennes: ORSB.

Chapter 15

Suicidal Behaviour in The Netherlands

E. Arensman, A. Kerkhof, M. W. Hengeveld & J. D.Mulder

Description of the catchment area

The area of Leiden is located on the coast of the North Sea in the western part of The Netherlands, which is a highly urbanised area with a very high population density, a high level of economic activity, and a comprehensive infrastructure. The catchment area can be divided into two districts: the Leiden urban area with 121,145 inhabitants, and the rural Bulb District with 263,443 inhabitants, with a total population of 384,588 (CBS, 2001)

Sample and method of data collection

Data on suicide are obtained from the Central Bureau for Statistics (CBS, 2001).

During the period 1989-1992, a monitoring study of medically treated suicide attempts was carried out in the area of Leiden in The Netherlands, as part of the WHO/ EURO Multicentre Study (Arensman, Kerkhof, Hengeveld, Mulder, 1994; Arensman, Kerkhof, Hengeveld, Mulder, 1995).

Between 1993 and 1999, the monitoring study could not be continued due to organisational problems and the absence of structural funding. Since 2000, the monitoring study in the area of Leiden has been started again, with 2000 being a pilot year. Apart from the area of Leiden, there are no other regions in The Netherlands where a systematic monitoring procedure has been used to register and follow patients who are referred to health care agencies following an act of non-fatal suicidal behaviour.

Results

Suicide

An update is presented on the prevalence of suicide specified by age in The Netherlands in the five-year period: 1995-1999. Considering all age groups, suicide rates were higher in the older age groups, which is in line with the findings in most other countries. During the five-year period the suicide rates were fairly stable in all age groups.

Table 1. Suicide rates per 100,000 population specified by age in The Netherlands, 1995-1999

Year	Age group						
	15-19	20-29	30-39	40-49	50-59	60-69	70+
1995	3.5	9.6	12.7	13.7	13.4	13.2	14.6
1996	4.0	9.8	12.7	14.1	14.1	12.0	17.5
1997	4.9	10.9	12.8	13.1	12.4	13.6	15.5
1998	4.3	8.9	12.5	12.5	13.9	12.1	15.7
1999	4.5	9.0	11.6	14.0	12.8	13.5	13.9

Source: Central Bureau for Statistics (CBS), 2001

Among those who commit suicide, two thirds were males, which is a stable finding, and similar to most other countries (Table 2). With regard to marital status, the majority of those who commit suicide are single (ca. 39%) or married (ca. 33%) and a relatively low percentage is divorced (ca.18%) or widowed (ca. 10%).

Table 2. Absolute number of suicides in The Netherlands, and distribution by gender and marital status in percentages

Year	Number of Suicides	Gender		Marital status			
	N	Males %	Females %	Single %	Married %	Divorced %	Widowed %
1995	1,511	66	34	40	35	16	9
1996	1,577	66	34	38	34	17	11
1997	1,570	66	34	39	33	18	10
1998	1,519	66	34	39	30	20	11
1999	1,517	67	33	40	32	18	10

Source: Central Bureau for Statistics (CBS), 2001

Nearly half of those who committed suicide used the method hanging or strangulation, ca. 16% used an overdose of medication, and ca. 11% jumped in front of a train. A relatively high percentage (ca. 21%) used other methods or are cases of suicide where the method was unknown. The distribution of suicide methods was stable over the five-year period.

Table 3. Distribution of suicides in The Netherlands by method, 1995-1999, in percentages

Year	Method of suicide				
	Hanging/ strangulation	Medication	Jumping in front of train	Drowning	Other/ unknown
	%	%	%	%	%
1995	43	16	11	8	21
1996	43	15	10	8	23
1997	42	16	11	8	22
1998	44	16	11	9	20
1999	43	17	11	8	21

Source: Central Bureau for Statistics (CBS), 2001

Attempted suicide

During the period 1989-1992, completed monitoring forms were collected on 793 suicide attempts (episodes), involving 690 persons. The total number of reports, including suicide attempts for which no additional demographic information was registered on a monitoring form by the participating agencies, comprised 1,166 suicide attempts (episodes).

Table 4 presents the number of suicide attempts reported by all participating persons, and the estimated number of actual suicide attempts per year, which was arrived at by means of extrapolation from available information. Through extrapolation[1], estimated annual person and episode rates per 100,000 population were calculated.

Table 4. The number of reported suicide attempts, number of suicide attempts after extrapolation, and suicide attempt rates per 100,000 population (persons and episodes), 1989-1992

	1989	1990	1991	1992
Suicide attempts				
Persons	214	261	257	255
Episodes	248	301	326	291
After extrapolation				
Persons	325	355	313	321
Episodes	377	409	398	367
Rates per 100,000				
Persons	111	120	105	107
Episodes	128	138	133	121
Estimation factor	1.52	1.36	1.22	1.26

[1] The estimation factor was calculated on the basis of the estimated annual percentage of reported suicide attempts by all participating agencies: 1989: 100/66 = 1.52; 1990: 100/73 = 1.36; 1991: 100/82 = 1.22; 1992: 100/79 = 1.26. The formula for extrapolation is the estimation factor x the reported number of suicide attempts.

No significant differences were found between the person and episode rates of suicide attempts for the four one-year periods. Due to the increased accuracy of the registration of suicide attempts in 1990, 1991, and 1992, the estimation factor in the last three years was lower than in the first year.

While no differences were found between the annual rates of attempted suicide for each age and sex group, these rates were calculated in terms of mean person and episode rates per 100,000 population for the entire four year period of the study. The mean annual person rate for men was 85/100,000, and for women this was 139/100,000. The mean annual episode rates for men and women were respectively 95/100,000 and 155/100,000. The ratio of female-male rates (persons) was 1.64. No difference was found between the mean age of women (35.8, SD ±14.1) and of men (36.1, SD ±15.4).

With regard to marital status, the highest mean annual attempted suicide rates for both men (191/100,000) and women (248/100,000) were found among divorced people, with higher rates among women. The lowest rates for both men (16/100,000) and women (39/100,000) were found among those who were widowed.

Looking at employment status, the highest mean annual attempted suicide rates were found among the unemployed, which is true for both men (322/100,000) and women (455/100,000). The rates among those who were disabled were also relatively high, men: 133/100,000 and women: 205/100,000.

Half (51%) of the suicide attempters had already had made at least one attempt prior to the index suicide attempt, and prospectively it was estimated that at least 25% made a repeated attempt during the four-year period. Most patients (76%) had taken an overdose of medication as method of the index suicide attempt, and among these more than two thirds ingested minor tranquilizers and sedatives.

We also made a comparison between suicide attempts (episodes), treated in a general hospital (n = 648) and those treated exclusively by General Practitioners (GPs) (n= 114). With regard to demographic characteristics, no significant difference was found. However, with regard to characteristics of suicidal behaviour, it appeared that people treated in a general hospital were more often repeaters (59%) compared to those treated by GPs (42%) (p < .01).

Peculiarities of the catchment area

Data from 1989-1992 also showed that about 15 percent of all medically referred suicide attempters were treated exclusively by GPs, and there were no further referrals to a general hospital (Arensman et al, 1995) This percentage is relatively high compared to other centres participating in the multicentre study, indicating that in the Leiden area, GPs are an important source of information in order to obtain a complete picture of the prevalence of medically treated suicide attempts.

References

Arensman E, Kerkhof AJFM, Hengeveld MW, Mulder JD (1994). The epidemiology of attempted suicide in the area of Leiden, The Netherlands, 1989-1992. In: AJFM Kerkhof, A Schmidtke, U Bille-Brahe, D DeLeo, J Lönnqvist (Eds.). *Attempted suicide in Europe. Findings from the multicentre study on parasuicide by the WHO Regional Office for Europe.* Leiden: DSWO Press.

Arensman E, Kerkhof AJFM, Hengeveld MW, Mulder JD (1995). Medically treated suicide attempts: a monitoring study of the epidemiology in the Netherlands. *Journal of Epidemiology and Community Health,* 49: 285-289.

Bille-Brahe U, Bjerke T, Crepet P, DeLeo D, Haring C, Hawton K, Kerkhof A, Lönnqvist J, Michel K, Philippe A, Pommereau X, Querejeta I, Salander Renberg E, Schmidtke A, Temesvary B, Wasserman D, Sampaio-Faria JG (1993). *WHO/EURO Multicentre study on parasuicide. Facts and figures.* Copenhagen: WHO Regional Office for Europe.

Bille-Brahe U (Ed.) (1999). *WHO/EURO Multicentre study on parasuicide. Facts and figures.* Copenhagen: WHO Regional Office for Europe.

Central Bureau for Statistics (CBS). (2001). *StatLine: Zelfdodingen Nederland: Leeftijd bij overlijden, burgerlijke staat, wijze van zelfdoding.* Voorburg: CBS.

Central Bureau for Statistics (CBS). (2001). *StatLine: Enquete Beroepsbevolking 1999.* Beroepsbevolking en werkloosheid, 1997/1999. Heerlen: CBS.

Central Bureau for Statistics (CBS). (2001). *StatLine: Gebieden in Nederland 2000.* Voorburg/ Heerlen: CBS.

Central Bureau for Statistics (CBS). (2001). *StatLine: Gezondheidskenmerken naar regio 1995/ 1999.* Voorburg/Heerlen: CBS.

Central Bureau for Statistics (CBS). (2001). *StatLine: Misdrijven/verdachten per politieregio.* Voorburg/Heerlen: CBS.

Schmidtke A, Bille-Brahe U, DeLeo D, Kerkhof A, Bjerke T, Crepet P, Haring C, Hawton K, Lönnqvist J, Michel K, Pommereau X, Querejeta I, Philippe A, Salander Renberg E, Temesvary B, Wasserman D, Fricke S, Weinacker B, Sampaio-Faria JG (1996). Attempted suicide in Europe: Rates, trends and sociodemographic characteristics of suicide attempters during the period 1989-1992. Results of the WHO/EURO Multicentre Study on Parasuicide. *Acta Psychiatrica Scandinavica,* 93: 327-338.

Chapter 16

Suicidal Behaviour in Germany

A. Schmidtke, B. Weinacker & C. Löhr

Description of the catchment area

The German area under study comprises the city and county of Wuerzburg. Wuerzburg is a governmental seat and centre of the administrative district (Regierungsbezirk) of Lower-Franconia (Unterfranken). It is located in the northern part of Bavaria, lying in southern Germany. Approximately 127,000 residents live within the 88 km² area of Wuerzburg. The county of Wuerzburg (the city itself excluded) covers 968 km² with 52 villages and approximately 156.000 residents. The entire catchment area covers 1.056 km² and has a population of 283,000 (1995-1999). The catchment area was before the reunification of Germany nearly representative for Western Germany (cf. Schmidtke, Fricke & Weinacker, 1994).

Sample and method of data collection

Official suicide mortality figures are obtained from the Statistical Bureau Germany. According to German law, every doctor can write a death certificate, however, there has to be an official investigation into the cause of death when the death is certified as unnatural, or suspected of being so. Due to the low autopsy rate in Germany (not higher than 5 %) the true rate of unknown death causes is assumed to be higher than the official rate.

The information on attempted suicides is based on the collected data of the referrals to a clinic or a medical institution (private doctor, health institution) in the catchment area. After a suicide attempt, most persons are admitted to the accident and emergency units of the University Clinic and then seen by a liaison doctor of the Psychiatric Clinic. All other clinics with facilities for transferred suicide attempters from the region were included. Due to the special German system with private doctors, a sample of private doctors and other health care facilities engaged in suicide prevention and aftercare was also included. For the years 1989 until 1994 the original sample, therefore, consisted of the Psychiatric Department of the University, the Psychiatric Clinic for Children and Adolescents of the University, two psychiatric state clinics, one municipal psychiatric clinic outside the catchment area, 14 general medical hospitals, 12 psychiatrists and neurologists, 19 general practitioners, 1 gynaecologist, 1 pediatrician, 7 specialists in internal medicine (8 of all these private doctors were also psychotherapists), 4 psychologists, and 16 other health institutions (e.g. hot line services, suicide and crisis centres, counselling services). For the years 1995 to 1999 the sample was reduced to the main clinics and a smaller sample of psychiatrists and neurologists and one hot line service.

The German translation of the monitoring form with some additional variables was applied. Additionally psychiatric diagnoses (ICD-9) made by psychiatric consultants were recorded. The ICD-9 classification system for psychiatric diagnoses was used, since this was the official classification system at the beginning of the project. The intent of suicide attempt was also rated according to the classification of Feuerlein (1971; e.g. serious suicide attempt, suicidal gesture and suicidal pause).

Results

Suicide

In 1999, the latest year for which nationwide data were available in Germany, 8,080 males and 3,077 females committed suicide. The total number (11,157) is higher than the number of deaths due to road accidents (6,910). Therefore, the suicide figures for males are 20.2 and for females 7.3. The male rate is lower than the European average, the female is similar to the European average.

The age distribution still follows the so-called "Hungarian pattern" (see figure 1). There is a strong correlation between suicide risk and age, with much higher suicide figures for both sexes in the elderly.

Over the last years the total suicide rates have been decreasing for males and females. In comparison with the average suicide rates for the 5-year period 1976–1980 the average suicide rate for the period 1995–1999 decreased by 34% for males and by

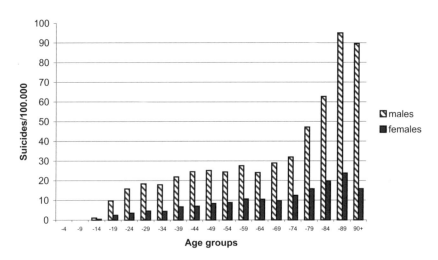

Figure 1. Suicide rates by age and gender, Wuerzburg

54% for females. (The decrease is similar for "West" and "East" Germany after the reunification).

The time series and age distribution shows some specific features. As in other countries, also in Germany a cohort-effect could be found for the birth-cohorts since the birth year 1932. Successive cohorts had in all age groups higher suicide rates than the previous birth cohorts. This cohort effect was observable in both parts of Germany. In the last years this cohort effect seemed to fade out.

The long term trends also show that over time there is a change in the age composition of the suicides. The percentage of suicides among males 60 years and older of the total number of suicides increased only slightly from 31% for the period 1952 – 1956 to 32% for the period 1995-1999 (the increase in the percentage of these age groups of the total male population for the same periods: 14% to 18%). However, the percentage of suicides for women older than 60 years increased from 31% to 48%, despite the fact that their percentage in the whole population increased only from 17% to 26%. Thus, at the moment nearly every second female suicide is a suicide by a women 60 years and older.

The most frequent suicide method in Germany is hanging (males: 58%; females: 41%). The second most frequent suicide method is self-poisoning (males: 12%; females 23%). It is noteworthy that the frequency of self-poisoning has been decreasing over time, especially among the elderly, whereas the "undetermined causes of death" increase (Schmidtke & Weinacker, 1991).

Suicide attempts

From 1st of December 1988 to 31st of December 1999, data for 1582 suicide attempt episodes committed by 1384 persons were collected. Thirty-eight percent of the suicide attempters were males. Ninety-three percent of the episodes were registered in a hospital, especially in intensive care units or directly in the psychiatric clinic. Only 8%

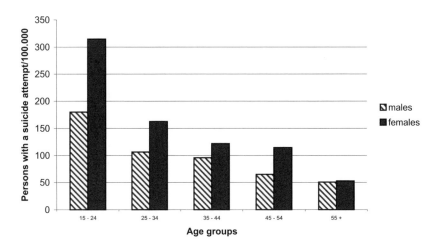

Figure 2. Rates of attempted suicide by age and gender, Wuerzburg

were not seen by a psychiatrist. The average age of the sample has not changed over the years: it is 36.5 years for males and 36.1 years for females.

Taking a correction factor into consideration (due to the sampling) the "real" suicide attempt rates for the last years were estimated: 1995: males 77/100,000, females 127/100,000; 1999: males: 90/100,000, females 116/100,000. In order to be more reliable, the age distribution and the age and sex-specific rates were computed for the sampling period (1995 -1999). Figure 2 shows these rates. The highest rates are found in the younger age groups, especially among younger females (15-24 years: 1995-1999 315/100,000). In contrast females aged 55 and older had only a suicide attempt rate of 53/100,000. These age distributions did not vary over the whole period.

The variances of the rates over the years are high, however, in general a long-term increasing trend for the total rates is observable. The increase for males between the periods 1989/1993–1995/1999 is 32 %; for females 18 % (see figure 3).

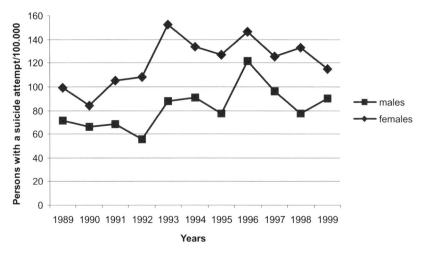

Figure 3. Rates of attempted suicide by gender, 1989-1999

Similar long-term trends were found for the various sex- and age-groups. Over the 11-year study period, the rates for most of the male age groups increased (e.g. in the age group 15-24 year-olds between the periods 1989/1993 to 1995/1999 to 44%, 25-34 year olds to 49%, and the age group 35-44 year olds to 45%, 45-54 year olds to 6%, and 55+ year olds to 23%). Among the females in most of the age groups, the rates also increased (15-24 year olds to 37 %, 25-34 year olds to 31 %, 45-54 year olds to 17 %, and 55+ year olds to 17%). The 35-44 year-old age group showed a decrease of 7%.

The suicide attempt methods are mostly the so-called "soft" methods. Since the beginning of the study, the method "poisoning" increased for males by 12% and comprises now almost two-thirds of all methods. For females an increase of 15% could be detected and poisoning now covers more than three-quarters of all methods. The method "cutting" (X 78) decreased for both males and females, but is still on second place (males: 19%; females: 10%). The third method is still "jumping" from a high place (X 80) but has a percentage under 10%, as at the beginning.

Epidemiological findings

General results

The percentage of non-German suicides (4%; males 4.2%, females 3.4%) is significantly lower than the percentage of non-Germans in the total population (9.8%; males 10.9%, females 8.8%). Also the mean age of "German" and "non-German" suicides is significantly different: 1998 males: Germans 52.0 years vs. non-Germans: 40.5 years, females: 58.2 years vs. 42.9 years.

The suicide rates differ significantly within the various states of the Federal Republic with significantly higher rates for the Eastern States Saxonia, Saxonia-Anhalt and Thuringia and lower rates for the Western states. The differences are more pronounced for the older age groups.

Of the suicide attempters 8% of the males and 6% of the females were not German.

The intention of the suicide attempt covaries with age and sex. More "seriously" rated suicide attempts are found in the older age groups and among males, while more demonstrative suicide attempts are prevalent in the younger age groups and among females. Thirty-four percent of the suicide attempts of the 15-29 year-old males are rated as "serious", 50% in the age group 30-54 year olds, and 59% in the age group 55+. For females, the percentages are 24%, 34%, and 57%, respectively. The suicidal act is rated as a gesture or demonstrative behaviour in 42% of all 15-29 year-old males, in 28 % of the 30-55 year-olds, and only in 24% of all persons 55 years and older. For females the percentages are 46%, 33 %, and 24 % (χ^2 for males 20.38; df = 8; p = .009; χ^2 for females = 49.64; df = 8; p<.001).

Seventy-two percent of all persons with suicide attempts received a psychiatric diagnosis – this has not changed in comparison with earlier years. Some were not seen by a specialist who could make a psychiatric diagnosis. The most prevalent diagnosis for males and females (23%) was "adjustment disorder" (ICD-9; 309); the second highest group was "affective disorders" (males: 17%, females: 21%). Fifteen percent of the males received a diagnosis of "addiction" (substance and alcohol) or "alcohol and substance abuse" (ICD-9; 303, 304 and 305) and fifteen percent received also a diagnosis of the group of "neuroses and personality disorders". Among females the third most frequent group of diagnoses was "neuroses and personality disorders" (19%), followed by "abnormal reactions to stress" (12%).

With regard to social variables a higher urban rate could be found. Compared with the population distribution (urban: 46%; rural: 50%), higher percentages of the suicide attempters live in the urban area: 67% of the males and 68% of the females resided in the city Wuerzburg at the time of the suicide attempt.

64% of male and female suicide attempters list "Catholic" as their formal religious membership, 18% of the males and 22% of the females "Protestant". Other religions were rare (3% "Muslim"); "no religion" was given by 8% of the males and 6% of the females. The percentage of suicide attempters with "no religion" has increased during the last years – in accordance with the population percentage.

Only 29% of the suicide attempters were married (suicide attempt rates for married males: 43/100,000; for females: 73/100,000). Eight percent of the males and 9% of the females were divorced (suicide attempt rates for divorced males: 194/100,000; for females: 260/100,000). Six percent of the males and 7% of the females were separated. A large proportion of suicide attempters usually lived alone (27% of the males and 23% of the females) and/or were never married (51% of the males and 47% of the females). The suicide attempt rate for never-married males was 73/100,000; for females: 122/100,000. However, adequate population figures were not available for all of these variables. Therefore, it was only possible to calculate rates for some variables.

A more detailed analysis of the household composition showed that social integration indicated through the living situation at the time of the suicide attempt often differed from the usual living situation. Fourteen percent of the males and 9% of the females changed their living conditions before the suicidal act: often from socially stable situations to unstable situations, or to institutions in a relatively short period before the suicidal act. For example, 34% of the "changers" changed to living alone; 10% changed to an institution.

For international comparisons, the different classifications of the national educational categories were recoded into three categories: low, middle, and high level of education. An average of 67% of the males and 51% of the females had only a low level of formal education. Only 20% of the males and 21% of the females were on the highest level of formal education. This does not coincide with the general population distribution. In the sample, persons with lower education are overrepresented. The picture is the same for vocational training: a high percentage of the male (35%) and female (51%) suicide attempters had no vocational training. Only 8% of the males and 4% of the females had the highest category of vocational training. These figures have been unchanged during the last years.

A relatively large proportion of the suicide attempters, 18% of the males and 9% of the females, were unemployed (suicide attempt rates for unemployed males and females 348/100,000; for employed males and females 83/100,000). 32% of the males and 50% of the female suicide attempters were economically inactive.

In relation to the economically active population (i.e. those who are able to work), the percentages of the unemployed suicide attempters were 27% for the males and 19% for the females. Also, a relatively high percentage of the suicide attempters had never had a job (males 12%; females 28%).

For international comparisons a classification of the social status into three classes was made. 48% of the males and 24% of the females with suicide attempts belonged to the lowest social class. Only 8% of the males and 5% of the females belonged to the highest class.

In-patient treatment was recommended in 61% of the cases of suicide attempts committed by males and 53% for those of females. Out-patient or community mental health institutions were recommended for males in 24% and for females in 35% of all cases. No aftercare was recommended for 16% of the males and 13% for the females.

Repetition

Thirty-one percent of all male and 38% of all female suicide attempters had made a previous suicide attempt. 9% of the males and 13% of the females committed one or more further suicide attempt(s) after their inclusion in the study. The analysis of all cases of the total sample revealed a repetition rate of the "first evers" of 17% among males and 22% among females within a 12-month period.

Comparisons between the persons with only one suicide attempt and persons with two or more suicide attempts showed a trend towards a lower mean age of the repeaters (males: 37.1 years versus 34.8 years; females: 37.2 years versus 34.5 years). The repeaters were not more often divorced or separated (persons with one suicide attempt vs repeaters: males: 16%/13%: females 16%/18%); however, the male repeaters were more often unemployed than male non-repeaters (male repeaters: 22% versus non-repeaters 16%; females: 9% versus 9%). In contrast to earlier results of this study suicide attempt methods did not differ significantly between non-repeaters and repeaters ("poisoning": male repeaters 53% vs. non-repeaters: 52%; female repeaters 69% vs. non-repeaters 75%; "cutting": male repeaters and non-repeaters 22%, females: repeaters 19% vs. 12% in non-repeaters).

Discussion

The general suicide rates in Germany are on the average below the European average (see chapter 4). The rates differ significantly within the various states with significantly higher rates for Saxonia, Saxonia-Anhalt and Thuringia and lower rates for the Western states. These differences of the suicide rates of the various states or regions have been known since the beginning of registration of suicide in German states (1877 and 1897; Winkler, 1960; Felber & Winiecki, 1998; Lester, 2000). The hypotheses to explain these differences are very speculative, when they do not refer to alcoholism and some sociological variables (Winkler, 1960).

"Non-German" suicides are significantly younger than the German suicides (males −11.5 years, females −15.3 years (Schmidtke, Weinacker & Löhr, 2000). This reflects perhaps a cultural difference in the treatment of the elderly in the families.

Also since the beginning of the registration of suicides the age distribution follows the "Hungarian pattern" (Schmidtke, Weinacker & Löhr, 2000). Similar to other European countries the suicide rates of the elderly are much higher than those of younger people, despite suicides among the younger age groups being the second most frequent cause of death after accidents. As in most countries also the male rates are significantly higher, the average ratio being 1:2.3 in the last years.

Over time the rates have been decreasing since the seventies. The overall suicide rate peaked in West-Germany in 1977 and in East-Germany in 1976 (Schmidtke & Weinacker, 1994). A previously found cohort effect similar to this found in other countries for the birth cohorts since 1932 with higher suicide rates in all age groups for successive cohorts (Häfner & Schmidtke, 1985), observable in both parts of Germany, seem to fade out in the last years (Schmidtke, Weinacker & Löhr, 2000).

The long term trends also show that over time there is a change in the age composition of the suicides. The percentage of suicides of males 60 years and older of the total number of suicides increased only slightly from 31% for the period 1952 – 1956 to 32% for the period 1995-1999 (the increase of the percentage of these age groups of the total male population for the same periods: 14% to 18%). However, the percentage of suicides for women older than 60 years increased from 31% to 48%, despite the fact that their percentage in the whole population increased only from 17% to 26%. Thus, at the moment nearly every second female suicide is a suicide by a women 60 years and older.

The average suicide rate for the last five available years (1995–1999) is for males 34% and for females 54% less than for the period 1976–1980. These decreases are similar for the "old" and the "new" states (the former GDR), even after the reunification Closer inspection of the data shows that this was generally true except for elderly men in the old states. This decrease of suicide rates was part of a steady pattern. Therefore, the decrease in the suicide rates after the reunification of Germany seems to be a continuation of the general trends since the late 1970s rather than a consequence of the reunification. In comparison to neighboring nations these decreases were not unique (Schmidtke et al., 1999). They were not anticipated in accordance with some of the economic and political trends in the new states. The unemployment rate in the New States has risen enormously (average 2000: 17.4%). In the New States women have also lost more economic and political resources since the reunification in comparison with women in the old states (Adler, 1996). The decrease also can not be attributed to a change in the death certification procedures after the reunification. On the other hand, in contrast to these economic and political changes, the reunification has led to a greater surge in religiosity in the new states than elsewhere. This may have reduced suicide rates accordingly (Lester, 1992; Stack, 1982, 1996)

An approximation of the female to the male suicide rates over time is not detectable. In some of the older age groups the differences even increased (Schmidtke, Weinacker & Löhr, 2000).

The typical German suicide method is "hanging" (Schmidtke, Weinacker & Löhr, 2000) with more than 80 % already in the younger age groups. In comparison with other countries it is nearly impossible to prevent in general this suicide method (particularly with reference to guns). In evaluating the changes of methods in Germany one has to take into account a covariation of the decrease of soft methods with an increase of undetermined deaths in the statistics (Schmidtke & Weinacker, 1991; Wiegand, 1987).

The German suicide attempt rates are below the European average. In general the same age and sex distribution as in other countries could be found (Schmidtke, Fricke & Weinacker, 1994). Over time, despite the high variance in the rates, in general a long-term increasing trend is observable. The increase amounts to 32% for males between the periods 1989/1993 – 1995/1999; for females for the same periods to 18%. A decrease would have possibly been attributed at least partly to a "fading out" of the monitoring system, up to now no valid hypotheses for these increases are available.

In comparison to previous years, where the suicide attempt rates of foreigners were lower (Feuerlein & Polanetzky, 1982; Häfner, 1980; Reuhl & Lutz, 1992), foreigners are no longer underrepresented since the percentage of foreigners has now increased and is more or less in accordance with the percentage of foreigners in the population. Therefore, the old hypotheses that over time the suicidal behaviour of foreigners (the in-Germany born generation of foreigners) will come more into line with the suicidal behaviour of Germans (Häfner, 1980) could be proven.

The percentage of people who received a psychiatric diagnosis has remained mainly the same (1989-1993: males: 78%, females: 70%; 1995-1999: males: 77%, females: 68%). The most prevalent diagnosis for both periods for males and females (23%) was "adjustment disorder" (ICD-9; 309); the second highest group of diagnoses "affective disorders". However, in reference to Lester (1972), it has to be considered that "adjustment disorders" as well as "abnormal reactions to stress" could possibly represent so-called "contaminated" diagnoses, describing only the suicidal act with other words. Therefore it is questionable whether the real rate of psychiatric disorders among suicide attempters is so high. There is also a notable increase of personality disorders (5%). The increase in these diagnoses can perhaps be attributed to a greater awareness of personality disorders due to the new multiaxial classification systems. In contrast to these findings, in the other 4 European centres which assessed psychiatric diagnoses "adjustment disorders" increased significantly (frequency for males: 24 %, females 31%) and the frequency of the diagnoses "personality disorders" and "neurotic depression" decreased.

The percentage of male suicide attempters living alone has increased during the last years about 12% whereas for females the percentage has almost remained the same. Perhaps this reflects the changes in living styles.

The higher percentage of urban suicide attempters in comparison to rural suicide attempters has remained the same. This fact is found in many studies on suicide attempters.

The percentage of unemployed suicide attempters has increased (for males +13%, females +3%). These differences reflect the rise in unemployment in Germany in this period (Germany: 1991 7.3% – 1999 11.7 %; Wuerzburg: 1991 3.9% – 1999 6.6%).

In general, as in other European catchment areas, suicide attempters seem in comparison to the general population to belong more often to the social categories which indicate social destabilization and poverty. Thus, this study has also provided additional evidence of a covariation of certain sociodemographic or socioeconomic conditions and the occurrence of attempted suicide in Germany (Welz, 1979, 1981, 1982; Breitmaier et al., 1986; Mösler, 1992; Mösler, Weidenhammer & Lungershausen, 1991; Häfner, 1998).

A positive result is that for males and for females the repetition rate decreased during the period of 1989 to 1999 from 49% to 37%. For males there was only a small decrease in repetition (43% to 35%). The repetition rate for females has decreased over time even though the percentage of high-risk groups – like the percentage of separated and divorced people and the unemployment rate has increased. The decrease of repetition is presumably caused due to the increase of therapeutic possibilities, more hotline services and crisis intervention agencies and the improvement of prevention strategies, mainly for persons who have already committed one suicide attempt.

References

Adler, M (1996). Impact of German unification on the status of women in the rural east and west. *Sociological Focus*, 29, 291 310.
Breitmaier, J, Becker, U, Kulessa, C, Böhme, K, Schäfer, D, & Drisch, E. (1986). Selbstvergiftungen in Heidelberg 1974-1980. Ergebnisse einer ökologischen Mehrebenenanalyse. In: F Specht und A Schmidtke (Eds.): *Selbstmordhandlungen bei Kindern und Jugendlichen.* Beiträge zur Erforschung selbstdestruktiven Verhaltens, Band 2. Regensburg: Roderer. S. 280-290.

Felber, W & Winiecki, P (1998). Suizide in der ehemaligen DDR zwischen 1961 und 1989 bisher unveröffentlichtes Material zur altersbezogenen Suizidalität. *Suizidprophylaxe*, 25, 42-49.

Feuerlein, W. (1971). Selbstmordversuch oder parasuizidale Handlung? *Nervenarzt*, *42*, 127-130.

Feuerlein, W & Polanetzki, P (1982). Selbstmordversuche bei Ausländern und Deutschen. Eine vergleichende Studie. *Crisis*, 3,63-77.

Häfner, H (1980). Psychiatrische Morbidität von Gastarbeitern in Mannheim. Epidemiologische Analyse einer Inanspruchnahmepopulation. *Nervenarzt*, 51, 672 – 683.

Häfner, H (1998). Arbeitslosigkeit und Suizidalität. *Suizidprophylaxe*, 97, 141 – 152.

Häfner, H & Schmidtke, A (1985). Do cohort effects influence suicide rates? *Archives of General Psychiatry*, 42, 926-927.

Lester, D (1972). *Why people kill themselves.* Springfield: Thomas.

Lester, D (2000). Explaining the regional variation of suicide in Germany. *Suizidprophylaxe*, 27, 67-69.

Mösler, T (1992). *Suizidhandlungen im Stadtgebiet Nürnberg.* Eine epidemiologische und ökologische Untersuchung über Häufigkeiten und Ursachen. (= Beiträge zur Erforschung selbstdestruktiven Verhaltens, Band 18.) Regensburg: Roderer.

Mösler, TA, Weidenhammer, W & Lungershausen, E (1991) Vergleich soziodemographischer Daten von selbstaggressiven mit fremdaggressiven Personen im Nürnberger Stadtgebiet. *Nervenheilkunde*, 10, 193 – 197.

Müller, P (1991) Suizid in Sachsen. Soziologische Annäherung an ein brisantes Thema. *MMG*, 16, 136-145.

Reuhl, J & Lutz, FU (1992). Suizide in einer westdeutschen Großstadt (1985-1989). *Versicherungsmedizin*, 44, 13 – 15.

Schmidtke, A, Fricke, S & Weinacker, B (1994). The epidemiology of attempted suicide in the Würzburg area, Germany 1989-1992. In: AJFM Kerkhof, A Schmidtke, U Bille-Brahe, D DeLeo & J Lönnqvist (Eds.). *Attempted suicide in Europe*. Leiden: DSWO Press, 159-174.

Schmidtke, A & Weinacker, B (1991). Covariation of suicides and undetermined deaths among elderly persons: a methodological study. *Crisis*, 12, 44 – 58.

Schmidtke, A & Weinacker, B (1994). Suizidalität in der Bundesrepublik und den einzelnen Bundesländern: Situation und Trends. *Suizidprophylaxe*, 21, 4-16.

Schmidtke, A, Weinacker, B & Löhr, C (2000). Epidemiologie der Suizidalität im 20. Jahrhundert. In: M Wolfersdorf & C Franke (Eds.). *Suizidforschung und Suizidprävention am Ende des 20. Jahrhunderts.* Regensburg: Roderer, 63-88.

Schmidtke, A, Weinacker, B, Stack, S & Lester, D (1999). The impact of the reunification of Germany on the suicide rate. *Archives of Suicide Research*, 5, 233-239.

Stack, S (1982). Suicide: a decade review of the sociological literature. *Deviant Behaviour*, 4, 41-66.

Stack, S (1996). *Sociological risk factors in suicide: A 15 year review.* Paper presented at the annual meeting of the Michigan Association of Suicidology, Lansing.

Welz, R (1979). *Selbstmordversuche in städtischen Lebenswelten.* Weinheim: Beltz.

Welz, R (1981). Epidemiologie und räumliche Verteilung von Selbstmordversuchen. In: R Welz & H Pohlmeier (Eds.). *Selbstmordhandlungen.* Weinheim: Beltz, 77-99.

Welz, R (1982). Räumliche Verteilung von Selbstmordversuchen in einer städtischen Region. In: LA Vaskovics (Eds.). *Raumbezogenheit sozialer Probleme.* Opladen: Westdeutscher Verlag, 250-272.

Wiegand, A (1987). Rückgang der Todesfälle durch Suizid in Berlin. *Suizidprophylaxe.* 14, 199-224.

Winkler, WF (1960). Über den Wandel in Häufigkeit, Bedingungen und Beurteilung des Suicids in der Nachkriegszeit. *Der Öffentliche Gesundheitsdienst*, 22, 135-145.

Chapter 17

Suicidal Behaviour in Switzerland

A. Schmidtke, B. Weinacker, C. Löhr, V. Waeber & K. Michel

Description of the catchment area

The Swiss area under study comprises the region of Berne. Berne and its agglomeration has a total population of 324,000 inhabitants. The catchment area differs little in the demographic and socioeconomic characteristics from the rest of the country (age and sex distribution, civil status, percentage of foreigners, distribution of working population into economic sectors such as farming, industry, services). The greater part of the inhabitants of the catchment area live in the urban area. The provision of in- and outpatient health care in Switzerland is funded by private insurance schemes, paid either directly to the provider or indirectly via patient. Hospitals are heavily subsidized by the state. Outpatient care is mainly provided by general practitioners and specialists working in their own private practices but also by "policlinics" usually attached to hospitals. For outpatient treatment, patients have to carry 10% of the costs from their own pocket. Pychiatric care is provided by several institutions: the university hospital (inpatient care), the social psychiatric clinic (inpatient crisis unit and outpatient care), the psychiatric university outpatient clinic with a 24-hour emergency psychiatric service (located at the general hospital, but providig outpatient care), and the university department for child and adolescent psychiatry (inpatient and outpatient care). Additionally, there is one private psychiatric hospital in the catchment area.

Sample and method of data collection

Switzerland is one of the countries in the world with a long tradition of registration of suicides. Since 1876, the Statistical Bureau collects nationwide data on suicide.

As in other European countries no official data on suicide attempts are available. The information on attempted suicide, therefore, is based as in the other centers on data collected within the study. The majority of suicide attempters admitted to the accident and emergency ward or to any other wards of the hospital were seen by the psychiatrist on duty. This was an ideal setting for the collection of data. In other hospitals and wards a trained person was responsible for supervision of data collection. The monitoring form was filled out shortly after admission of the patients, either by doctors or members of the nursing staff. The research team visited the hospitals regularly and checked the medical records for unreported cases. Furthermore, general practitioners were contacted either personally or in writing. Of the 369 general practitioners and internists in the catchment area 83 (22,4%) agreed to participate. In addition, 57 practicing psychologists were contacted and 18 (31,5%) provide data. Data were available for the period 1989 – 1990, and 1993 – 1998.

Results

Suicides

In 2000, the latest year for which nationwide data are available in Switzerland, 1378 persons committed suicide. The suicide figures are 27.3 for males and 8.6 for females. The sex ratio males to females for suicide in Switzerland was in 1989 2.4:1, 1998 3.2:1 (see figure 1).

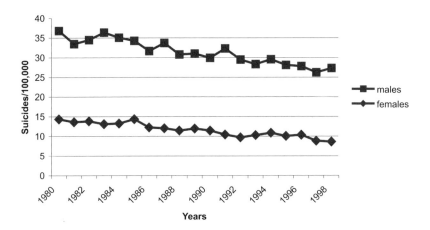

Figure 1. Suicide rates by gender over time for Switzerland

For Switzerland it is possible to compute long-term trends. Using Box-Jenkins analyses already Häfner & Schmidtke showed that on the long run, no significant trends over time were detectable. The increases or decreases are mostly short-time, e.g. affecting only shorter periods of time. In the last years, the Swiss suicide rate has been decreasing.

Attempted suicide

The majority of cases (85%) were reported from the general hospitals, 11% from psychiatric hospitals, and only 3% of all cases were reported by general practitioners and hardly any by practising psychologist. These figures, however, are not representative of the actual distribution of the type of treatment suicide attempters receive because in many cases there was an overlap of reporting from various sources. No attempt was made to record all the subsequent contacts with health care facilities if a patient was referred from one institution to another. Even if the cooperating general practitioners did not report all cases it is unlikely that this could have affected the total of all cases. Therefore, the estimation is that the data represent 90% of all cases seen in medical institutions.

During the two assessment periods from 1989 to 1990 and from 1993 to 1998 a total of 1714 suicide attempts were recorded. These events involved 1432 persons. The event/person ratio from these figures therefore is 1.20 over all years.

The highest rates per 100,000 were found in the first year for women aged 20-24 (374) and for men aged 25-29 (309). The average rates for both years (age 15+) were 157 for women and 121 for men (see figure 2).

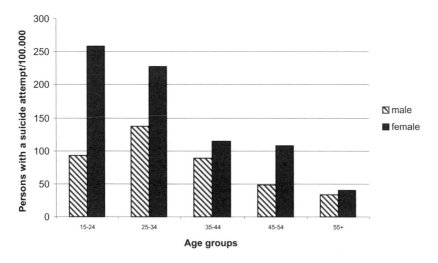

Figure 2. Rates of attempted suicide by age and gender, Berne, 1995-1999

The rates of attempted suicide are highest for the group of the economically active but unemployed persons. However, because of the small numbers this rate should not be overvalued. The rates are 95 for the employed and 129 for the economically inactive.

5 percent of the men and 13 percent of the women never had a job. Nine percent (males) and 3% (female) were self-employed while 87% (m) and 84% (f) were employed. Therefore, the rates per 100,000 for employed persons were 167 and those for the self-employed 108.

The rates per 100,000 were highest for divorced persons: 200 for men and 288 for women. For unmarried (including "cohabiting") persons they were 116 (m) and 143 (f), for married (including separated) persons 65 (m) and 93 (f), for widowed persons 100 (m) and 103 (f).

In the usual living arrangements few differences between men and women were found. Twenty-seven percent of the persons lived alone, 14% with their parents, 27%

(m) and 25% (f) with a partner without children, 16% with a partner and children. Five percent of the women lived with a child only. Five percent of all patients lived in an institution.

Using the general population statistics rates per 100,000 of attempted suicide were calculated for persons living alone (167), for those living alone with children (163), those living with a partner only (109) and for persons living with partner and children (71).

Persons were assigned to three categories according to the level of education when leaving school: (1) primary school and special schools (77%), (2) secondary school (11%) and (3) high school (Gymnasium) and other higher schools (12%).

Rates per 100,000 were highest for those who finished secondary school, 185, compared to 111 with the lowest and 82 with the highest level of schooling.

Vocational training: Because our categories are not directly comparable with those of the general population statistics, it was not possible to calculate the rates of attempted suicide for the different groups. In contrast to the first two years of assessment, persons without a formal work training are no longer overrepresented in our population (1989-1990: 32%; 1989-1998: 12%).

58% were considered as economically active (i.e. not of school age, retired, disabied, etcetera). Out of this group 62% of all men and 48% of all women were employed while 7% of all men and 3% of all women were unemployed. Thirty-one percent of the men and 49% of the women were econornically inactive.

There were little differences in the rates of attempted suicide between the various religious groups. Those who had no religious denomination represented 6% and the rate of attempted sucide was 108. Sixty-two percent were protestants, with a rate of 92. The 25% catholics had a rate of 107, and the 7 percent with another religion 149/100,000.

An average of 23% of the men and 18% of the women were of foreign nationality, which is slightly higher than the percentage of foreigners in Switzerland (19%). Foreigners had higher rates of attempted suicide than the Swiss: the rates per 100,000 were 121 (m) and 170 (f) for foreigners compared to 98 (m) and 117 (f) for the Swiss population. There was no significant difference between the distribution of the persons by the country of birth and the distribution by nationality.

The majority of persons attempting suicide (66% of the men and 65% of the women) lived in the City of Berne (about 136,000 inhabitants). About 25% changed their address within the previous year: 10% of the men and 11% of the women had moved within the catchment area, 13% (m) and 9% (f) had moved within Switzerland and 2% (m) and 3% (f) had previously lived abroad. However, no population data were available on the mobility of the population in the catchment area.

Fiftyfour percent (m) and 46% (f) of all attempts were first attempts. Seventeen percent of the males and 21% of the females had made an attempt within the previous 12 months.

Twelve percent of the males and 13% of the males made further attempts after the first attempt was assessed, most of them within the following year. As mentioned in the introductory remarks we have to take into account that certain frequent repeaters (e.g. those cutting their wrists) were discharged without having been registered for our study. We therefore expect that if all repeaters were included the true rate of repetition would be higher.

When more than one method was used (which was the case in 36.6 percent (m), and 32.8 percent (f), respectively), the method considered the most dangerous was taken. Drugs and alcohol added up to 56.1 percent of the events carried out by men and to 76.0 percent of those carried out by women. When the methods used in combination were included (adding up to a total of 1915 methods) the picture is somewhat different: drugs and alcohol represent 66 percent of all the methods used by men and 81 percent of those used by women. This indicates that drugs and alcohol are commonly combined with other methods (e.g. cutting). There was a significant sex difference in the distribution of the methods ($\chi^2 = 119,14$, df = 23, p<.001). Notable differences were found in the use of psychotropic drugs (45.6 percent of methods used by men compared to 63.8 percent of methods used by women). Cutting was more often used by men (21.3% (m) versus 13% (f)), also hanging and suffocating were relatively more often used by men (5.3% (m) versus 1.4% (f)).

Men were more likely to be referred or kept in inpatient care (51% (m) versus 45% (f)), including both general and psychiatric hospital care. Outpatient care was recommended in 17 percent (m) and 26 percent (f), respectively. In 14% (m) and 15% (f) patients were discharged without recommended aftercare. It should be noted that these are recommendations for treatment shortly after the event, usually by the consultation psychiatrist. We do not know how in how many cases these recommendations were actually followed.

Discussion

The catchment area includes mainly an urban but also a rural population and there is no difference in the distribution of the population into the three economic sectors (farming, industry, services) compared to Switzerland as a whole. Sex and age distribution are similar, but average income and the proportion of foreigners are both slightly higher in Berne. Therefore, it appears that Berne and its agglomeration can be considered representative for Switzerland regarding the main sociodemographic variables.

The fluctuation of the number of recorded suicide attempts between the first and the second year was surprising. Independently from these numbers it was noted that in the same year the number of referrals to the consultation service of our psychiatric clinic had dropped considerably, indicating a true reduction of the numbers of medically treated suicide attempters. Also, our efforts to gather lost cases were the same in both years. We therefore believe that this drop in the incidence is unlikely to be an artefact.

Surprisingly, only few reports were received from the cooperating general practitioners. Enquiries confirmed that general practitioners in private practice are rarely confronted with attempted suicide. A similar finding was reported by Walther and Noack (1993). In Berne, most suicide attempters or their relatives call an ambulance via emergency number and no general practitioner has to be involved. Also, patients are not enrolled with a general practitioner but are free in their choice of a health care provider.

Generally, reporting was reliable and we believe that the extrapolation of the recorded data with a factor of 1.1 is realistic. However, it may be that in the case of frequent repeaters sometimes not all events have been reported and therefore, the true event/persons ratio might be somewhat higher.

The total rates of attempted suicide are higher than the rates found by Zumbrunnen et al. (1990) in Geneva. However, this was to be expected as their cases were recorded at the university hospital only. Compared with other centres of the WHO/EURO Multicentre Study on Parasuicide (see Chapter 13) the mean person rates are lower than the average rates across all centres. This is noteworthy because the rate of completed suicide in Switzerland is clearly above average and ranges among the European countries with the highest suicide rates. The sex ratio female/male for persons attempting suicide was 1.53 for 1989 and 1.34 for 1990 which is dose to the median of all participating centres (1.5:1). For comparison: the sex ratio for completed suicide in Switzerland was 2.4 m/f (1989).

The highest event and person rates for men are found in the age groups 25-29 and for women in the age groups 15-29. The differences between men and women are most marked in the 15-19 age group.

Using the demographic data available on the catchment area population (Bundesamt für Statistik, 1993) we were able to calculate rates of attempted suicide for various sociodemographic risk populations. Categories and their definitions were not always similar and we therefore had to limit ourselves to those variables where a comparison of general population data with our data seemed adequate. Divorced persons had rates above average while married persons had low rates. Similarly, persons living without partner (with or without a child at home) had higher rates than those living with a partner. Those living with a partner and children had the lowest rates. Surprisingly, persons who had finished school at a secondary school level had increased rates of attempted suicide while those who had attended primary school or a high school had lower rates. The high rates of those at school or in training can be explained with the young age which by itself is a potent risk factor. Unskilled workers probably have an increased risk of attempted suicide although we were unable to calculate rates. Self-employed persons had lower rates than employees. And, last, foreigners had higher rates than the Swiss. Many of these findings are consistent with those reported by others, for example by Hawton and Catalan (1987), but a direct comparison of the results with those of other centres of the WHO/EURO Multicentre Study will now enable us to determine if there are risk factors specific for our country.

Drug overdoses were the most common method, accounting for 52% (m) and 70% (f) of the methods, followed by cutting and jumping from high places. Alcohol was recorded as the only method in ca. 5% but was altogether found in 24.7% of all events, usually in combination with another method. A more detailed analysis of the methods used by the same patient population (Michel et al., 1991) showed that in over 40% of the overdoses a combination of several drugs had been taken. Benzodiazepines nearly represented 50% of all the drugs taken, followed by antidepressants (11%). Analgetics are relatively rarely used (9.6%). It is interesting to note that the patterns of drugs used differ considerably between different countries, for example, in Britain, paracetamol is the drug used most frequently (Hawton and Fagg, 1992). Availability of drugs obviously plays a major role and this would be another important area for further comparison because this factor could easily be influenced.

Acknowledgements

Our thanks to the many persons in the different institutions who gave their best to fill in the forms and to Ch. Knecht, I. Kohler, Ch. Jaeggi and M. Sturzenegger who worked for the project in various stages.

This project could only be realized because of the financial support by the Schweizerischer Nationalfonds zur Förderung der wissenschaftlichen Forschung, Projekt Number 32-25379.88.

References

Bundesamt für Statistik (1993). *Info à la Carte*. Bern.

Hawton K & Catalan, J (1987). *Attempted suicide. A practical guide to its nature and management*. Oxford: Oxford Medical Publications.

Hawton K & Fagg J (1992). Trends in deliberate self-poisoning and self-injury in Oxford, 1976-1990. *British Medical Journal*, 304: 1409-1411.

Michel K, Knecht Ch., Kohler I, & Sturzenegger M (1991). Suizidversuche in der Agglomeration Bern. *Schweiz. Med Wochenschrift*, 121: 1133-1130.

Michel K, Waeber V, Valach L, Arestegui G & Spuhler T (1994). A comparison of the drugs taken in fatal and nonfatal self-poisoning. *Acta Psychiatrica Scandinavica, 90*, 184-189.

Platt S, Bille-Brahe, U, Kerkhof A, Schmidtke, A, Bjerke, Crepet P, De Leo D, Haring C, Lönnqvist J. Michel K, Philippe A, Pommereau X, Querejetä, Salander-Renberg E, Temesvary, B, Wasserman D & Sampaio Faria J (1992). Parasuicide in Europe: the WHO/EURO Multicentre Study on Parasuicide. 1. Introduction and preliminary analysis for 1989. *Acta Psychiatrica Scandinavica*, 85: 97-104.

Spuhler Th & Michel K (1993). Suizid. In W Weiss (Ed.), *Gesundheit in der Schweiz*. Zürich: Seismo Verlag.

Walther F, & Noack H (1994). *Suizid und Suizidversuch in der ärztlichen Praxis*. Dissertation, University of Bern, Switzerland.

Zumbrunnen R, Madoni F & Volterra V (1990). Compared patterns of parasuicide in two European cities: Bologna (Italy) and Geneva (Switzerland). In G Ferrari, M Bellini, & P Crepet (Eds.), *Suicidal behavior and risk factors*. Bologna: Monduzzi Editore.

Eastern Europe

Chapter 18

Suicidal Behaviour in Lithuania

D. Gailienė

Description of the area

Lithuania is situated near the Baltic Sea and has a present population of approximately 3.5 million inhabitants. When the USSR disintegrated in 1991, the independent state of Lithuania was recognized by the world.

Sample and method of data collection

The first epidemiological data on suicide in Lithuania was obtainable from 1924, when suicide was categorized in accordance with international classification (XVII codes 163-171), and before World War II it was therefore possible to compare suicide rates in the Baltic States with rates in Western Europe. There were some differences between the three Baltic countries, and suicide rates were especially low in Lithuania, the average rate in 1924-1939 being 8.1/100,000 (Gailienė, 1999).

Data on suicide in Lithuania between 1940 and 1945 are missing. Data on the period between 1946 and 1961 are fragmented and somewhat unreliable (Gailienė, Domanskiene, Keturakis, 1995). The first reliable data from the period of Soviet occupation is from 1962. An abridged classification of causes of death based on the regular versions of the ICD-8 and ICD-9 was used. Before 1988, data regarding mortality due to suicides were kept secret in the former USSR. A qualitative and quantitative review of routines for classification and registration of suicide showed that the data used were, however, reliable for Baltic republics (Wasserman, Värnik, 1998). Procedure for registering causes of death did not change in the Baltic States after the restoration of their independence in 1990. Since 1998, classification based on ICD-10 has been used, and data on suicide mortality is obtainable from the Lithuanian Department of Statistics.

Attempted suicides are not registered regularly in Lithuania.

Results

Suicide

Over the last ten years, suicide has grown to become a serious social and public health problem for Lithuania. According to the WHO database, Lithuania, beside Estonia,

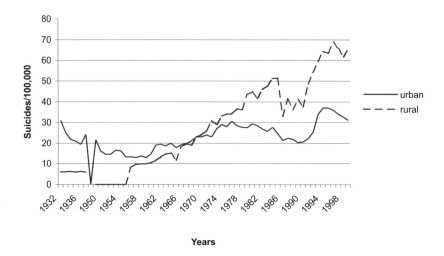

Figure 1. Suicide rates in Lithuania 1932-1998 by areas

Latvia and Russia, has one of the highest registered suicide rates in the world where in recent years, the rate has reached approximately 42 per 100,000.

In the pre-war independent state of Lithuania, suicide rates were low (Figure 1), but during the Soviet occupation, rates started to grow rapidly. At the beginning of the period 1962 and 1990, the suicide rate in Lithuania was 15.8 per 100,000 (25.6 for men and 7.3 for women). By 1984, the rates had increase by 27% to 35.9 per 100,000 (by 39% for men and by 7.9% for women).

At the beginning of political reforms in the Soviet Union – the perestrojka – in 1986, the Lithuanian rate of suicide fell abruptly by 25% to 25.1/100,000. Between 1984 and 1988, suicide rates had continued to decrease as in all the 15 republics of Soviet Union. The decrease varied from 5.3% in Armenia to 37.9% in Belarus, and for the whole of USSR, the suicide rate was reduced by 34.5% (Värnik, 1997).

In Lithuania, political reforms influenced men in particular, and male suicide rates decreased by 14%, compared to a decrease of only 1.4% for women. During the years 1987-1990, rates remained more or less on the same level.

Since the beginning of the 1990s, and during a period of radical social and economical reforms, suicide rates increased dramatically from 25.9 per 100,000 in 1990 to 46.4 per 100,000 in 1996. The rapid changes in society after 1990 influenced all groups of citizens aged 15 and over, but had the greatest effect on men aged 20-24 and women aged 50-59 years where rates of suicide increased by 81% and 7%, respectively. After 1996, the increasing trend was replaced by decreasing rates (from 46.4 per 100,000 in 1996 to 41.90 per 100,000 in 1999), but the Lithuanian rate remained among the highest in the western world.

In pre-war Lithuania, the gender ratio (m/f) was 2.3:1. During the Soviet occupation, the male rate varied markedly, while the female rate remained relatively stable. Therefore, the increase in the total rate in 1991 and 1996 was mainly due to the marked increase in male suicides. During the last five years, the sex ratio has been 4.5:1.

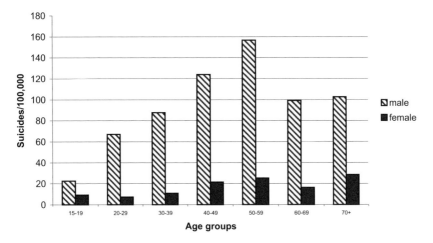

Figure 2. Suicide rates by age and gender in Lithuania 1998

Figure 2 shows that the risk of suicide is increased with age for women, but for men it is peaking among the 40-59 years old, with the main high-risk group being the middle-aged men.

In pre-war Lithuania, frequency of suicide was 4-5 times higher in the urban areas than in the rural parts. During the period 1970-1999, this changed somewhat, and in 1997, a little more than half (53%) of all suicides occurred in the larger cities, while close to half (47%) took place in the rural areas. In Lithuanian villages, however, rates remained higher than in the cities, the ratio being 2:1.

Hanging was the most common method of suicide in Lithuania among both men and women (89% and 75% respectively). Self-harm by firearms is more common for males (3.4%, 0.8%) while self-poisoning is more common among females (10.6%, 1.8%, respectively).

Conclusion

The variations in the rate of suicide in Lithuania are strongly associated with the socio-political changes that have taken place. Since the pre-war period, the number of suicides in the rural areas has increased 9-10 times, while in urban areas the number has changed insignificantly. The Soviet regime inflicted the greatest damage on the Lithuanian country to the extend that people in the rural areas were physically and psychologically exhausted due to the forced collectivism, and most people strived to push their children into the cities, where they were supposed to have better prospects.

Men seem to have been more affected by the changing socio-political conditions than women, and this also seems to be the ease during the transitional period after the regaining of independence (1991-1996). Although all groups of citizens aged 15 and over were affected, rates in rural areas remained high (Stankuniene, Jasilionis, Krumiņš, 1999).

References

Gailiené D (1999). Suicide Trends in Lithuania. *Revue Baltique*, 1999, 14 : 131-137.
Gailiené D, Domanskiene V, Keturakis V (1995). Suicide in Lithuania. *Archives of Suicide research* 1 (3): 149-158.
Stankuniene V, Jasilionis D, Kruminš J (1999). Social Differences in Mortality, Morbidity and Health-Related behaviour during Transition: Research findings in the three Baltic Countries. *Revue Baltique*, 14: 9-36.
Värnik A (1997). Suicide in the Baltic Countries and in the Former Republics of the USSR. Stockholm: Gotab.
Wasserman D, Värnik A (1998). Reliability of statistics on violent death and suicide in the former USSR, 1970 – 1990. *Acta Psychiatrica Scandinavica*, 98 (Suppl. 394): 34-41.

Chapter 19

Suicidal Behaviour in Slovenia

O. T. Grad, U. Groleger & A. Zavasnik

Description of the catchment area

Slovenia is a small central European country that became independent only in 1991. The catchment area under study by the centre in Ljubljana includes the capital of Slovenia and its suburbs with a total population of 273,180 and a female to male ratio of 1.10. The population of the catchment area over the age of 15 years totals 231,883 with a female to male ratio of 1.13.

Sample and method of data collection

Data on suicide are collected by the State Police, who report directly to the National Register of Suicide at the University Psychiatric Hospital. The attempted suicide data presented in this text were collected from 1995 up to and including 1998.

Results

Suicide

The average suicide rate for the whole population in the decade 1985 – 1994 was 31 per 100,000 (Marusic, 1999), while the highest ever suicide rate was found to be 35.8 per 100,000 in the year 1984 (Milcinski & Virant, 1985).

In 1998, suicide rates for Slovenia were 59.9 per 100,000 for males and 15.8 per 100,000 for females. In the same year, suicide rates in Ljubljana were 52.4 per 100,000 for males and 18.7 per 100,000 for females, the gender ratio (m/f) being 2.8. Rates were calculated for age groups 15 years and older.

An average profile of a Slovenian who commits suicide, is a man (the average gender ratio being 3.5 m/f) in his late forties (49.8 years of age), who used hanging as the method for the suicidal act (62.5%), had problems in his partnership (divorced or widowed), had a low level of education and had problems with alcohol or some other substance – either being dependent, addicted and/or being drunk at the time of the event (26%), and usually had some additional problems with health (Milcinski et al, 1998).

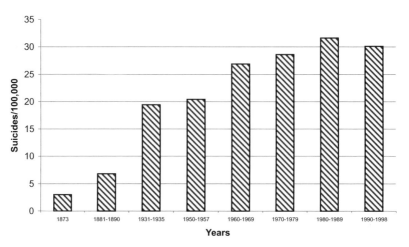

Figure 1. Suicide rates in Slovenia from 1873 – 1998

Attempted suicide

In Ljubljana catchment area in 1998, annual rates for medically treated suicide attempts suicides (events) were 82.7 per 100,000 for males and 83.7 per 100,000 for females. The attempted suicide to completed suicide ratio was 1.58 for males and 4.48 for females. The difference was significant ($\chi^2 = 13.79$, p = 0.0002). The gender ratio (m/f) was 0.988. No significant changes in attempted suicide rates were observed during the period of monitoring (1995 to 1998).

Through the period, 757 cases of attempted suicide were registered, of which 373 (49.3%) were committed by men and 384 (50.7%) by women. The event to person ratio was 1.2 with 333 men (53.3%) and 292 women (46.7%). The average age was 38.2 years (SD 18.40), among women, the mean age was 38.6 years (SD 19.11), and among men was 37.8 years (SD 17.57). The difference was not significant.

Epidemiological findings

General results

In our sample not all known socio-demographic suicide risk factors were confirmed. The majority of the catchment area (88.2%) was of Slovene nationality and there were no significant gender differences. Close to half (46.6%) of the attempters were never married, 17.5% were widowed, separated or divorced, and 35.7% were either married or cohabitating. There were no significant differences between the genders.

The same was true for education level, where less then half (45.7%) had a middle and 10.2% a high education. At the time of the event, 30.3% were living with their parents, 36% with their partners and 25% alone or in an institution (retirement homes,

correction facilities). Gender differences were statistically significant (for all categories, $\chi^2 = 59.941$, p < 0.001), women were more often living with partners, while men
more often lived alone at the time of the event ($\chi^2 = 6.57$, p=0.01). Men were far more
likely than women (19.9%, 4.8%, respectively) to be staying at an institution ($\chi^2 =$
38.02, p < 0.001). Less than one third of the whole sample was living with their parents
at the time of the event, however the difference between genders was not significant
(men 31.9%, women 28.7%).

Economic status was found to be significantly different for men and for women (χ^2
= 12.811, p = 0.002). More men (26.9%) than women (16.1%) were unemployed at the
time of the event, and more women (52.8%) than men (42.5) were inactive. About one
third of both male and female suicide attempters were employed and active at the time
of the event. Significant gender differences are summarized in Table 1.

The method used during the suicide attempt differed significantly between the genders ($\chi^2 = 1.4375$, p < 0.001). More women (51.2%) than men (30.4%) had poisoned

Table 1. Characteristics of suicide attempters by gender

	male	female	χ^2 (p)
Civil status			
Never married vs. married or cohabiting	52.8% vs. 32.2%	42.0% vs. 38.6%	4.37 (0.036)
Never married vs. widowed, divorced, separated	52.8% vs. 15.0%	42.0% vs. 19.4%	3.85 (0.05)
Married or cohabiting vs. widowed, divorced, separated	32.2% vs. 15.0%	38.5% vs. 19.4%	Ns
Usual household			
Living alone vs. with partner	15.2% vs. 32.2%	21.3% vs. 40.9%	Ns
Living alone vs. with parents	15.2% vs. 34.8%	21.3% vs. 32.9%	Ns
Living alone vs. in institution	15.2% vs. 17.4%	21.3% vs. 4.5%	20.79 (0.0000)
With partner vs. institution	32.2% vs. 17.4%	40.9% vs. 4.5%	22.48 (0.0000)
With parents vs. institution	34.8% vs. 17.4%	32.9% vs. 4.5%	14.18 (0.0002)
Education			
Low vs. middle vs. high	42.6%/46.2%/11.3%	45.3%/45.3%/9.4%	Ns
Professional vs. secondary	20.9% vs. 23.4%	10.0% vs. 34.7%	13.80 (0.0002)
Economic status			
Unemployed vs. inactive	23.9% vs. 43.2%	15.2% vs. 51.8%	7.38 (0.007)
Nationality			
Slovene vs. others	95% vs. 5%	96.5% vs. 3.5%	Ns
Accompanying person			
Family, friend vs. official	41.3% vs. 55.4%	59.2% vs 34.3%	16.72 (0.0000)
Method			
+Non-violent* vs. +violent*	44.7% vs. 39.6%	74.3% vs. 14.6%	85.60 (0.0000)

themselves by benzodiazepine, hypnotics, antidepressants and antipsychotics. Also, more women (12.6%) than men (6%) had used analgesics, antipyretics or antirheumatics.

So-called 'soft methods' were used in 74.3 per cent of all cases of female suicide attempts, while 44.7 per cent of all male suicide attempts were committed by a 'violent' method (χ^2 = 94.52, p = 0.0000). Poisoning by carbon monoxide was seen among men in only 9 cases, and in six cases the attempter had tried to drown him/herself, and pesticides or some other chemicals had been used in 18 cases.

According to available data, the sample was divided in four groups according to the pattern of repetition: (1) prospective repeaters, who repeated the attempt after the index attempt; (2) first evers, who had made no attempts neither before nor after the index attempt; (3) retrospective repeaters with a history of attempts prior to the index attempt; and (4) attempters with an unknown history of previous attempts. In all four groups there were significant differences between genders (χ^2 = 21.932, p = 0.000).

Eighty-four attempters repeated the attempt after the index attempt, and of these, 46 (54.8%) were men and 38 (45.2%) were women. Thirty (35.7%) repeaters repeated the attempt twice, and 40% three times. The gender ratio (f/m) for those repeating the attempt after the index attempt was 0.83. For the first-ever group the ratio was 1.26, but the difference was not statistically significant (χ^2 = 2.94, p = 0.087). Among those who had only made suicide attempts prior to the index attempt, the gender ratio (f/m) was higher (1.44), and the difference between the genders statistically significant (χ^2 = 5.44, p = 0.02).

Checking the differences between the first-evers and the repeaters (table 2), no significant differences were found in regard to mean age and gender. The majority of first-evers (80%) were treated in the hospital, compared to 69% of repeaters, who were more often treated as outpatients (23%) or not treated at all (8%). There were no differences between the groups regarding nationality, marital status and usual household. However, significant differences were found in regards to the level of education, where the first-

Table 2. Attempted suicide in first-evers vs. repeaters

Civil status	first-evers	repeaters	χ^2 (p)
Single vs. partner	64.6% vs. 35%	64% vs. 36%	Ns
Usual household			
Living alone vs. with others	19.7% vs. 71.7%	13.7% vs. 72.6%	Ns
Education			
Low vs. middle vs. high	43.9%/48.8%/7.3%	47.1%/37.1%/15.7%	5.91 (0.05)
University vs. secondary	7% vs. 32.9%	13.2% vs. 23.5%	4.05 (0.044)
Economic status			
Employed/unemployed/inactive	34.3%/14.8%/50.9%	25%/31.3%/43.8%	11.39 (0.003)
Nationality			
Slovene vs. others	95.3% vs. 4.7%	93.4% vs. 6.6%	Ns
Method			
Non-violent vs. violent	59.8% vs. 24.1%	58.5% vs. 27.1%	Ns

evers were over-represented among those on the middle education level (48.8%). Also, there were significant differences regarding employment status ($\chi^2 = 11.393$, p =0.003), wherein 31.3% of repeaters were unemployed compared to 14.8% of the first-evers. Finally, there were no significant differences between first-evers and repeaters in regard to the method used.

Peculiarities of the catchment area

Since 1974, a special crisis intervention unit for suicide attempters and people in varying sorts of life crisis has been organized at the University Psychiatric Hospital of Ljubljana. Since 1980 many telephone crisis lines have started operating to help people in immedate crisis, and regular seminars for the teachers at primary and secondary schools on how to recognize and react to a suicidal child or adolescent have been developed. As well as this, seminars for GPs, a special program for suicide survivors, and information brochures for the media on how the media should report on suicide have been distributed. National and international research on suicide and attempted suicide has also been going on throughout the years.

The official number of suicide attempts is almost the same as the number of suicides, while the gender ratio of attempted suicide is 1:1. It is believed however, that the number of suicide attempts is highly underestimated, and this has been supported by the Slovenian data in the WHO/EURO Multicentre Study on Suicidal Behaviour. In the catchment area of Ljubljana that represents Slovenia in this study, it was found that there were five times more attempted suicides monitored than in the years previous to entering the study.

Conclusion

Suicide and suicide attempts are considered a serious problem in Slovenia, with the rates being among the highest in Europe. This research has found out that there are even more suicide attempts than usually reported. This fact and all the details found within the project will help us to plan, implement and evaluate the preventive activities in the future.

References

Grad OT (1995). Why is the incidence of suicide in Slovenia one of the highest in Europe. In: OT Grad (Ed.). *How to reduce suicide in Slovenia.* Proposal for the national programme for suicide prevention in Slovenia. WHO Regional Office for Europe.

Marusic A (1999). Suicide in Slovenia: Lessons for cross-cultural psychiatry. *International Review of Psychiatry.* 11: 212-218.

Milcinski L & Virant-Jaklic M (1986). *Samomor in samomorilni poskus v Sloveniji v letu 1985.* (Suicide and suicide attempt in Slovenia in 1985). Ljubljana: Psihiatricna klinika Ljubljana.

Milcinski L, Virant-Jaklic M, Jeraj T (1998). *Samomor in samomorilni poskus v Sloveniji leta 1996.* (Suicide and suicide attempt in Slovenia in 1996). Ljubljana: Psihiatricna klinika Ljubljana.

Statistical Office of the Republic of Slovenia (1999). *Statistical Yearbook of the Republic of Slovenia,* Ljubljana.

Chapter 20

Suicidal Behaviour in the Federal Republic of Yugoslavia (Serbia and Montenegro)

S. Selakovic-Bursic

Description of the catchment area

The city of Novi Sad is located in the north of Yugoslavia (and Serbia), spread out in the Pannonian plains on both sides of the river Danube. It lies about 100 km south of Hungary, 150 km west of Romania and about 40 km east of Croatia. It is the provincial capital of Vojvodina, Serbia's northern province, populated by about 2 million people. It is also the economic, administrative and educational centre of the region. The population of Novi Sad itself is about 300,000. For more than 40 years Novi Sad has been a university centre, today comprising of nearly 20 various faculties with about 30,000 students.

Novi Sad is the second largest city (next to Belgrade) of present Yugoslavia, not only in population, but also in the economic sense. Besides agriculture, which is one of the major areas of economiy, it is also a big industrial centre.

The health care system has, as in the whole country, undergone some very turbulent changes in recent years. A decade ago, in former Yugoslavia, it was entirely state managed, with no private practice possibilities and with health insurance that entitled full health coverage, which meant that everything (medication, inpatient and outpatient care) was free of charge for the individual. In the following years, with all the social upheavals and deteriorating economy, the health care system also changed significantly – for the worse. Private practices appeared and developed, while the public health deteriorated in quality, since the state lacked funds to support it. Fewer services were available through public health care, while private practices are not covered by health insurance of any kind, so the individual has to pay for them in full. The supply of medications in state owned hospitals and pharmacies has also decreased over the last decade, again for the same reasons, shortage of money. As the result, many privately owned pharmacies started up, offering a full range of medications (again, without the coverage of health insurance). Private pharmacies sell drugs without medical prescription and verbal requests for drugs, including all psychopharmaceuticals, are sufficient. This means, in practice, that even a teenager or a child can get sedatives or hypnotics just like any over-the-counter drug. Currently, the state is making an effort to eradicate this practice, but unless the overall situation of the state health care system and drug supply improves, this is not likely to happen.

In terms of outpatient health care, there are nearly 50 outpatient health centres in the municipality of Novi Sad. They offer services of general practitioners, as well as specialists in nearly all branches of medicine. Inpatient services are all grouped in a single

Clinical Centre, with a capacity of about 1200 beds, consisting of various specialized units. The second inpatient facility is the Military Hospital, and contains almost a couple of hundred beds, mostly for patients with surgical and internal medical problems.

Sample and method of data collection

Data on suicide is obtained from the Statistical Yearbook of Yugoslavia, Federal Statistics Office.

There is no register of suicide attempts either for the whole country or for the catchment area. Therefore the situation must be judged only on the basis of individual studies. For the area of Novi Sad, the fact that there is no single unit for treatment of all suicide attempts represents a further difficulty. Instead, depending on the methods used, these cases are treated at various departments (surgical, internal medicine, psychiatry, etc.).

In this overview on attempted suicide, we shall be dealing with the Clinical Centre only, since the Institutes for Cardiovascular Diseases, Oncology and Pulmology hardly ever treat suicidal patients, and their number in these institutions is negligible. The Military Hospital is under the jurisdiction of military health authorities and thus the data for suicidal behaviour are not available to civilians.

Our sample consisted of patients referred to the Clinical Centre because of a suicide attempt. When their state was not perceived as life threatening, they were given treatment and then sent home, or, they were hospitalized at the in-patient department.

After having gained permission from the clinic directors, collection of the sample was achieved through identifying suicide attempts in patient files. Some units still did not have computerized data collection systems, so admission book files had to be searched manually. Due to the fact that clinics did not have identical logbooks kept, data were not identical for each Clinic. In some cases the data were very simple and insufficient, and in some places, books were not possible to obtain for various reasons (including unavailability and poor recording systems).

The time interval covered in this survey spanned 5 years from 1995-1999. The survey did not cover outpatient health centres as it was thought that the great majority of general practitioners would refer suicidal patients to the Clinical Centre and would not attempt to treat them themselves. As well as this, the procedure of contacting all health-centres was too long and cumbersome and there were insufficient staff to carry out this task.

By collecting the sample in this way, it is possible that a small percentage of cases were left out – namely those whose suicidal behaviour was perceived as not serious or life threatening, so that it could have been dealt with at home or on an outpatient basis.

Results

Suicide

Looking at overall numbers of suicides for the whole country, Yugoslavia is a country somewhere in the 'golden middle' as far as suicide rates are concerned, having a rate of

16.4 per 100,000 (Nikolic, 1991). In the past decade, though, very dramatic changes took place in the society and it is interesting to see how these changes affected suicide rates. By looking at these numbers, we have to remember that the country is no longer the same as of 1991, where Federal Republic of Yugoslavia now represents Serbia and Montenegro. Therefore, we shall look at the number of suicides from 1991 onwards, where the last available official data is provided only for the year 1997.

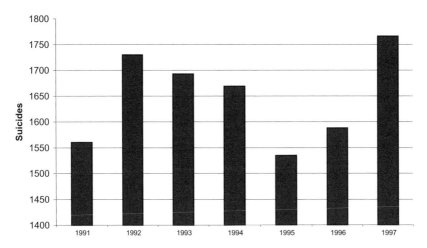

Source: Statistical yearbook of Yugoslavia 1999, Federal Statistics OfficeSource: Statistical yearbook of Yugoslavia 1999, Federal Statistics Office

Figure 1. Number of suicides. 1991-1997

Taking into account that according to the last census performed in 1991, Serbia and Montenegro had about 12 million inhabitants an average rate of 14.4 per 100,000 may be calculated for 1992, decreasing to 12.7 per 100,000 in 1995 and then rising to 14.7 per 100,000 in 1997.

Figure 2 shows oscillations in various age groups. Those over 55 years old show the highest rise in the years 1992 and 1993, which was the year of unprecedented economic crisis, with hyper inflation of this kind hardly seen in the history of mankind.

This impacted upon nearly all social strata, but those affected the most were the retired. Pensions during the last months of 1993 were insufficient to meet basic needs, so the rise of suicides in this group can be correlated to the decrease in their average monthly income (Biro & Selakovic-Bursic, 1996). On the other hand, there was an increase in suicides among younger age groups, particularly 15-24 year olds in 1997.

The cause for it may be related to many factors. For example, the political situation which gave young people no perspective for employment and living a normal life, a general increase in criminal and aggressive behaviour and the increased availability of firearms – the final answers to this remain yet to be given. Incidentally, the use of firearms as a suicide method has increased from a merely 7.1% in 1990, to 15.7% in

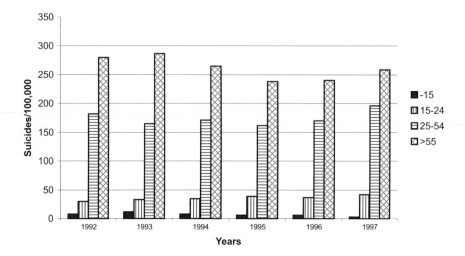

Figure 2. Suicide rates by age, Yugoslavia 1992-1997

1997 (Statistical yearbook of Yugoslavia, 1999). Undoubtedly, this is the result of the easy availability of weapons due to ongoing wars in the area since 1991.

The 'golden middle' image changes remarkably if we look at Yugoslav provinces separately. Here the province of Vojvodina, whose capital is Novi Sad, stands out as the area with the highest suicide rate per 100,000 for decades: from 22.4 in the sixties (Kapamadzija, 1967), 27.4 in 1989 (Nikolic, 1991) to over 30 in 1993 (Pokrajinski Zavod za statistiku). This is associated with the level of economic development and standard of living. Vojvodina is among the most economically developed areas in former Yugoslavia and also has the highest standard of living in the present Yugoslavia. Another key issue relates to the population structure, where societies with a predominantly younger population, like Kosovo, appear to be at a low risk of suicide (Biro and Selakovic-Bursic, 1996), whereas the population of Vojvodina is characterized by high percentage of the elderly and consequently, by high suicide rates.

Attempted suicide

A study that analyzed suicide attempts in Novi Sad area in the first years of this decade (Selakovic-Bursic et al., 1995) showed that the number of hospitalized suicide attempters steadily decreased since 1989, with the most marked decrease in 1993. During that year the number of hospitalizations because of suicide attempts decreased by nearly two thirds compared to 1989. Again, this can be connected to economic factors, including the fact it was a year of hyper inflation and low standard of living which led to an increase in self-destructive behaviour and completed suicides. In this study, adolescents (up to 20 years of age) were the most numerous group. Among them, male suicide attempts increased in the period 1991-1993 from 16% to 28%. The diagnosis of alcoholism was dominant in males (25%), but also an increase in depressive disorders, while in females there was an increase in psychotic disorders during this period.

Table 1. Number and rate of attempted suicide, 1995-99

Year	Number of attempts	Rate
1995	151	43
1996	92	26
1997	191	55
1998	161	46
1999	204	58

It is surprising to see that the highest rate of attempted suicide occured in the latest year (1999), since it is the year of the NATO bombing, whereas the rate of completed suicides, according to still unofficial data dropped significantly. Whether any of these suicide attempts had anything to do with the stress, anxiety and trauma of bombing needs to be established by a further investigation of each individual case.

If we look at the gender structure of the attempters, the domination of female gender is obvious for all years observed. However, the number of male attempts has been constantly on the rise since 1997, so that in 1998 the ratio male: female attempt was nearly 1:1.

The age distribution of persons attempting suicide shows that the most numerous are persons aged 15-19 years, followed by those aged 19-24 years. After that, numbers steadily decrease with age, with slight exception for age group 44-49 years, which showed an unexpected rise. Looking at gender once again, young men aged 19-24 years attempted suicide the most often, and even outnumbered females in this age group, while females aged 14-19 years outnumbered by far the males in that group. A question

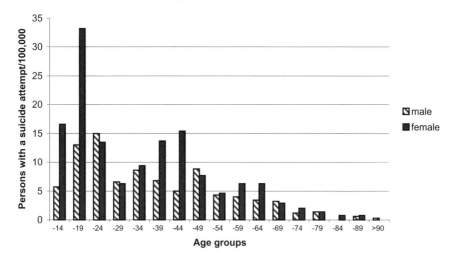

Figure 3. Rates of attempted suicide per 100,000 for males and females in age groups

that pops up here is whether the increase in male suicide attempts in this age group had anything to do with the threat of war, military conscription or regular military service (mandatory in Yugoslavia). Again, the answer demands a more detailed knowledge of each individual case.

Finally, when observing the prevalence of suicide attempt methods employed the findings are not surprising. About 73 per cent of all attempts were by overdoses (although these include intoxication with pesticides in about 2 per cent), followed by 16 per cent by wrist cutting. The third most common suicide attempt method was hanging (3%).

Due to the fact that many individuals who attempt to end their life endure a short period of unconsciousness before being taken to hospital, such persons often have no recollection of their suicide attempt and cannot explain their suicidal behaviour. Among those who completed suicide, hanging was by far the most common method utilised in Novi Sad and the country as a whole.

Peculiarities of the Novi Sad catchment area

This area is special and indeed different from the southern parts of the country in that it has a much higher rate of suicide. Its rate is double the rate of Serbia proper (parts of Serbia south of the Danube), almost triple the rate of Montenegro (which was 11 per 100,000) and many times higher than the rate of Kosovo (although the rates for Kosovo have not been available since 1991). The elderly dominate the population structure and suicides among this age group are also the most frequent in this area. In the last decade the number of elderly suicides has increased significantly, which is probably related to difficult economic conditions throughout the country. The most common method of suicide is hanging, although in the last several years the use of firearms has increased greatly (due to its availability caused by wars).

Concerning suicide attempts, there is a lot to be improved in regard to the maintaining regional record and the organization of health care services, such as intensive care units for suicide attempters. The rate of suicide attempts in Novi Sad is roughly twice that of completed suicides. Even though females are dominant in this group, there has been a significant rise in male attempts in the last two years, so that in the 19-24 year age group males outnumbered females. The most common method of suicide attempt was overdose, followed by wrist cutting, and a third small percentage (3%) of suicide attempts by hanging. Trends in suicide attempts appear to be rising every year, as do the trends for suicides – with the exception of 1999 when the total number of suicides decreased, as a probable result of NATO bombing in the country, although these figures have not yet been officially released.

Conclusion

The area of Novi Sad and Vojvodina is characterized by high suicide rates, which are increasing. The group most at risk is the elderly. Suicide attempts show fluctuations, with a significant drop in 1993, the year of extreme economic hardship, but with a constant increase thereafter. Particularly dominant is the increase in young male suicide attempts in the last two years.

There is a need for improved services for the suicidal in the Novi Sad area, starting from better intervention and postvention facilities, to developing an entirely new strategy for suicide prevention, which, at the present time, is largely non-existent.

References

Biro M, Selakovic-Bursic S (1996). Suicide, aggression and war. *Archives of Suicide Research* 2: 75-79.

Dem 2 podaci (1998). Novi Sad: Pokrajinski Zavod za statistiku.

Kapamadzija B (1967). *Samoubistvo u Vojvodini sa posebnim osvrtom na odnos samoubistva i alkoholizma,* Doktorska disertacija. Novi Sad: Medicinski fakultet.

Nikolic D, Dimitrijevic D (1991). Samoubistva u Jugoslaviji. Beograd: Savezni Zavod za zdravstvenu zastitu.

Selakovic-Bursic S, Borisev L, Vuckovic N, Mitrovic D (1995). Uticaj drustvene krize na dinamiku suicidalnog ponasanja. In Kulauzov M (Ed.), *Stremljenja i naucna dostignuca u medicini.* Novi Sad: Medicinski fakultet.

Statistical Yearbook of Yugoslavia (1999). Beograd: Federal Statistical Office.

Chapter 21

Suicidal Behaviour in the Ukraine

A. Mokhovikov & V. Rozanov

Description of the catchment area

The catchment area of Odessa is situated in the south of Ukraine on the coast of the Black Sea. Odessa is a centre of the Odessa Region, which is one of the 25 administrative regions in Ukraine (including the Republic of Crimea) with a population more than 5% of that of the whole country (2.63 million people in 1990 and about 2.2 million in 1999). Nearly one half of the population of the region lives in the Odessa City. It is one of the biggest cities in the country, the most important seaport, and a large industrial, scientific and cultural centre. It has a population of 1,046,400. The Odessa catchment area covers the city centre and the suburban areas.

Sample and method of data collection

The data on suicide was obtained from the Ministry of Health of the Ukraine, Center of Statistics, and analyzed by researchers from the Ukrainian Institute of Social and Forensic Psychiatry and Odessa WHO Multicentre Study group. The calculation of the rates for the years 1991-2000 was based on the mid-year population data, also supplied by the regional statistical department.

Data on attempted suicide are provided due to collaboration with the Odessa municipal ambulance. Unfortunately, in 1998-2000 the registration was not complete and our data therefore had to be seen as estimates only. Nevertheless, in the period of 2001-2002, when suicide attempt registration card for ambulance was introduced and registration procedures for ambulance staff were implemented, so more valid data have been obtained. The calculation of the rates for the years 1988-2000 is based on the mid-year population data supplied by the Ukrainian Statistical Committee in Kiev.

Results

Suicide

Previously, Odessa was known for its high suicide rates and was ranked as the area with the third highest suicide rates in the Russian Empire, after Moscow and St. Petersburg.

Before World War I, the rate of suicide per 100,000 in Odessa in 1913, was 33.0, while in Moscow and in St. Petersburg, rates of suicide were 21.0 and 29.0, respectively. Then for a long period, suicidal behaviour was a closed topic and no statistical information was available, even to specialists.

Table 1. Suicides number and rate in Ukraine in 1988 – 1998

Year	Number of suicides	Suicide rate per 100,000 of population	Percentage relative to 1988
1988	9,792	19.0	100
1989	10,934	21.1	111
1990	10,693	20.6	108
1991	10,743	20.7	108
1992	11,731	22.5	118
1993	12,541	24.0	126
1994	13,907	26.8	141
1995	14,587	28.3	149
1996	15,258	29.9	157
1997	14,973	29.4	155
1998	14,860	29.6	156
1999	14,452	29.1	153
2000	14,600	29.6	156

As can be seen from table 1, the frequency of suicide has increased markedly during the last decade (by approximately 56%), which places Ukraine among the top ten countries in the world with the highest suicide rates.

Completed suicides are committed 4.9 times more frequently by men than by women. The sex ratio (m/f) is even higher in the rural areas, where the male suicide rate is 6.2 times higher than that the female rate, while in the cities it is 5.3 times higher.

The frequency of suicide is lowest in the Western part of Ukraine and highest in the Eastern part. Central and Southern parts have practically the same rates, and are more similar to rates in the Eastern part. High suicide rates were registered particularly in the areas that were polluted as a result of the Chernobyl disaster, namely Sumy, Chernigov, Zhitomir, and Vinnitsa regions.

During the 11 years under study, the lowest rates of suicide were registered in practically all regions of Western Ukraine, which may be the result of the fact that these regions and cities are more agricultural and less polluted by the Chernobyl disaster. This difference may also be attributed to socio-cultural peculiarities of the Western Ukraine.

Unfortunately, data on suicide by age and gender do not exist at the national level. Data from the Odessa region, which are higher than the average for the whole country, have shown that the risk of suicide peaks among 20-59-year-old men, while for women it increases with age and reaches its maximum among those older than 60 years.

Hanging is by far the most often used method for suicide – both in the Odessa area and in Ukraine as a whole.

Attempted suicide

During the period 1998-2002, 1794 suicide attempts were registered; 818 (45.6%) were committed by men and 976 (54.4%) by women. The distribution of the age and gender of suicide attempters in 2002 is shown in figure 1.

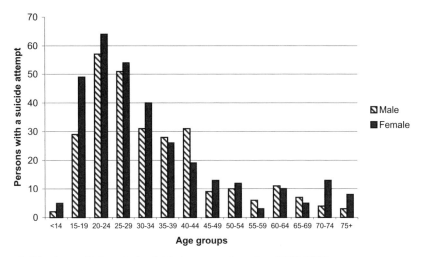

Figure 1. Numbers of attempted suicide by age and gender, 1998-2002

Though presented in absolute figures, these data give a clear understanding of the situation: the risk of attempted suicide is high among the young, especially among 15-19 year old women, and – to some degree – among women aged 30-34 years old. Among the very young, (<14 years and 15-19 years) and among the aged (70years and more), females constitute the absolute majority, while among 40-44 year olds, men out number women.

In 607 cases of attempted suicide in 2002, the method used was clearly stated in the ambulance files, and from these, 50.7% were cases of self-poisoning by pills (mainly hypnotics and sedatives), 33.1% constituted self-cutting, 5.1% self-poisoning with pesticides, acids and caustics, 4.6% jumping, 4.3% hanging, and 2.2% were use of firearms and other methods.

A distinct seasonality could be seen – there were more suicide attempts in spring and summer. The highest rates were registered in April, June and July, there was also a rise in September with sharp diminishing in November and December. From social factors it could be noticed that separation, lower education and poor economic status were risk factors of suicidal behaviour as registered by our suicide attempts monitoring.

Peculiarities of the catchment area

Prevention programs supported by authorities or specialized medical and psychological aid facilities are largely non-existent in Odessa. The examples of prevention are the activity of volunteer crisis telephone lines that function according the principles and practice of the Samaritans, and some non-government institutions, which focus on risk groups such as military personnel, prisoners, females who suffered violence and people in crisis states. Recently much efforts are done to train GPs, ambulance doctors and family physicians in identifying suicide risk and management of suicidal patients. Local network of trained medical doctors is created. Within the frame of WHO European network on suicide attempts monitoring and prevention a family resource on preventing suicide in youth and adolescents is developed, published and distributed while contacting suicide attempters and their families. A WHO resource on suicide prevention for GPs is translated into Russian and distributed within the medical community.

Conclusion

The average Ukrainian rates of completed suicide are among the ten highest in the world. There are, however, marked differences between various regions, with the western part having low rates, and the eastern part high rates. In the area of Odessa in the south, the rate is also high and steadily increasing. Data on attempted suicide confirm the usual pattern with regard to age, gender distribution, and suicide attempt methods.

Continuation of monitoring suicide attempts is highly needed, and there is a great necessity for the further development of prevention activities and better services for people at risk. The local program on suicide prevention should be developed, public awareness measures, as well as destigmatization measures are a high priority.

References

Kryzhanovskaya L, Pilyagina G (1999). Suicidal Behaviour in the Ukraine, *Crisis* 24: 184-190.
Mokhovikov A (1994). Suicide in the Ukraine, *Crisis*, 15/3: 137.
Mokhovikov A, Donets O (1996). Suicide in the Ukraine: Epidemiology, Knowledge and Attitudes of the Population. *Crisis*, 17/3: 128-134.
Panina N, Golovakha E (1999). *Tendencies in the Development of the Ukrainian Society (1994-1998)*. Kiev: Nat. Academy of Sciences.
Population of Ukraine. (1995). Kiev: Ministry of Statistics of Ukraine.
Rozanov VA, Mokhovikov AN, Stiliha R (2002). Successful model of suicide prevention in the Ukraine military environment *Crisis,* 23/4: 171.
Rozanov VA, Zaharov S, Zhuzhulenko PN (2003) Suicide attempts monitoring in Odessa within the European suicide prevention network: XXII World Congress of IASP (Stockholm, Sweden, September 10-14, 2003).

Chapter 22

Suicidal Behaviour in Hungary

S. Fekete, B. Temesváry & P. Osvath

Description of the catchment areas

In Hungary, two catchment areas have been under study, namely the Szeged area and the Pecs area. The Szeged centre collected data from 1989 till 1992, and at the Pecs centre monitoring started in 1997. Both catchment areas include mainly an urban, but also a rural population, and there were no differences regarding main economic variables, compared to Hungary as a whole. Gender and age distributions were similar, and it therefore appears that the Pecs and Szeged areas and their surroundings can be considered to be representative of Hungary as a whole with regard to the main sociodemographic variables.

Sample and method of data collection

At both centres, information on attempted suicide is based on referrals to the main general hospital. Information on demographic characteristics of suicide attempters was registered through a monitoring system. Relatively complete information was collected for patients referred to, and assessed by, the general hospital psychiatric service. On the basis of information from the emergency services and from both out- and in-patient facilities, it was estimated that the percentage of reported suicide attempts in the three year period amounted to 70% of all medically treated suicide attempts in the Pecs catchment area. Data on the general population in the catchment area was derived from national, regional, and municipal bureaus of statistics. Generally, reporting was reliable and we believe that the extrapolation of the recorded data in Pecs with a factor of 1.4 is realistic. In the Szeged centre all cases of attempted suicides have been registered, so the estimation factor was 1. From previous experience we know that the number of cases dealt with solely by general practitioners in our area, and not referred to hospital, is probably quite small. We have, of course, no idea of the number of episodes which occur in the community and do not come to medical attention.

Results

Suicide

Traditionally, suicide mortality has been very high in Hungary, and despite a slight decreasing trend during recent years – from 45 per 100,000 in 1985 to 40 per 100,000 in 1992 and 33 per 100,000 in 1998, the overall rate is still high compared to other western countries. The gender ratio (m:f) for completed suicide in Hungary is 3.17:1.

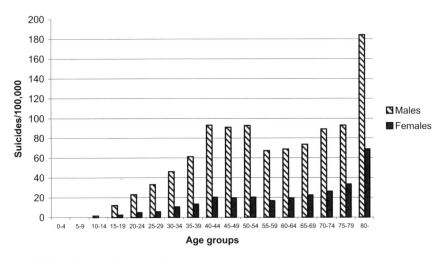

Figure 1. Suicide rates by sex and age

Attempted suicide

In 1998, the mean annual rates of medically treated suicide attempts (events) in Pecs were 196 per 100,000 for men and 321 per 100,000 for women, and in Szeged during the period 1989-92 the average male rates were 89.9 per 100,000 and female rates 222 per 100,000. In both cities the risk group for suicide were the young (15-39 years).

In the catchment area of Pecs, 849 cases of attempted suicide were registered in the period 1 July 1997 to 30 June 2000. Of the sample, 529 (62.3%) suicide attempts were made by women and 320 (37.7%) by men. The gender ratio (f/m) for events was 1.65, for persons 1.55. The event:person ratio was 1.17:1 for the men and 1.24:1 for women. The mean age was 34.85 years (16-79, SD:12.98) for men and 36.63 years (14-86, SD:16.3) for women.

Drug overdoses were the most common of the methods of suicide attempt in Pecs, accounting for 62% of male attempts and 79% of female, followed by cutting and jumping from high places. Alcohol was recorded as the only method in 1%, but had been consumed in connection with 19% of male and 12% of female events. A more detailed analysis showed that benzodiazepines were used in about 57% of cases of self-

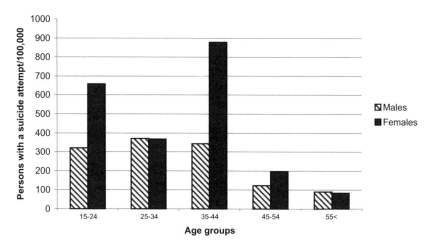

Figure 2. Rates of attempted suicide by age and gender

poisoning, followed by antidepressants. Analgesics were used relatively rarely (7%). Availability of drugs obviously plays a major role and this would be another important area for further studies as this factor could easily be influenced (Fekete et al., 2000). Results of the analyses also showed that in the Szedged area in particular, pesticides were often used for self-poisoning (Michel et al., 2000).

About one half of the attempters (51.6% of the men and 51.2% of the women) had made attempts previous to the index attempt, and 26.3% and 26.8%, respectively, had done so within the last previous year. The proportion of repetition after the index attempt was 17.2% among men and 19.5% among women. Two-thirds of male repeaters and one half of females made the first repeated attempt within six months after the index suicide attempt.

Epidemiological findings

General results

For both suicide and attempted suicide, the risk group comprised people being divorced, unemployed or disabled, or who had achieved low levels of education. The rates of attempted suicide were highest among those unemployed. Divorced persons had rates above average while married persons had low rates. Persons living without a partner had higher rates than those living with a partner. Those living with a partner and children had the lowest rates.

There were little differences in the rates of attempted suicide between the various religious denominations, albeit more protestants than catholics attempted in the Szeged area.

Table 1. Main differences between male and female suicide attempters

males	Sign. (p)	females
– migration inside region (16.3%)	0.037	– migration inside (11.9%) and outside (4 vs 1.9%) region
– never married (38.1 vs 29.3%)	0.002	– divorced (15.9 vs 11.3%). widowed (9.1 vs 2.5%)
– living with parents (31.6 vs 20%)0	0	– living with partner and children (29.1 vs 21.3%).
– living alone (16.9 vs 7.8%)		– alone with children (13.8 vs 2.8%)
– lower lever of education (57.5 vs 51.%)	NS	– higher level (48.9 vs 42.5%)
– more unemployment (33.8 vs 18.8%)	0	– more economically inactive (51 vs 31.3%)
– age group: – 20-39 (65.3 vs 18.4%) – 50-64 (11.3 vs. 8.2%)	0	– age group: – 15-19 (14.4 vs 6.3%) – 40-49 (21 vs 15%) – over 65 (9 vs 2.2%)
– more cutting (13.3 vs 7.7%). hanging (4.1 vs 0.85%) and alcohol intox. (19.78 vs 11.3%)	0.008	– more poisoning (75.5 vs 58.7%)
– meprobamate (16.9 vs 8.5%)		– benzodiazepine (64.8 vs 58.4%)
– antipsychotics (5 vs 3.6%)		– barbiturates (1.35 vs 0.77%)
		– sleeping pills (2.5 vs 1.15%)
– more alcohol abuse (16.85 vs 6.46%) and psychotic disorder (3.74 vs 1.44%)	0.001	– more depressive (16.73 vs 10.48%) and adjustment disorder (53.9 vs 48.1%)

There were no significant differences between male first-evers and repeaters except that first-evers were suffering more often from alcohol and drug abuse and adjustment disorder, whereas male repeaters more often suffered from psychotic disorders, affective disorders and personality disorders.

Female first-evers were characterized by more outpatient treatment, self-poisoning method, and adjustment and psychotic disorders. They were most often in the age brackets 15-29 years or 60 years and over. Female repeaters had more often been hospitalized, were more often aged 30-44 years, and more often used hanging as a method of suicide attempt. Finally, such females more often suffered from alcohol abuse and personality disorders.

The aftercare offered to patients following their attempts most often included inpatient admission (68%), or outpatient or community mental health care (32%), as opposed to other agencies (0%), and return to general practitioner care (0%). The rate of inpatient admission following attempts is considerably higher than in many other European centres. Analyses had shown that patients in Pecs and Szeged were characterized relatively often by comorbid conditions, and a higher frequency of inpatient care, which, in part, may the relatively high proportion of suicide attempters in Hungary that suffer from a major mental illness.

Conclusion

Contrary to the Hungarian rates of completed suicide, which are among the highest in the Western world, rates of attempted suicide are not much higher than the European average (Schmidtke et al., 1996; Fekete et al., 2000). A plausible explanation for this phenomenon might be that in Hungary, the suicidal acts are more serious and violent than in other countries, thus resulting in a higher mortality rate (Szadoczky, Rihmer et al. 2000). The rates of repetition of attempted suicide are higher in the two catchment areas than in the other European areas under study. This may reflect a relatively high frequency of major mental health problems found in the population of suicide attempters. Indications from findings in Pecs, which suggests that modelling and social transmission of suicidal behaviour, as well as a high consumption of alcohol, along with choice of some particularly lethal suicidal methods in Szeged such as pesticides, seem to play an important role in the Hungarian culture.

References

Bille-Brahe U, Kerkhof A, DeLeo D et al. (1996) A repetition-prediction study on European attempted suicide populations. *Crisis*, 17/1.

Fekete S, Jegessy A, Osvath P (2000). Choice of method and lethality in suicide behaviour: overdoses during a 14 years period in Baranya region, Hungary. *European Neuropsychopharmacology*. 10. (Suppl 3): 267.

Fekete S, Osvath P (2000). Diagnosis and prevention in the suicidal behaviour. Data of three years experiences in Pecs within the WHO\EU multicenter study on attempted suicide, *Orvosi Hetilap*, 141, 45: 2427-2431.

Michel K, Ballinari P, Bille-Brahe U, Temesvary B et al. (2000). Methods used for attempted suicide: results of the WHO/EURO Multicentre Study on Attempted suicide. *Social Psychiatry and Psychiatric Epidemiology*, 35:156-163.

Osvath P, Fekete S, Michel K. (2001). Contacts of suicide attempters with health care services in Pecs and Bern in the WHO/EURO Multicentre Study on Attempted suicide. *International Journal of Psychiatry in Clinical Practice*, in press.

Platt S, Bille-Brahe U, Kerkhof A, Schmidtke A, Temesvary B et al. (1992). Attempted suicide in Europe: the WHO/EURO multicentre study on attempted suicide. I. Introduction and preliminary analyses for 1989. *Acta Psychiatrica Scandinavica* 85: 97-104.

Schmidtke A, Bille-Brahe U, DeLeo D, Kerkhof A, Temesvary B et al. (1996). Attempted suicide in Europe: rates, trends and sociodemographic characteristics of suicide attempters during the period 1989-1992. *Acta Psychiatrica Scandinavica* 93: 327-338.

Szadoczky J, Vitrai J, Rihmer Z, Füredi J (2000). Suicide attempts in the Hungarian adult population. *European Psychiatry* 15: 343-347.

Chapter 23

Suicidal Behaviour in Estonia

A. Värnik, O. Küpersepp, T. Marandi & E. Palo

Description of the catchment area

The catchment area of the Estonian centre comprises of the city of Tallinn, the capital of Estonia, that is seated in the Northern region. Roughly one third of the people of Estonia live in the city. In 1999, of the 409,961 inhabitants, 46% were men and 54% women. Twenty per cent of the population were children below the age of 16 years, 60% were of working age, and 29% of the age of retirement. The population is gradually diminishing.

Close to 60% of the population of Tallinn is Estonian, and a large minority is Russian. The religion for Estonians is mainly Protestant, but the Russian groups belong to the Russian Orthodox Church. The state language is Estonian. The catchment area is an urban, relatively well-developed district, and is not considered to be representative of Estonia as a whole.

Sample and method of data collection

The 1989 reforms in the USSR opened the doors of the statistical offices, and information on suicide that had been kept secret for decades, became available to researchers (Värnik, 1997).

After a pilot study had been carried out by the Tallinn Centre over four months (September-December) in 1995, monitoring of attempted suicides began in 1996. The database includes all suicide attempts committed by residents of Tallinn, 15 years or older, and admitted to health care after the attempt for the period of 1996-1999.

Data was gathered through the collection of standardized forms filled in at hospitals by the Emergency Ambulance Service and via case records sorted by medical staff. Furthermore, when possible, the patients were interviewed. Team members, who regularly checked the hospital's daily record of all receptions, updated the list of attempted suicides. At the end of each year of the study, the list was controlled by scanning the hospital patient-register for admissions where the diagnoses might cover a suicide attempt. Medical records from archives were then used to identify possible cases of suicide attempts. Also, a team member and a specialist from the hospital's statistical department looked through the files for medically treated patients.

The crude annual rate of attempted suicide per 100,000 inhabitants aged 15 years and older was calculated by the use of the mid-year surveys of permanent inhabitants of Tallinn. Annual averages were calculated as pooled rates (Estonian Statistical Committee).

Results

Suicide

The frequency of suicide in Estonia is characterized by rather stable, high rates during the years 1970-1984 (the stagnation period in the former USSR), and by an S-shaped profile (fall-rise-fall) in the period 1985-1999 (the period of political and socio-economic reforms). The lowest rate was registered in 1988 and the highest in 1994 (24.5 per 100,000 and 41.0 per 100,000, respectively), with the fluctuation in male rates reflecting the turbulent historical events.

The steady declining trend of suicide rates continued during the period under study (1996-1999) from 37.5 to 32.4 per 100,000 (Värnik et al.2001, Värnik et al 1997).

The rate of suicide in the Tallinn catchment area, which is below the national rate, decreased from 28.87 per 100,000 in 1996 to 27.1 per 100,000 in 1999. The curve is slightly U-shaped, reaching a minimum of 25.1 per 100,000 in 1997.

The gender ratio (m:f) during the period of the study was 5.1:1 in Estonia and 4.3:1 in Tallinn. The lower suicide rates in Tallinn are due to the male rates being relatively lower than the national male rates (Värnik et al. 2000).

Age-specific rates of suicide in Estonia in 1999 (latest year available data), are shown in Figure 1.

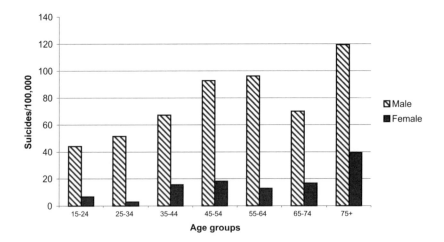

Figure 1. Suicide rates by sex and age, 1999.

In general, male rates of suicide increased by age, except for the 65-74 year olds. High rates were found in particular among the oldest (75 years and over). For women too, a bimodal distribution was found, with peaks among the 45-54 years old and again among those 75 years or older.

The reliability of diagnostics and registration of suicide (ICD-10: X60BX84) in Estonia is considered to be good (Wasserman et al., 1998).

Suicide attempts

During the period under study (1996-1999), a total of 2,518 suicide attempters, 1,320 men (52.4%) and 1,198 women (47.6%), were registered in the catchment area. The total number of events was 2,825, committed by 1,481 men and 1,344 women. The annual number of male attempters for 1996 and 1999 varied from 313 per 100,000 to 338 per 100,000 respectively, and from 270 per 100,000 to 338 per 100,000 for females attempters. In 1996, the ratio events:persons was 1.1:1, and in 1999 it was 1.2:1.

Table 1. Number and rates of suicide attempters (persons 15+) and attempts (events) in Tallinn

	1996		1997		1998		1999		1996-99	
	N	R	N	R	N	R	N	R	N	R
Males										
Persons	335	171.9	334	174.2	338	178.4	313	166.7	1,320	172.8
Events	355	182.2	357	186.2	389	205.3	380	202.4	1,481	194.0
Females										
Persons	338	147.5	270	119.4	289	129.0	301	135.5	1,198	132.8
Events	357	155.8	307	135.7	330	147.3	350	157.5	1,344	149.1
Both genders										
Persons	673	158.7	604	144.5	627	151.7	614	149.8	2,518	151.2
Events	712	167.9	667	158.9	719	173.9	730	178.1	2,825	169.7

Table 1 shows the annual person-based rates of suicide attempts for both genders during the period under study. The annual male rate varied between 166.7 and 178.4 and the female rate from 119.4 to 147.5. The average person-based rate for the whole period was 172.8 for men and 132.8 for women.

Table 2. Annual average number and proportion of suicide attempts by age and gender in Tallinn 1996-1999

	15-24	25-34	35-44	45-54	55+
Male	116	85	65	35	28
%	35.2	25.8	19.8	10.5	8.5
Female	112	57	55	35	41
%	37.2	19.1	18.4	11.6	13.5
Both genders	228	143	120	70	69
%	36.1	22.6	19.1	11.0	10.9

Table 2 shows the average number and the proportion of total suicide attempters in various age groups during the period under study. The average age-specific incidence of the registered suicide attempts showed a clear decrease with age. Among both men and women, young people in the age group of 15-24 years accounted for the highest proportion of suicide attempts.

Mean age-specific rates by gender are shown in figure 2. For both genders, the rates were by far highest among the 15-24 years old (399 per 100,000) whereafter the rates were continually decreasing by age.

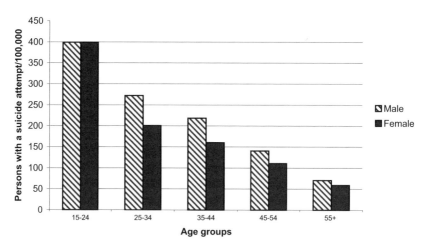

Figure 2. Rates of attempted suicide by sex and age

Non-fatal repetition (event:person ratio) during the monitoring period was 1.1:1 for both genders. In 1999, the ratio increased to 1.2 for both genders. By December 2000, 157 suicide attempters (6.2%) were dead; of these 27 men and 19 women had died by suicide, 23 men and 12 women in an accident, and 41 men and 35 women of other causes (Table 3).

Table 3. The outcome after four years of suicide attempt in Tallinn

	Male		Female		Both genders	
	N	%	N	%	N	%
Still alive	1,229	93	1,132	94	2,361	94
Died by suicide	27	2	19	2	46	2
Died by accident	23	2	12	1	35	1
Died by other causes	41	3	35	3	76	3
Total	1,320	100	1,198	100	2,518	100

In the Tallinn area, the so-called soft methods were used most often (56.8%), especially by women (72.1%). Self-poisoning by drugs (X60-X64) counted for 51.9% of all cases, and by other chemical substances (X65-69) for 4.9%. For men, the most common method was cutting with sharp objects (48.0%) and then self-poisoning by drugs. Intoxication by alcohol (X65) was excluded from the register because of the uncertainty of the intention. If added, the group would have comprised 25% of the attempters (Table 4).

Table 4. Method of suicide attempts (events) in Tallinn in percentage for 1996-1999

	Male	Female	Total
'Soft' methods:			
Medicines X60-64)	37.5	67.9	51.9
Chemical substances (X66-69)	5.6	4.2	4.9
'Hard' methods:			
Hanging/strangulation (X70)	3.6	1.9	2.8
Cutting (X78)	48.0	23.4	36.3
Jumping from high place (X80)	2.7	1.4	2.1
Other	2.6	1.3	2.0
Total	100.0	100.0	100.0

Peculiarities of the catchment area

In general, the frequency of attempted suicide in the Tallinn catchment area was quite similar to the frequencies found in the other European areas under study. However contrary to other areas, male rates of attempted suicide in Tallinn were higher than female rates. The only centre with similar findings was Helsinki (Schmidtke et al. 1994a).

The methods used by female suicide attempters were more or less similar to those used by women in other catchment areas. For male suicide attempters however, violent methods were chosen more often. Also a relatively great number of males (48.0%) and females (23.4%) attempted suicide through cutting themselves (Schmidke et al. 1994b).

Conclusion

Suicidal behaviour is a serious public health problem in Estonia (WHO 1999). The monitoring study of attempted suicide gives a picture of approximately one third of attempted suicides in the population of Estonia. The relatively high rates of attempted suicide followed by marked decreases in 1988 and 1997 may be explained by the socio-political changes that have taken place (Noor, 1993).

References

Noor H (1993). Attempted suicide incidence in the Changing Society of Estonia Political Aspects of Mental Health. In: B Strauss, C Bahne Bahnson, H Spiedel (Eds), *New Societies New Models in Medicine*. Stuttgart – New York: Schattauer Press, 38-43.

Schmidtke A, Bille-Brahe U, DeLeo D, Kerkhof A, Bjerke T, Crepet P, Deisenhammer K, Hawton K, Lönnqvist J, Michel K, Pommereau X, Querejeta I, Philippe A, Salander Renberg E, Temesvary B, Wasserman D, Sampaio-Faria JG, Weinacker B (1994a). Rates and Trends of Attempted Suicide in Europe. In: Kerkof et al. (Eds), *Attempted suicide in Europe,* pp.209-230. DSWO Press: Leiden.

Schmidtke A, Bille-Brahe U, Kerkhof A, DeLeo D, Bjerke T, Crepet P, Haring C, Hawton K, Lönnqvist J, Michel K, Pommereau X, Querejeta I, Salander Renberg E, Temesvary B, Wasserman D, Sampaio-Faria JG, Frike S (1994b). Sociademographic characteristics of suicide attempters in Europe. In: Kerkhof et al. (Eds), *Attempted suicide in Europe,* pp.231-241. DSWO Press: Leiden.

Värnik A (1997). *Suicide in the Baltic countries and in the former republics of the USSR.* Doctoral diss., Stockholm

Värnik A, Kõlves K, Palo E, Tooding LM (2001). Estonian suicide curve has taken S-Shape, *Estonian doctor,* 3: 81-85.

Värnik A, Tooding LM, Palo E, Wasserman D (2000). Suicide Trends in the Baltic States, 1970-1997. *Trames,* 4(54 per 49): 1, 79-90.

Wasserman D, Värnik A (1998). Reliability of Statistics on Violent Death and Suicide in the Former USSR, 1970-90. *Acta Psychiatrica Scandinavia,* (Suppl. 394): 34-4.

Chapter 24

Suicidal Behaviour in Latvia

S. Udrasa & J. Logins

Description of the catchment area

Latvia is one of the three Baltic countries situated on the East Coast of the Baltic Sea, between Estonia and Lithuania with a total population of 2,404,926 inhabitants (July, 2000). About 69% of the population live in urban and 31% in rural areas. At present Latvia covers 64,589 km². The average population density is 38.1 inhabitants per km².

Administratively the country of Latvia is divided into 26 regions which cover a total of 469 smaller rural districts. There are 56 towns, seven of which have a city status.

Historically Latvia has been made up of 4 parts, still existing, each with its specific historical and cultural tradition – Kurzeme (the western part of Latvia), Zemgale (the Zemgale Plain, Augszeme – Upland), Vidzeme (the central and northen part of Latvia, including Riga) and Latgale (the eastern part of Latvia).

Sample and method of data collection

Data on suicide and attempted suicide was obtained from the Demographical year-books of the Central Statistical Bureau, from the Emergency Medical Services in Riga, the Riga Psychoneurological Hospital, and from the Mental Health Care centre in Latvia.

Results

Suicide

The overall suicide rate in the country, during the last 30 years, has shown significant fluctuations. During the years 1974-1984, the rates were rather stable (31.8-34.3 per 100,000 population a year), in the period 1985-1991 a decrease took place, (23.1-29.4 per 100,000), in the years 1992-1995 there was again a marked increase (34.9-42.5 per 100,000) and then a decline took place during the years 1996-2000 (369-31.4 per 100,000).

The variations in the total suicide rates are mainly due to marked changes in the male rates, while the female rates were stable during the last 30 years (10.8-16.8 per 100,000).

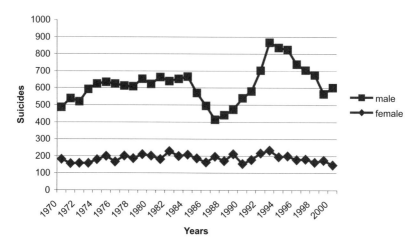

Figure 1. Raw figures of suicide by sex, 1970–2000

As in most other countries, Latvian rates of suicide increase with age, although rates are also high during the economically active life period, namely among the 40-59 year olds (55-56 per 100,000 in 1998, 44-52 per 100,000 in 1999, 42-53 per 100,000 in 2000).

Attempted suicide

Data on attempted suicide is only available for the years 1998-2000. Rates cannot be calculated, but based on the actual number of suicide attempts, it seems that the fre-

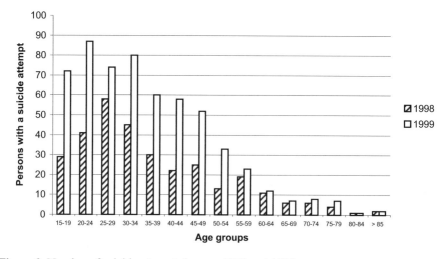

Figure 2. Number of suicide attempts by age, 1998 and 1999

quency is higher in the cities than in the rural areas. One may think that this phenomenon is connected with the particular socio-economical situation.

Apparently, among men, fewer attempts took place in 1999 than in 1998 and 2000 respectively, while in 1999 the frequency increased among women.

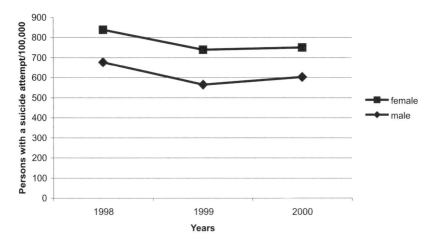

Figure 3. Number of suicide attempts by sex, 1998-2000

Peculiarities of the catchment area

The increase in the frequency of both suicide and suicide attempts, especially in the 15 to 19 year age group, may indicate a shortcoming of social guaranties and social security provided by the state for the young after graduating from secondary school. Namely, there are no ties between secondary school settings such as high schools and vocational schools, and employers. Calculation, planning and forecasting of the work market's demands do not take place, along with a demand for middle-level employees with secondary or technical secondary education. There could be several possible reasons for this including the fact that employers have no need for employees with a middle-level education, employers are not satisfied with the educational level of the young (15-19 year olds), and there exists a demand for specialists with higher education but not for personnel with only a secondary level. Also, the variation in the frequencies of suicide and attempted suicide are closely interconnected with the socio-economic situation in the country.

Conclusion

After 'developed socialism' and economic stability was proclaimed in the former USSR (including Latvia) in 1970-80s, a decrease in suicide rates was observed until 1988.

The 1990s brought to Latvia, along with freedom and independence, privatization of property and recession in economics with unemployment. For the former Soviet people, who had been accustomed to social stability, meeting with the realities of the free market with its merciless competition, demands for better qualifications and learning of foreign languages, as well as knowledge and skills of high technology and management was a clash. There were many winners, but also many losers. The rates of suicide kept increasing until 1995, whereafter a decrease has taken place.

The fluctuations of the Latvian rates of suicide and attempted suicide during the last 30 years testifies to the importance of these phenomena as indicators of changing psychological and social and economical realities of the society in transition.

Southern Europe

Chapter 25

Suicidal Behaviour in Spain (Basque Country)

*I. Querejeta, J. Ballesteros, R. Benito, B. Alegría, A. Sánchez, M. Ruiz,
S. Barrio & M. J. Alberdi*

Description of the catchment area

Guipuzcoa is the smallest Basque territory with an extent of 1996 km², and is the smallest province in Spain. Most of the population in Guipuzcoa live in towns. For the purpose of this study, the area of Bidasoa was selected, using the name of the river that crosses it. This area is located just on the border of France and Navarra. Some of the towns included in this area formally belong to the Autonomous Community of Navarra, but they use the health services in Guipuzcoa. The area has 112,813 residents aged 15 years and over (1986 local census), and the population of the area has the same structure as the rest of the province.

Sample and method of data collection

The data on suicide presented here should be considered as estimates, due to the fact that official statistics exist only to a limited degree and the present data therefore had to be obtained from various studies.

The monitoring of suicide attempters was carried out from the period 1st of January 1989 to 31st of December 1991. All cases referred to the emergency services were registered and interviewed, and all admissions at the three general hospitals in the area under diagnoses that might cover a suicidal act, were considered. Also out-patient community health centres, primary care units (GPs), the local clinical emergency service, and the main private clinic took part in the monitoring. Before starting the project, all health facilities working in the area were contacted and trained in attending to suicide attempters and taking them to the hospital.

Results

Suicide

Although there have been many changes in public opinion since Durkheim studied the influence of religion on this behaviour (Berrios et al.,1990), some negative attitudes towards suicidal behaviour still contribute to an underestimation of the number of sui-cides. In many cases, suicidal behaviour is hidden by the relatives, and this too contrib-utes to an underestimation of the phenomenon. It should be noted that in Spain, mental health services were introduced in the National Health System only 15 years ago. Prob-ably for these reasons, statistics on suicide in Spain show very few cases and that na-tional and local data are not in agreement.

Here, data will be presented on suicide in the Basque Country, Guipúzcoa being one of its three provinces. National data will also be considered.

The estimated rate of suicide in the Basque Country was about 2.9 per 100,000 in 1980 and 6.36 per 100,000 in 1991, which was markedly lower compared with rates in other European countries. The rate increased during the period 1980-1987, then fol-lowed a period of stabilisation and an increase thereafter during years 1996-1998 (Eustat. Instituto Vasco de Estadistica. 1991, 1999). It should be noted that the small number of suicides means that even small changes in the numerators may have disproportionate effects on the rate.

Figure 1 shows the rate of suicide by gender in the Basque Country in the years 1988-1998. As in most other countries, suicide rates were higher for men than for women.

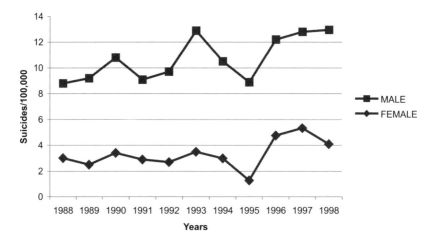

Figure 1. Suicide rates by gender, Basque country, 1988-1998

Figure 2 shows the rates by gender and age in the Basque Country for the year 1998, which is the last year available. The same figures are available for the years 1996 and 1997.

An age-period-cohort analysis of the frequencies of suicide in the period 1961-1981 showed that the risk of suicide increased by age for both genders (Ballesteros J et al., 1992).

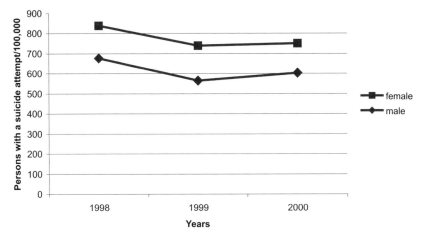

Figure 2. Suicide rates by age and gender, Basque country, 1998

Attempted suicide

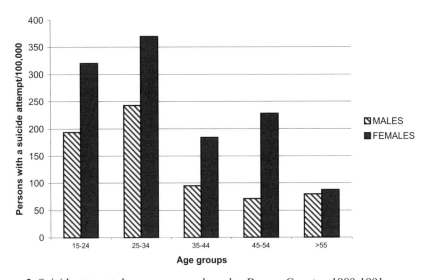

Figure 3. Suicide attempts by age group and gender, Basque Country, 1989-1991

In all, 235 cases of suicide attempts were registered during the years 1989,1990 and 1991. Figure 3 shows the rate of attempted suicide (persons) by sex and gender. In all age groups women were at a higher risk than men.

The most common method used for attempting suicide was self-poisoning (73%), mainly by barbiturates and sedatives, and analgesics (11.4%). In most cases, only one method was used; if more than one was used, alcohol was the most common accompanying method.

After a preliminary study of data (Querejeta et al, 1990), it was found that in Guipuzcoa, almost one half of suicide attempters (45%) registered in 1989 had attempted suicide prior to the index attempt (Kreitman et al., 1988), and 13% repeated the attempt during the follow-up period.

Epidemiological findings

General results

The general profile of the suicide attempters in the catchment area were characterised as being female (57.7%), young (15-34 years 65.8%), single (45%) and unemployed (69.7%).

Conclusion

The frequency of suicide in the Basque Country is comparatively low, but with an increasing trend during the last years. As to attempted suicide, however, there has been a tendency towards decreasing frequencies during the period under study. The highest risk of attempted suicide was observed among those in the youngest age groups, especially young women, where the risk was 1.3 times higher than for young men.

The risk of repetition after the index attempt seemed to correlate with attempts made within 12 months prior to the index attempt, and also with the treatment received at the hospital. More studies are necessary, especially with regard to completed suicide, to improve our knowledge about this kind of behaviour.

Chapter 26

Suicidal Behaviour in Italy

G. Meneghel, P. Scocco, E. Colucci, M. Marini, P. Marietta, W. Padoani,
M. Dello Buono & D. DeLeo

Description of the catchment area

The area covered by our study is the town of Padua, which together with eighteen minor communes surrounding it, comes under the local health unit, *ULSS 16*, of the Veneto region. This region also hosts the Faculty of Medicine of the University of Padua. The district in question is well populated (378,900 inhabitants, 378,98 km²), but we chose to limit our study to the population of the town of Padua in order to obtain more reliable information. The area we studied therefore extends over a total of 92.95 km² and has a density of 2,527 inhabitants/km². According to data from the municipal statistics office, on 31 December 1989, Padua recorded 199,199 inhabitants 15 years and over, of whom 47% were male and 53% were female. The total population on 31 December 1999 was 186,898, of whom 46.8% were male and 53.2% were female.

Comparisons by age, sex and marital status of the population in the catchment area with that of the Veneto region and Italy as a whole showed equal distribution patterns in the three areas. It can therefore be affirmed that the Padua area satisfies the relative criteria to be considered a representative sample of the Veneto region and Italy itself for the monitoring of attempted suicide.

Sample and method of data collection

Data on the suicides occurring in the study period (1989-1999) were collected from the Institute of Public Health in Padua. This institute is part of the local health unit and records all deaths on a yearly basis, including information on their causes and many of the socio-demographic variables. This information is then sent to the National Institute of Statistics in Rome and contributes to national demographical data.

Data on attempted suicide were obtained from the medical and surgical casualty department and the general hospital wards, the emergency psychiatric service, the psychiatric diagnosis and treatment services, the anaesthetic and intensive care services at the University Hospital and Padua Geriatric Hospital.

The monitoring form was administered to all persons treated at each of the above mentioned centres for non-lethal, self-inflicted injuries, with the exception of drug addicts suffering from accidental overdose and subjects presenting suicidal threats.

Three research operators collected data daily from the above mentioned hospital structures.

During the years 1989-1992, the researchers also obtained data from the 177 GPs working in the Padua territory. The GPs were contacted by phone every two months with the aim of including possible cases of attempted suicide that had been recorded by them, but not referred to a general hospital emergency ward. This approach has subsequently been terminated since it was unable to add any further epidemiological information to what had already been detected at the level of the general hospital.

Results

Suicide

During our study period (1989-1999) there were 252 suicides among the subjects living in Padua, of whom 168 were males (66%) and 84 were females (34%). The distribution of these suicides over the study period is identified in Table 1.

Table 1. Number and rates per 100,000 of suicide, 1989-1999

Year	Males		Females		Total	
	Number	Rate (per 100,000)	Number	Rate (per 100,000)	Number	Rate (per 100,000)
1989	14	15	8	7.5	22	11
1990	13	14	7	6.6	20	10
1991	9	9.7	7	6.6	16	8.1
1992	14	16	6	5.7	20	10.7
1993	18	19.8	7	6.7	25	12.8
1994	16	17.9	7	6.8	23	12
1995	19	21.5	8	7.9	27	14.2
1996	16	18.2	10	9.9	26	13.7
1997	17	19.4	6	6	23	12.2
1998	16	18.3	9	9	25	13.3
1999	16	18.3	9	9	25	13.3

Attempted suicide

During the 11 years period under study (1989-1999), it has been possible to record data related to 1559 attempted suicide committed by residents in the city of Padua. The 1,559 attempts were performed by 1,214 persons, thus supporting an event/person ratio of 1.28 (1.27 for males and 1.29 for females). Table 2 shows the ratio event/person of every year during the period under study.

Table 2. Event/person ratio of attempted suicide, 1989-1999

Year	Males	Females	Total
1989	1.01	1.05	1.04
1990	1.2	1.15	1.17
1991	1.25	1.25	1.25
1992	1.41	1.33	1.36
1993	1.2	1.18	1.19
1994	1.09	1.55	1.39
1995	1.13	1.21	1.18
1996	1.57	1.48	1.51
1997	1.2	1.3	1.25
1998	1.66	1.48	1.51
1999	1.43	1.55	1.50

Of the total sample of 1,214 attempters, 446 were men (36.7%) and 768 women; the sex ratio (f/m) being 1.72.

Table 3. Attempted suicide by gender, 1989-1999

Year	Males			Females			Total	
	Number	% of sample	Rate (per 100,000)	Number	% of sample	Rate (per 100,000)	Number	Rate (per 100,000)
1989	60	34.5	64.66	114	65.5	107.12	174	87.35
1990	44	34.9	47.60	82	65.1	77.40	126	63.52
1991	40	33.3	43.49	80	66.7	76.00	120	60.85
1992	51	38.6	55.75	81	61.4	77.45	132	67.33
1993	34	31.2	37.54	75	68.8	72.36	109	56.12
1994	21	34.4	23.6	40	65.6	39.1	61	31.89
1995	36	35.3	40.88	66	64.7	65.18	102	53.88
1996	35	40.2	39.88	52	59.8	51.59	87	46.14
1997	53	49.1	60.58	55	50.9	54.87	108	57.53
1998	33	36.3	37.89	58	63.7	58.21	91	48.73
1999	39	37.5	44.68	65	62.5	65.24	104	55.64

The age distribution of the suicide attempters is shown in Table 4. The main age of the total sample was 41.14 years of age (SD = 18.6, range 15-98). Statistically signifi-cant difference for gender was found: 69.5% of the female attempters were below the age of 50 years old, as against 55.1 of the male attempters. Furthermore, compared to men, women were more concentrated in the youngest age group (15-19), while there were more men in the age groups 25-34 and 40-44 (χ^2 = 28.356, p< .008). Among attempters older than 45, gender distribution was similar.

Table 4. Attempted suicide by age, average 1989-1999

Age	Number	Percentage of total sample
15-19	22	7.6
20-24	148	12.3
25-29	169	14.0
30-34	160	13.3
35-39	98	8.1
40-44	84	7.0
45-49	93	7.7
50-54	81	6.7
55-59	50	4.1
60-64	49	4.1
65-69	52	4.3
70-74	48	4.0
75-79	29	2.4
80+	52	4.3
Missing data	9	0.7

Epidemiological findings

General results

Of the total sample, 345 attempters (48.3%) were single, 56 (7.8%) were widowed, 64 (9%) separated or divorced, and 249 (34.9%) were married (34.9%). In 500 cases (41.2%), information were missing. Significant differences were observed between the male and the female attempters: men were more often single, while women were more often widowed (χ^2 =9.303, p<.025).

With regard to household composition at the time of suicide attempt, 87 (12.6%) of the attempters were living alone, 34 (4.9%) were living with one or more children, 111 (16%) with their partner, 132 (19.1%) with both partner and children, 250 (36.1%) with their parents, 40 (5.8%) with relatives or friends, and 35 of the attempters (5.1%) stayed at an institution, while in 3 cases (0.4%) living conditions was defined as 'other' (missing data= 522; 43% of the total sample). There were significant differences between the female and the male attempters; women were more often living with children and/or partner and children, while men more often lived with a partner without children (χ^2 = 2.459, p<.003).

About two thirds of the suicide attempters (63.1%) had only completed compulsory education (low educational level), 30.3% had finished high school (middle level), and 6.6% had university degrees (high educational level). Data were missing in 590 cases (48.6% of the total sample). We did not find any significant differences between the two sexes (χ^2 = 1.458; p = 0.482).

As to employment, 252 of the attempters (35.8%) were economically active and in work at the time of the attempted suicide; 115 (16.3%) were unemployed, and 337 (47.9%) were economically inactive, being students, housewives or pensioners (missing data = 510; 42% of the total sample). The difference between the genders was statistically significant; more women were economically inactive and more men unemployed ($\chi^2 = 31.037$; $p < .000$).

Table 5 shows the choice of suicide methods of the suicide attempters.

Table 5. Methods used in suicide attempts

Method	Number	Percentage
Poisoning		
Non-narcotic analgesics, anti-inflammatory and anti-rheumatic agents	40	2.6
Barbiturates, other sedatives, hypnotics and other psychotrophic agents	904	58
Opiods, nacotics and psychodyslectics	10	0.6
Other drugs used for central nervous system	27	1.7
Other drugs and medicine	42	2.7
Alcohol	3	0.2
Petrol derivatives, solvents and their vapours, pseticides, herbicides and other agricultural toxics	110	7.1
Drowning	31	2.0
Firearms	4	0.3
Burning	5	0.3
Wrist cutting with sharp objects	173	11.1
Jumping from heights	42	2.7
Running out in front of a vehicle	12	0.8
MISSING DATA	133	8.5

Most attempters had used non-violent methods: in 1026 cases (71.9%), the attempter had taken an overdose of drugs (in particular, sedatives or hypnotics), while 28.1% (400 cases) had used more violent methods. More men had used violent methods, women more often used non-violent methods ($\chi^2 = 44.775$, $p < .000$).

Of the 1,214 subjects constituting the total sample of suicide attempters, 407 (63.1%) had no history of previous suicide attempts, 88 (13.6%) had attempted suicide once or more times attempts prior to the 12 months leading up to the index episode, 101 (15.7%) within the 12 months prior to the index episode, and 49 (7.6%) had made one or more previous suicide attempts, but at an unknown time (missing data for 569 attempters (46.9%).

The frequency of previous attempts differed significantly between the genders ($\chi^2 = 13.738$, $p<.003$): 66.1% of the women claimed never to have attempted suicide before the index attempt versus 57.1% of the men. Furthermore, 21.7% of the male sample had attempted suicide some time during the 12 months preceding the index attempt, against only 12.6% of the female sample.

By following each of the attempters for an average period of 12 months after the index event, we noted that 16.5% (235 cases) of the sample had repeated the attempt within the period (missing data = 132; 8.5% of the total sample of events). This evaluation was not performed for those who had attempted suicide in 1999 since data for 2000 were not yet available.

The frequency of repetition during the 11 years under study was rather high; only 1,031 of the attempters (35%) had only made one attempt. Of the total sample, 117 of the attempters (9.6%) were minor repeaters (less than 3 repeats), and 66 (5.4%) were major repeaters (3 or more attempts). In general, the average time between the index event and the subsequent attempt was 410 days (SD = 562, range 0-3116). There were, however, significant differences between the genders (f = 5.349, p<.021); on the average, males attempters (123 cases) repeated the attempt within 340 days after the index episode (i.e. within one year), while the female attempters (222 cases) on the average repeated the attempt after 449 days (i.e. after one year). Furthermore, the analyses showed that the more numerous the episodes of repetition, the shorter the interval between the episodes.

Suicide attempts were slightly more frequent during springtime and summer, but the difference in the distribution of suicide attempts throughout the year was not significant, nor was there any corelation between time of the year and gender or method. As to the time of the day, 63% of the attempts took place between 8.00am and 8.00pm (missing data =3 50; 28.8% of the sample). We found no significant differences between sexes.

Conclusion

Contrary to the rates of suicide that were slightly increasing during the period under study, there was a decreasing trend in the rates of attempted suicide. In all the years, except for in 1997, the female rates were markedly higher than the male rates, the sex ratio (f/m) being 1.72. The majority of the suicide attempters in the Padua catchment area was below the age of 50 years and close to 40% were young people 20-34 years old. This age group is notoriously more affected by personal or work problems and social maladjustment (Beautrais et al, 1997; Negron et al, 1997). This was particularly true for male suicide attempters, a high percentage of them being unemployed (Platt, 1984). Many of the very young women (15-19 years old) were economically inactive as e.g. housekeepers, something that may be partly due to the demographic distribution of the population in Padua and to the fact that the majority of the suicide attempters was on a low educational level. The suicide attempters were also characterized by a high percentage of single men and widows. While living with children seemed to be a protective factor when women were concerned, the reverse seemed to be true for men.

The choice of method by the attempters in the catchment area is in line with what is shown in the literature (e.g. Schmidtke et al, 1996), self-poisoning being the common method used by both male and female suicide attempters and in all age groups. At the index attempt, about two thirds were 1st evers; looking, however at the whole period under study, it turned out that only about one third had never made more than the index attempt.

References

Beautrais AL, Joyce PR, Mulder RT (1997). Precipitating factors and life events in serious suicide attempts among youths aged 13 through 24 years. *Journal of the American Academy of Child and Adolescent Psychiatry* 36: 1543-1551.

Negron R, Piacentrini J, Graee F et al. (1997). Microanalysis of adolescent suicide attempters and ideators during the acute suicidal episode. *Journal of the American Academy for Child and Adolescent Psychiatry* 36: 1512-1519.

Platt S (1984): Unemployement and suicidal behaviour: A review of the literature. *Social Science and Medicine* 19: 93-115.

Schmidtke A, Bille-Brahe U, DeLeo D et al. (1996). Attempted suicide in Europe: Rates, trends and socio-demographic characteristics of suicide attempters during the period 1989-1992. Results of the WHO/EURO Multicentre Study on Attempted suicide. *Acta Psychiatrica Scandinavica* 93: 327-338.

Chapter 27

Suicidal Behaviour in Greece

A. J. Botsis, A. Kapsali, N. Vaidakis & C. N. Stefanis

Description of the catchment area

The Greece catchment area comprises the island of Evia. Evia lies east of the coast of Attiki, where Athens, the capital of Greece, is situated. It is separated from the mainland of the country by a canal, which at its narrowest is 10-20 meters broad. The capital city of Evia is Chalkida, 80 kms from Athens. Chalkida has 80,000 inhabitants, whereas the whole island of Evia has 205,208 inhabitants, and comprises 2 per cent of the entire population of Greece. Close to one third of the island (30%) is urban, 27% semi-urban, and 43% rural. The great majority of the inhabitants are Christian Orthodox with only few Muslim families. As to demographic, social and health characteristics, the catchment area is considered to be representative of the whole country.

Sample and method of data collection

Data on suicide are obtained from the National Statistics. The 'real' suicide rate is, however, thought to be much higher, with under-reporting mainly due to the negative attitude towards suicidal behaviour held by the Christian Orthodox Church. Suicide victims are not tolerated by the Church, and a person who has committed suicide is not permitted to be buried in Christian soil. The stigmatization also has serious social consequences for the survivors.

After 4 months of planning and preparation, the monitoring study started 1st May 2000. All suicide attempters treated at the health care services of the island were registered. The health care services of the island include the Chalkida General County Hospital (CGCH), the Community Mental Health Center (CMHC), and one small private hospital. The Community Mental Health Center is the only psychiatric service on the island, which cooperates with the General County Hospital as well as with the five Primary Care Medical Centers. Two psychologists and one social worker were trained in data collection using the monitoring form. During the first year of monitoring, the whole group involved in the study met every month.

Calculation of an estimation factor of 1.13 was based on reports obtained during the month of December 2000 from doctors working in private practice or at private hospitals.

Results

Suicide

The National Statistics reported that in 1998 the suicide rate for the country was 4.03 per 100,000 inhabitants, the female rate being 1.69 per 100,000 and the male rate 6.23 per 100,000.

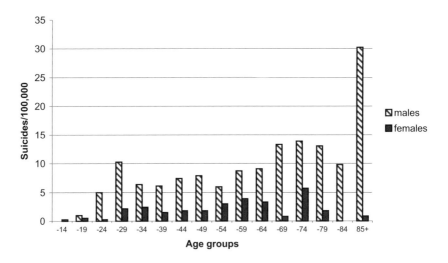

Figure 1. Suicide rates by age groups and gender, 1998

The rate of suicide for the island of Evia was 3.9 per 100,000. The sex ratio (m/f) varied with age: 33.55:1 among the elderly older than 85 years, 16.24:1 among the 65-69 year old age group, 20:1 among the 20-24 years old, and as low as 1.87:1 among the 15-19 years old. This finding is in line with results obtained from other studies (Plutchik et al, 1996). The frequency of suicide in the catchment area is similar to the frequency in the Greek population as a whole.

Attempted suicide

During the first year of the study, 102 suicide attempts were registered (78 by women and 24 by men). Taking into account the estimation factor, the number of suicide attempts was 115 (88 by women and 27 by men).

The age and gender distribution of the estimated 115 suicide attempts is presented in figure 2.

The estimated rate of attempted suicide (events) was 56.04 per 100,000, which means that the number of suicide attempts is 14.36 times higher than the number of completed suicide. The estimated female rate of attempted suicide was 86.34 per 100,000, and

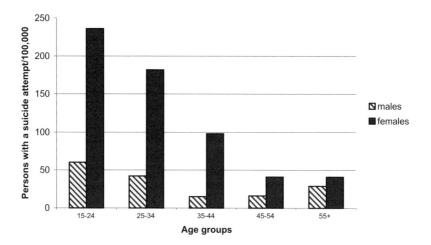

Figure 2. Rates of attempted suicide by age and gender

26.16 per 100,000 among males. The overall sex ratio (f/m) was 3.3:1, but there were marked variations between age groups. For example, the ratio among the 35-44 years old was 6.54:1, among the 25-34 years old was 4.34:1, among the 15-24 years old 3.94:1, and finally, as low as 1.41:1 among the age group older than 55 years.

Of the registered suicide attempters, eight had attempted suicide by using a violent method (five men and three women), while the other 94 had used a non-violent method. The majority of those who had used a non-violent method had taken an overdose of medicine.

Conclusion

The official rates of suicide in Greece are low, but it is argued that for religious and social reasons the real frequency remains underestimated. An indication of this could be that, according to our study, the ratio of suicide attempt:suicide is as high as 15:1.

The fact that many social changes have taken place in Greece during the last ten years indicates that suicidal behaviour in the coming decade will be a problem of great concern. About half of the Greek population are now living in Attika, which means that the region will be suffering from problems usual in big cities, such as social isolation and the breakdown of the social support system. Another problem is that since 1990 many migrants have moved into the country, and it is estimated that 9-10% of the population are now immigrants. It is expected that the convergance of Greece into a multicultural society will, at least in the beginning, cause difficulties that may result in potential suicide risk factors.

References

National Statistic Service: Suicide rates in Greece in 1998.

Plutchik R, Botsis AJ, Bakur-Weiner M, Kennedy G (1996). Clinical measurement of suicidality and coping in late life. In: G Kennedy (ed.). *Depression and Suicide in Late Life: Critical Issues in Treatment, Research and Public Policy.* pp 83-102. New York: Wiley.

Other Participating Centres

Chapter 28

Suicidal Behaviour in Turkey

I. Sayil & H. Devrimci-Özguven

Description of the catchment area

The Turkish area under study, Mamak, is a district in Ankara, which is the capital and the second largest city of Turkey. Mamak, being one of the leading districts of Ankara, is located in the North-Eastern part of Ankara. Some parts are included in the old city, but most of the catchment area is a newly settled part of the city. Especially since the 1960s, there have been many immigrants, and the district of Mamak has been growing fast into one of the most heterogeneous and colourful parts of Ankara. This mirrors, to some extent, Turkey as a whole. The exact ethnic structure of Mamak is not known. It is, however, known that the district has attracted many people from all over Turkey, and that the county today represents the overall ethnic structure of Turkey. It is supposed that most of the people living in Mamak are Muslims, and that Mamak represents the whole country with regard to social structure.

According to the census in 1990, Mamak had 410,359 inhabitants of which 269,367 were aged 15 years or older (DIE 1993a). The population of Mamak is a young population with the majority between the ages of 10 and 30 years. The sex ratio (m/f) is close to 1/1. The socio-demographic characteristics of Mamak are basically similar to those of Ankara and to Turkey as a whole.

Sample and method of data collection

The suicide statistics for Turkey have been collected and published by the State Institute of Statistics Republic of Turkey since 1962. The source of these data is the "Suicide Statistics Forms" filled in by the police. The determination of whether a death is a suicide or not is based on reports from hospitals and police records.

The monitoring of attempted suicide started on the 1 April 1998, involving all the general hospital wards and the primary care units in the catchment area. In addition to the two hospitals and the primary care units in the area, three more hospitals near Mamak were included in the study in case suicide attempters from the area should contact these centres.

Information on suicide attempts treated at the emergency rooms and mental health clinics were registered on monitoring forms by house staff nurses, who had been specifically trained in completing the forms. Three staff members gathered the forms every week from the Crisis Centre and incomplete data were checked and recorded by the staff.

In addition, all medical and police records from 5 hospitals in Mamak and the Police Headquarters records were checked. The control showed that not all suicide attempters had been registered and, furthermore, that the medical records, the hospital police records and records of the police headquarters were not concordant. Some cases not hitherto registered were identified, and in the end it was estimated that 75.34% of all hospital treated suicide attempters were registered and reported to the centre. After the first 3 months, primary care units and one of the five hospitals in the catchment area were excluded from the study since no suicide attempts from Mamak were ever treated in these units or at the hospital.

Due to a shortage of staff, the registration was, from the beginning, carried out in two intervals of three and six-month-periods. For the estimation of the "true" suicide attempt rates, estimation factors were therefore calculated. The estimation factor was 1. 3, 2 and 2 for 1998, 1999 and 2000, respectively. For the computation of rates and for the analysis of socio-demographic variables, demographic statistics of the catchment area were obtained from State Institute of Statistics (DIE 1993a, DIE 1993c).

Results

Suicide

Data on suicide is only available for Ankara and Turkey as a whole and not for Mamak.

In Turkey, the suicide rate in 1998 (the last available year) was 3.9 per 100,000 for men and 2.7 per 100,000 for women (DIE 2000), the gender ratio (m/f) being 1.4.

The risk of suicide increased by age, with the male rate peaking among those aged 75 years and older (10.6 per 100,000). Among women, however, the highest rate was found to be among the 15-24 year olds (6.4 per 100,000) and then among the 25-29 year olds (3.6 per 100,000) and the 65-74 year olds (3.3 per 100,000).

Hanging was the most frequently used method of suicide by both men and women, employed by 45% of men and 36% of women. Shooting was the next most frequent method used among men (30%), whereas among women, self-poisoning was used by 27%, while only 20% of the women invoked their own death through shooting. Ten per cent of the men and 11% of the women committed suicide by jumping from a high place.

During the last years, the suicide rate have been increasing in Turkey. In 1989, the rate was 2.5 per 100,000 for men and 1.6 per 100,000 for women (DIE 1991). Thus, by 1998 rates had increased by 56% for men and 41% for women.

In Ankara, the rate in 1998 was 6.6 per 100,000 for men and 3.5 per 100,000 for women. The gender ratio (m/f) was 1.9. The distribution of age was similar to the distribution throughout the whole country, but the small number of suicides, especially among the elderly, should be kept in mind when age-specific rates are calculated. The rates of suicide among young women were high (7.4 per 100,000 among the 15-24 years old).

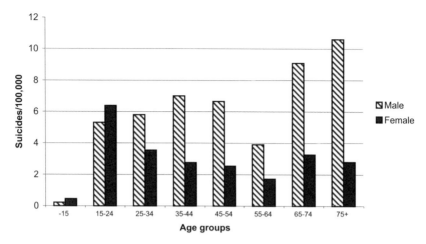

Figure 1. Suicide rates by age and gender in Turkey, 1998

Rates of suicide were higher in Ankara than in Turkey as a whole, but the age distribution and the gender ratio were more or less the same, and the choice of method followed the pattern throughout the whole country.

Suicide attempts

During the two and a half year period of monitoring (from 1 April 1998 to 30 June 2000), 298 suicide attempts were registered.

Of these, 208 were women and 90 men, the gender ratio (f/m) being 2.3. The mean age of male attempters was 27.88 ± 10.81 years, and ranged from 15 to 55; whereas the

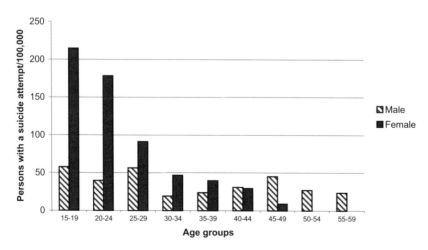

Figure 2. Rates of attempted suicide by age and gender, 1998-2000

mean age of female attempters was 22.99 ± 6.54 years, ranging from 15 to 48 years with the difference between genders being statistically significant (t=30.52, p<0.000).

The mean rate of annual suicide attempts for the total group was 63.36 per 100,000, for men it was 37.53/100,000 and for women 90.80/100,000. The gender ratio (f/m) was 2.4.

Figure 2 shows that young women are at a particularly high risk of attempted suicide, with rates reaching 214.6 per 100,000 among 15-19 year olds and 178.5 per 100,000 among 20-24 year olds. Although much lower, the male rate of attempted suicide are highest among the very young also; among the 15-19 year olds the rate was 57.8/100,000 and among the 25-29 year olds 56.7/100,000. It is noteworthy that in Mamak, suicide attempts were not registered by women older than 48 years or by men above the age of 55 years.

Figure 3 shows the changes in the frequency of attempted suicide rates during the years 1998-2000. Male rates increased by more than 23.78%, and female rates by 22.36%, with an overall increase taking place in most age groups. However, the highest increases took place among females aged 15-19 years old and males aged 20-24 years. It should be noted, however, that an investigation period of only three years is not long enough to allow for proper trend analyses.

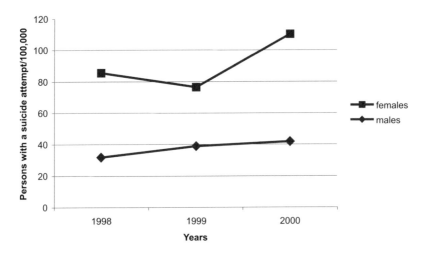

Figure 3. Rates of attempted suicide, 1998-2000

Generally, the methods used for the attempt were most often so-called "soft methods". Self-poisoning was by far the most often used method by both men and women (76.7% and 97.2, respectively). Close to sixteen per cent (15.6%) of men and 22.6% of women had taken overdoses of psychotropic drugs, and 52.2% of men and 68.3% of women had used other drugs. More than one fifth of men (22.0%) and 3.9% of women had used "alcohol" as their second or third method of attempting suicide. Cutting was the next most frequent choice of method used among men (8.9%), while only 2.4% of the women used this method.

The methods chosen did not co-vary significantly with age, in that all age groups used "soft methods" most often. The use of alcohol, however, was most frequent among younger people, but as a second or third method.

Epidemiological findings

General results

In Mamak, more than half of the suicide attempters were single, 53.4% of men and 52.9% of women had never been married, while 32.7% of men and 34.6% of women were married (mostly their first marriage). Keeping in mind that marital status is age-related, age-specific analyses were carried out, showing (as expected) that the percentage of single persons diminished with age. Specifically, only 17.2% of men and 11.1% of women aged 25 years and older were single, and as age increased so did the percentage of persons who were married. In accord, only 3.4% of the men, and 24.1% of the women below the age of 25 years were married. The percentage, who had experienced marital breakdown also increased with age, where 13.8% of men 8.4% of women older that 25 years were divorced or separated, while only 6.9% and 3.7%, respectively, of counterparts were below the age of 25 years.

The majority of the suicide attempters (70.6% of men and 75.9% of women) were living with partner or others (e.g. parents, partner, other relatives, and friends), and only 3.4% of the men and 2.6% of the women were usually living alone. Few men (1.7%) and few women (2.6%) were living alone with child(ren). Finally, 5.2% and 0.6%, respectively, were staying in hostels. For some (13.6% and 11.1%, respectively), the living conditions had changed immediately prior to the suicide attempt.

On the average, 30.5% of male and 26.6% of female attempters had no or little formal education. Close to half of men (57.6%) and two thirds of women (64.9%) were educated on a middle level, and only 10.2% of men and 8.4% of women were highly educated. There were no significant differences between the genders.

An average of 32.2% of all male and 16.9% of all female suicide attempters were unemployed. With regard to economically active persons, calculated in relation to the overall numbers of people who were economically active, 43.2% of male and 40.6% of female attempters were unemployed, and 22.0% of men and 57.1% of women were economically inactive. The inactive group was mainly composed of students and housewives. Taking into account the fact that many people up to 25 years of age are economically inactive (e.g. apprentices, students, or those having not finished vocational training), this variable was also analyzed separately for persons 25 years or older. Even then an average of 50.0% of the economically active men were unemployed, and 55.6% of the women economically inactive.

All the registered suicide attempters were Muslims, and the religious affiliation among suicide attempters did not differ significantly from that in the general population.

Table 1. The socio-demographic variables of suicide attempters by gender

	Male	Female	Total
Marital status in relation to sex			
Never married	53.4% (n=31)	52.9% (n=81)	54.5% (n=112)
Widowed, divorced, separated	12.0% (n=7)	9.1% (n=14)	9.9% (n=21)
Married	32.7% (n=19)	34.6% (n=53)	34.1% (n=72)
Cases who had attempted to suicide before in relation to sex			
Persons who had attempted to suicide within the last 12 months	15.3% (n=9)	7.8% (n=12)	9.9% (n=21)
Persons who had attempted to suicide more than 12 months ago	10.2% (n=6)	7.1% (n=11)	8.0% (n=17)
Persons who had attempted to suicide in unknown date	11.9% (n=7)	6.5% (n=10)	8.0% (n=17)
Persons who had not attempted to suicide before	62.7% (n=37)	76.6% (n=118)	72.8% (n=155)
Level of education in relation to sex			
Lowest level	30.5% (n=18)	26.6% (n=41)	27.7% (n=59)
Middle level	57.6% (n=34)	64.9% (n=100)	62.9% (n=134)
Highest level	10.2% (n=6)	8.4% (n=13)	8.9% (n=19)
Employment status in relation to sex			
Economically active, employed	42.4% (n=25)	24.7% (n=38)	29.6% (n=63)
Economically active, unemployed	32.2% (n=19)	16.9% (n=26)	21.1% (n=45)
Economically inactive	22.0% (n=13)	57.1% (n=88)	47.4% (n=101)
The household composition			
Living alone	3.4% (n=2)	2.6% (n=4)	2.8% (n=6)
Living alone with children	1.7% (n=1)	2.6% (n=4)	2.4% (n=5)
Living with partner and children	13.8% (n=8)	11.7% (n=18)	12.3% (n=26)
Living with partner without children	15.5% (n=9)	22.7% (n=35)	20.8% (n=44)
Living with parents	51.7% (n=30)	50.0% (n=77)	50.5% (n=107)
Living with other relatives/friends	3.4% (n=2)	3.2% (n=5)	3.3% (n=7)
Other	10.3% (n=6)	7.1% (n=11)	8.0% (n=17)

The majority of the attempters had no history of previous suicide attempts (62.7% of male and and 76.6% of the female attempters). An average of 37.4% of the men and 21.4% of the women had attempted suicide prior to the index attempt and of these, 40.9% and 36.4%, respectively, had done so within the last 12 months. Previous suicide attempts were more common among the male than among female attempters. ($\chi^2 = 5.23$, p<0.05).

Among the first-evers of the index attempt, only 1 male and 3 females repeated the attempt once or more during the observation period. Comparisons between those, who had made one or more suicide attempts prior to the index attempt and those who had not, showed no difference between the two groups in regard to the mean age (24.27 ±

8.06 vs. 23.61 ± 7.51) or the choice of method. The female repeaters were, however, more often divorced or separated (12.2% vs. 3.4%), slightly more often unemployed (18.2% vs.16.9%), and more often economically active (36.4% vs. 21.2%). The male repeaters were less often divorced or separated (4.8% vs. 13.5%), but more often educated at the lowest level (36.4% vs. 27.0%). None of the differences were, however, statistically significant.

Questions on aftercare were included in the monitoring form in 1998 and 1999. Inpatient care was recommended for 38.6% of male attempters and 30.8% of female attempters, out-patient care for 40.9% and 49.5%, respectively, and no further treatment was recommended for 18.2% of male attempters and 17.6% of female attempters.

Conclusion

The rate of suicide in Turkey has been relatively low compared to most other countries, but during the last ten years, a marked increase has been taking place. As in other countries the risk of suicide among men is increasing with age, but among especially women, the young, are most at risk.

As in other countries, attempted suicide is most common among women (Schmidtke et al 1996, Bille-Brahe 1998). The highest age-specific rate was found among 15-24 year old women and 15-29 year old men. This confirms the common notion that suicide attempts, especially the more dramatic ones, occur most often among teenagers and young adults. However, this simple inverse relationship between age and suicide attempts appears to be less valid for men whereby among male attempters, a second peak is found in those aged 45-49 years olds. The frequency of previous suicide attempts were found to be low for both genders, and the repetition rate in the year following the index attempt was very low too.

Compared with the other European areas under study, both rates of suicide and attempted suicide are relatively low in the catchment area being studied by the Mamak centre (Schmidtke et al., 1996; Bille-Brahe et al., 1998). As in the other catchment areas, attempted suicide is most common among women, but gender ratio (f/m) in Mamak is relatively high. It is noteworthy that no women over the age of 48 years and no men over the age of 55 years in the Mamak catchment area had ever attempted suicide.

References

Arikan Z, Cosar B, Candansayar S, Isik E (1996). The alcoholism prevalence in a semi-urban area (Turkish). *Kriz Dergisi*, 4(2): 93-101.
Bille-Brahe U, Schmidtke A, Kerkhof AJFM, DeLeo D, Lönnqvist J, Platt S, Faria JS (1995). Background and introduction to the WHO/Euro Multicentre Study on Attempted suicide. *Crisis:* 16(2): 72-84.
Bille-Brahe U, Kerkhof A, DeLeo D, Schmidtke A, Crepet P, Hawton K, Hjelmeland H, Lönnqvist J, Michel K, Salander Renberg E, Wasserman D (1998). *Report on the WHO/Euro multicentre study on attempted suicide 1988-1997.* Odense: Centre for Suicidological Research.

Bille-Brahe U (1999). *WHO/EURO Multicentre Study on Attempted suicide. Facts and Figures.* Second Edition. Copenhagen: World Health Organisation

Diekstra RFW (1993). The epidemiology of suicide and attempted suicide. *Acta Psychiatrica Scandinavica* (Suppl), 371:9-20.

DIE (Devlet Istatistik Enstitüsü- State Institute of Statistics Prime Ministry Republic of Turkey) (2000) *Suicide Statistics 1998.* Ankara: State Institute of Statistics, Printing Division.

DIE (Devlet Istatistik Enstitüsü- State Institute of Statistics Prime Ministry Republic of Turkey) (1991) *Suicide Statistics 1989.* Ankara: State Institute of Statistics, Printing Division.

DIE (Devlet Istatistik Enstitüsü- State Institute of Statistics Prime Ministry Republic of Turkey) (1993a) *Census of Population Social and Economic Characteristics, Province Ankara 1990.* Ankara: State Institute of Statistics, Printing Division.

DIE (Devlet Istatistik Enstitüsü- State Institute of Statistics Prime Ministry Republic of Turkey) (1993b) *Justice Statistics 1990.* Ankara: State Institute of Statistics, Printing Division.

DIE (Devlet Istatistik Enstitüsü- State Institute of Statistics Prime Ministry Republic of Turkey) (1993c) *Census of Population Social and Economic Characteristics 1990.* Ankara: State Institute of Statistics, Printing Division.

Kerkhof A, Schmidtke A, Bille-Brahe U, DeLeo D, Lönnqvist J (1994). *Attempted Suicide in Europe.* Leiden: DSWO Press.

Platt S, Bille-Brahe U, Kerkhof A et al. (1992). Attempted suicide in Europe: The WHO/EURO Multicentre Study on Attempted suicide. I.Introduction and preliminary analysis for 1989. *Acta Psychiatrica Scandinavica,* 85: 97-104.

Sayil I, Oral A, Güney S, Ayhan N, Ayhan Ö, Devrimci H (1993). A Study on the attempted suicides in Ankara (Turkish). *Kriz Dergisi* 1(2): 56-61.

Sayil I (1997) Review of suicide studies in Turkey. *Crisis,* 18:124-127.

Sayil I, Berksun O, Palabiyikoglu R, Oral A, Haran S, Güney S, Binici S, Geçim S, Yücat T, Beder A, Özayar H, Büyükçelik D, Özgüven HD (1998). Attempted suicides in Ankara in 1995. *Crisis,* 19:47-48.

Sayil I, Gögüs AK, Sözer Y, Ceyhun B (1990). Attitudes of clinicians toward suicide in Turkey. In: G Ferrari, M Bellini, P Crepet (ed). *Suicidal Behaviour and Risk Factors* pp.803-809. Bologna: Monduzzi .

Schmidtke A, Bille-Brahe U, DeLeo D, Kerkhof A, Bjerke T, Crepet P, Haring C, Hawton K, Lönnqvist J, Michel K, Pommereau X, Querejeta I, Philippe I, Salander Renberg E, Temesvary B, Wasserman D, Fricke S, Weinacker B, Sampaio-Faria JG (1996). Attempted suicide in Europe: rates, trends and sociodemographic characteristics of suicide attempters during the period 1989-1992. Results of the WHO/Euro multicentre study on attempted suicide. *Acta Psychiatrica Scandinavica,* 93: 327-338.

Sözer Y, Ceyhun B, Gögüs AK, Sayil I (1991). The attitudes of the physicians toward the suicide (Turkish). 27th National Congress of Psychiatry, Oral presentation, The Congress Book, 6-9 October 1991, Antalya.

WHO-World Health Organisation (1992) Health-for-all targets. The health policy for Europe. Summary of the updated edition. September 1991. Copenhagen: World Health Organisation. EUR ICP HSC 013, 1992.

Chapter 29

Suicidal Behaviour in Israel

D. Stein, E. Lublinsky, D. Sobol-Havia, J.Asherov, L. Lazarevitch & A. Apter

Description of the catchment area

The catchment area under study comprises the two neighbouring cities, Holon and Bat Yam, in the center of Israel with a population of 283,000 inhabitants 15 years and older (mean for 1990-1998, Central Israeli Bureau of Statistics). The area comprises about 1.3 per cent of the area and 5.4 per cent of the population of Israel. The population is mostly Jewish (98%). On a socio-economic status scale ranking 188 local authorities in which 1 represents the lowest status and 188 the highest, Bat Yam is ranked 132, and Holon 152. The two cities are fairly representative of the urban population in the center of Israel (CBS 1990-1998).

Sample and methods of data collection

The study population consisted of all subjects attempting suicide who were treated at the Edith Wolfson Medical Center, Holon between the years 1990-1998. The center is the only emergency service for Holon and Bat Yam.

Exclusion criteria of the study population included suicidal subjects treated at the Edith Wolfson Medical Center who were not inhabitants of Holon and Bat Yam.

From 1990, every indivdual admitted to the emergency service of the Edith Wolfson Medical Center because of attempted suicide was interviewed by the nursing staff with a structured interview based on the requirements of the Central Israeli Bureau of Statistics (Central Bureau of Statistics, 1995). The survey was anonymous. Data were collected on gender, age, place of residency, place of birth, date of the suicide attempt, motive for the act, method (both according to a structured list), number of suicide attempts throughout the research period, and next care following the assessment at the emergency service.

From 1997, the nursing staff of the emergency service administered in addition to the previous questionnaire, the Hebrew translation of the WHO monitoring form for the evaluation of suicidal behavior (Platt et al., 1992). This instrument includes data relating to marital status, usual household composition (e.g., living with parents, spouse, alone, etc.), change of address in the year preceding the parasuicidal event, economical status including unemployment, level of education, and previous suicidal behavior. Due to limitations in space, data related to care following the assessment at the emergency service, as well as data concerning repeated and previous attempts are not presented here.

The rates of attempted suicide were calculated according to the number of people engaged in this behavior, and according to the number of suicide events occurring during a specific period. Between-group differences were calculated by chi-square analysis and the analysis of variance (ANOVA). A log linear model was used for the analysis of the correlation of the suicide parameter in question with two or more socio-demographic variables. All analyses were performed using BMPD statistical software. An estimation factor (EF) was calculated for the best estimation that approximates the "real" number of people who attempted suicide in the catchment area of Holon and Bat Yam according to the instructions of the WHO/EURO Multicenter Study on Suicidal Behavior. This factor takes into consideration the percentage of Holon and Bat Yam residents who attempted suicide and were treated at the Edith Wolfson Medical Center during a certain period of time (M), and the percentage of Holon and Bat Yam residents who attempted suicide and were treated at other facilities during the same period (N). Specifically, EF=100-[M-M+N)*100]. The EF for the present study was calculated as 1.25. All results presented take into consideration this EF.

Results

Suicide

Analysis of the suicide rates for the cities of Holon and Bat Yam for the years 1990-1995 showed inconsistent changes between 5-10/100,000 for females, whereas for males, an increase from 10 to 20/100,000 was noted between 1990-1992, with a constant annual decrease to rates between 12-15/100,000 thereafter.

Attempted suicide

During the period between 1990-1998, a total of 1,774 individuals over the age of 15 years in the cities of Holon and Bat Yam were reported to have attempted suicide, and the total number of suicide attempts was 2,150. The mean age of these individuals was 34.51 years (SD=18.78; range 10-93). The group consisted of 621 males (31.2%) and 1330 females (66.8%) (no gender was mentioned for 40 cases). The difference between the mean age of the male (37.92 ± 19.04 years) and female suicide attempters (33.00 ± 18.52 years) was significant [F(1,1893)=27.33; p<.001].

The mean annual rate of suicide attempts for the period between 1990-1998 among individuals over the age of 15 was 88/100,000 for males, and 180/100,000 for females. Comparison of Holon and Bat Yam with the other 16 European centers of the WHO/ EURO Multicenter Study places our group in 8th place for males, and 9th place for females. The suicide rate for Holon and Bat Yam for persons over the age of 15 years during the period of 1990-1995 was 18/ 100,000 for males, and 8/ 100, 000 for females, suggesting the attempted suicide/suicide ratio to be 5:1 for males and 22:1 for females.

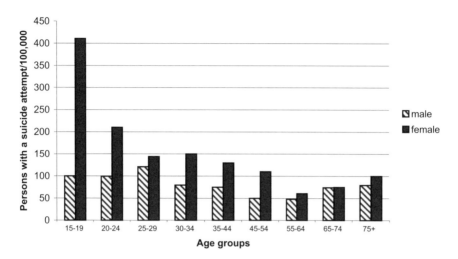

Figure 1. Rates of attempted suicide per 100,000 by age and gender, Holon & Bat Yam, Total 1990-1998

Among males, the highest rate was shown for the ages of 25-29 years (121.4 per 100,000), with a second smaller peak after the age of 65. For females, the highest rate was shown for the ages of 15-19 years (411 per 100,000). By contrast, the suicide rate for both male and female residents of Holon and Bat Yam was found to increase with age.

Except for the age range of 65-74, female subjects had a constantly higher rate of attempted suicide than males (Figure 1). The highest female/male ratio was shown for the age range of 15-19 (4.2), and the mean female/male ratio for all age groups was 1.8. By contrast, for completed suicide, the mean male-female ratio for the population of Holon and Bat Yam during the period between 1990-1995 was 2.1.

Considering the changes in the rate of suicide attempts for Holon and Bat Yam between 1990-1998 for each gender separately, it was shown that among females the rates were highest in 1990, with a yearly decrease thereafter, with the lowest rates being recorded for 1998. The changes among males, although similar in their direction, were less robust. A further analysis for females by age groups, showed the decrease in the rate of attempted suicide to be related particularly to the age group of 15-19 years, from around 500-600/100,000 in 1990 –1992, to rates around 350/100,000 thereafter.

Epidemiological findings

General results

Twenty six percent of the suicide attempters were married; the rest were either single (50%), divorced (12%), separated (3%), or widowed (9%). Current data for the total population of Holon and Bat Yam exist only for divorce. Comparison of the two groups showed the suicide attempters to include a significantly greater percentage of divorced subjects (12% vs. 4.9%, respectively; $\chi^2(1) = 41.98$; p < .001). Analysis of the usual household composition demonstrated that 72% of the suicide attempters lived with another person (e.g., parents, spouse, friends), 23% lived alone or were single parents, and 5% lived in an institution. By contrast, only 9% of the overall residents of the cities of Holon and Bat Yam lived alone or were single parents [$\chi^2(2) = 24.7$; p < .001].

Eleven percent of the suicide attempters were employed, 62% were economically non-active, and 27% were unemployed. These findings are significantly different from the total population of the cities of Holon and Bat Yam, for whom the rate of employment was 54%, of economic inactivity 44%, and of unemployment 2% [$\chi^2(2) = 557$; p < .0001].

Twenty six percent of the suicide attempters finished 8 years of schooling, 60% had a highschool education, and 14% studied in a university or a similar institution. Nationwide data for the total Jewish Israeli population showed respective rates of 18%, 50%, and 32%, suggesting that a smaller percentage of the suicidal individuals had an above highschool level of education.

The most prominent motive for attempted suicide was depression (31.9%), followed by conflicts with family members (27.9%). The percentages for other motives, including conflicts with friends, difficulties in school or at work, mental disorder other than depression, and separation events were in the range of 5-7% each. Analysis of the two most prominent motives for attempted suicide for each gender by age, revealed a significant effect of age [$\chi^2(121) = 498.20$; p < .0001], gender [$\chi^2(11) = 81.81$; p < .0001], and the interaction between these variables [$\chi^2(77) = 105.86$; p < .02]. The main motive for both male and female children (50%) and adolescents (36-44%) was conflicts with family members. By contrast, depression emerged as the most prominent motive for all other age groups, increasing from 30-40% in younger age groups, to 60-80% in the ages of 65 and over.

Use of medications emerged as the most prevalent method, accounting for almost 90% of all suicide attempts. Other less frequent methods included cutting (5.8%), poisoning (3.3%), jumping (1.4%), and the use of alcohol (1.2%) (the overall percentage of methods is greater than 100%, as several subjects have used more than one method). Analysis of the suicidal methods as "soft" (all types of poisoning and cutting), and "hard" (jumping, hanging, drowning and fire setting) by age and gender revealed that both males (94.2%) and females (97.3%), used mainly "soft" methods. Nevertheless, a significantly greater percentage of males (5.3%) used "hard" methods, compared with females (2.1%) [$\chi^2(1) = 9.58$; p < .002].

Conclusion

The results of the present study suggest that the rate of suicide attempts among both male and female residents of Holon and Bat Yam is in a middle rank order position when compared with the other 16 centers participating in the WHO/EURO Multicenter Study on Suicidal Behaviour. Most of the socio-demographic risk factors for attempted suicide reported in the present study were similar to those reported in previous studies of the WHO/EURO project and elsewhere. These include the smaller attempted suicide/suicide ratio among males, and the greater rate of female gender, younger age groups, and an elevated female/male ratio among younger suicide attempters. Our study has also shown a greater prevalence of subjects divorced, living alone, being economically non-active or unemployed, and having a lower education level among suicide attempters, compared with the total population of the catchment area (Gunnell, Brooks & Peters, 1996; Roy, 1995; Schmidtke et al., 1996).

Data related to specific aspects of suicidal behavior have, for the most part, shown important consistencies in our findings with previous reports. These relate particularly to the considerable overrepresentation of the use of medications and overall "soft" methods, the greater rate of "hard" methods among males, and the lack of influence of age on the choice of the parasuicidal method (Roy, 1995; Schmidtke et al., 1996). Although in keeping with previous studies, conflicts with significant others were considered as an important motive for attempting suicide, particularly for children and adolescents. Depression was of particular relevance in our cohort but not in others, whereas the opposite was found for alcoholism and drug abuse (Hawton et al, 1997). The overrepresentation of the motive of depression in our study probably reflects its inclusion under the category of motives unlike other studies (Platt et al., 1992), as we have not assessed directly the association of attempted suicide with mental disturbance. This also explains the low rate of "other mental disorders" in our cohort. The low rate of substance abuse among Israeli suicide attempters is related to the relatively lower rate of alcohol and drug use in Israel, compared with many countries in Europe and the Americas (Levav & Aisenberg, 1989).

The rate of attempted suicide in Holon and Bat Yam showed an almost constant decrease from 1990-1998. Schmidtke and colleagues (1996) have argued that such ongoing decreasing trends could be attributed to a "fading out" process of the monitoring by the interviewing staff. This seems, however, not to be the case in the present study, as separate analyses of males and females by age showed different trends for different cohorts, with the decrease being most prominent among female adolescents, particularly after 1992. We suggest that the high rates of attempted suicide in the years 1990-1992 are associated with the immigration of around 400,000 Jews from the former USSR to Israel during 1988-1990. About 9.5% of the residents of Holon and Bat Yam are former USSR immigrants, who joined the cities from 1990 on (Central Israeli Bureau of Statistics, 1990-1998). Immigration has been largely associated with an increase in attempted suicide, and is of particular relevance for adolescents of Russian origin, because of identity crises, loss of familial and social support, and a sense of estrangement in the new country (Ponizovsky, Safro, Ginath, & Ritsner, 1997). This assumption is further substantiated by the overrepresentation of subjects of European descent among suicide attempters, compared with the population of Holon and Bat Yam at large, and by the presentation of a similar trend also among suicidal males (the American immigration during that period was relatively negligible).

In conclusion, our study in the cities of Holon and Bat Yam in Israel confirms the importance of many of the risk factors for attempted suicide shown in other countries. The project is planned to continue for at least several more years, to further verify our findings and to study the influence of several important socio-demographic processes on attempted suicide such as immigration, establishing peace with the neighboring Arab countries, and the recent rise of aggression and violence in the Israeli population.

References

Beautris AL, Joyce PR, Mulder RT, Fergusson DM, Deavoll BJ & Nightingale SK (1996). Prevalence and comorbidity of mental disorders in persons making suicide attempts: a case-control study. *American Journal of Psychiatry*, 153: 1009-1014.

Central Bureau of Statistics (1990-1998). *Statistical Abstracts of Israel.* Jerusalem: Central Bureau of Statistics.

Central Bureau of Statistics (1995). *Statistical Abstracts of Israel.* Jerusalem: Central Bureau of Statistics.

Gunnell DJ, Brooks J & Peters TJ (1996). Epidemiology and patterns of hospital use after attempted suicide in the south west of England. *Journal of Epidemiology and Community Health*, 50: 24-29.

Hawton K, Fagg J, Simkin S, Bale E & Bond A (1997). Trends in deliberate self-harm in Oxford, 1985-1995. *British Journal of Psychiatry*, 171: 556-560.

Hintikka J, Viinamäki H, Tanskanen A, Kontula O & Koskela K (1998). Suicidal ideation and attempted suicide in the Finnish general population. *Acta Psychiatrica Scandinavica,* 98: 23-27.

Hjelmeland H & Bjerke T (1996). Attempted suicide in the country of S-Trdelag, Norway. General epidemiology and psychological factors. *Social Psychiatry and Psychiatric Epidemiology*, 31: 272-283.

Levav I & Aisenberg E (1989). The epidemiology of suicide in Israel: international and intranational comparisons. *Suicide and Life Threatening Behavior* 19: 184-200.

Platt S, Bille-Brahe U, Kerkhof A et al. (1992). Attempted suicide in Europe: the WHO/EURO Multicentre Study on Parasuicide. 1. Introduction and preliminary analysis for 1989. *Acta Psychiatrica Scandinavica*, 85: 97-104.

Ponizovsky A, Safro S, Ginath Y & Ritzner M (1997). Suicide ideation among recent immigrants: An epidemiological study. *Israel Journal of Psychiatry and related Sciences*, 34: 139-148.

Roy A. (1995). Suicide. In HI Kaplan & BD Sadock (Eds.). *Comprehensive textbook of psychiatry,* 6th edition (pp. 1739-1752). Baltimore: Williams and Wilkins.

Schmidtke A, Bille-Brahe U, DeLeo D, Kerkhof A, Bjerke T, Crepet P, Haring C, Hawton K, Lönnqvist J, Michel K, Pommereau X, Querejeta I, Philippe I, Salander Renberg E, Temesváry B, Wasserman D, Fricke S, Weinacker B & Sampaio-Faria JG (1996). Attempted suicide in Europe: Rates, trends and sociodemographic characteristics of suicide attempters during the period 1989-1992. Results of the WHO/EURO Multicentre Study on Attempted suicide. *Acta Psychiatrica Scandinavica*, 93: 327-338.

Stein D, Apter A, Retzoni G, Har-Even D & Avidan G (1998). The association between recurrent suicidal behavior and negative affective conditions among adolescents. *Journal of the American Academy of Child and Adolescent Psychiatry* 37: 488-494.

World Health Organization (1992). *ICD-10 Classification of mental disorders.* Geneva: World Health Organization.

Invited Papers

Chapter 30

Suicidal Behaviour in Asturias (Spain)

*J. Bobes, P. A. Sáiz, M. P. G-Portilla, M. T. Bascarán, S. Martínez,
B. Paredes & M. Bousoño*

Epidemiology of suicide in Spain

Numerous methodological stumbling blocks, derived in most cases from information sources limit the measuring of the true extent of the problem of suicide and suicide attempts. Many authors therefore point out that in most countries, including Spain, the true incidence is underestimated (Soto Loza and Ruiz Otazo, 1995), and consequently, official figures usually represent only the tip of the iceberg. Hence, a tremendous number of suicides are hidden, and it is often difficult to establish if a particular death is the consequence of an act of suicide or accidental, particularly because families, for varying reasons, are often interested in hiding the voluntary death of one of its members.

Fortunately, however, there are more and more epidemiological studies both in Spain and world-wide that allow us to obtain a better indication of the true reality of this phenomenon.

The World Health Organisation (WHO) (1991) classifies community suicide rates as low, average, high, and very high, based on the number of suicides that have occurred per 100,000 inhabitants per year. Figures of less than 5 per 100,000 inhabitants per year are considered low, between 5 and 15 average, between 15 and 30 high, and more than 30 very high.

In Spain, statistics on suicide have been kept continuously since the beginning of the century, thus complying with the Royal Decree dated 8 September 1906. The National Institute of Statistics (INE) currently publishes suicide data on an annual basis. These data are provided by the Courts of Instruction and sent to the Provincial Delegations.

According to the data published by the INE (1998), the mean suicide rate in Spain between 1987 and 1996 was 6.18 per 100,000 inhabitants (6.91 in 1996), with remarkable differences between provinces (figure 1).

Lugo is the province having the highest rate (16.9 per 100,000) and Valencia the lowest (3.1 per 100,000). Of the 50 provinces described, only Lugo has a rate considered to be 'high' according to the WHO classification, 10 provinces (Badajoz, Barcelona, Granada, Guipúzcoa, Huelva, Madrid, La Rioja, Santa Cruz de Tenerife, Valencia y Valladolid) have low rates and the rest have average suicide rates.

A comparison by age groups manifests the same trend observed in most Western countries; that is, as age increases, so do suicide rates, such that the highest rates are observed in both males and females in the over 65 years of age groups (Figure 2).

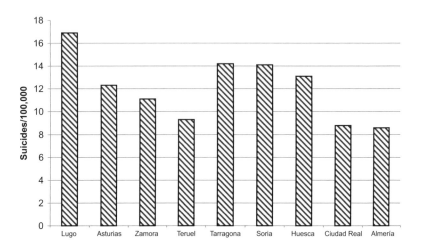

Figure 1. Suicide rates in Spain, 1992-1996

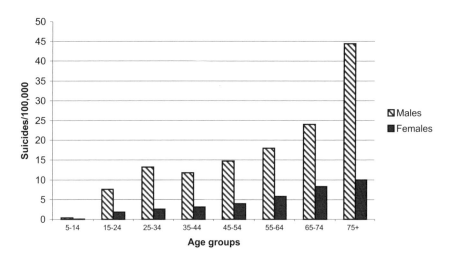

Figure 2. Suicide rates by age and sex, Spain 1994

With regard to sex, it is worthwhile to note that in all age groups, the highest rates of suicide are given for males, with male:female ratios that fluctuated in 1994, from 2.9:1 (for the 65-74 years of age group) to 5.1:1 (for the 25-34 years of age group), with a mean ratio of 3.9:1 (WHO, 1999).

However, the figures for actual suicides are undoubtedly higher as we can deduce from different epidemiological research studies offering mean rates ranging from 10-15 completed suicides per 100,000 inhabitants. Much higher rates are seen in the elderly population, since the over 60 years of age population in Spain account for around 40 to 50% of all suicides (Bobes et al, 1997a).

Evolution of trends in suicidal behaviour

It is difficult to assess the evolution of trends in suicidal behaviour over long periods of time for methodological reasons; nevertheless, we will attempt to present the changes that have taken place in Spain over the last several years, and will perhaps aid in understanding how this phenomenon has evolved.

At a European level there are several countries, Spain among them, that have gathered statistical data over long periods of time (at least 100 years), thus providing a more global view of the evolution of suicide.

In Spain, a gradual rise in the number of suicides (an increase of 51.1% in males and 42.3% in females; mean increase of 50.0%) can be observed during the second half of the twentieth century.

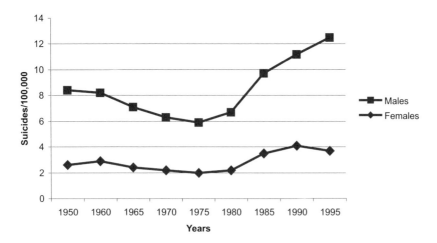

Figure 3. Suicide rates by sex in Spain, 1950 – 1995

This increase is particularly noticeable during the last decade and has affected both sexes in a similar way. The male:female ratio of suicides has remained stable throughout this period, at about 2.9:1 (WHO, 1999).

As far as provinces are considered, this clear rising trend in suicidal behaviours can also be seen as opposed to a decrease observed in the average rates from 1976-1980 through 1990-1994 (INE, 1995) in only four provinces (Granada, Málaga, Santa Cruz de Tenerife and Valencia).

Suicide in Asturias

Asturias is a region located in the north of Spain, consisting of a single province with a population of approximately 1,100,000 inhabitants. The mean suicide rates in Asturias have varied throughout this century with regard to the Spanish mean rates. This variation currently establishes Asturias as a frontrunner in the "suicide race" in the country (Bobes et al, 1997b).

Various studies have been conducted in the region in recent years to determine the "reality" of suicide in the community. Specifically, the three most important municipalities have been studied in depth:

- Gijon, was studied from 1975-1986. This municipality has the largest population (approximately 325,000 inhabitants) and during the study period it was considered half urban, half rural (Díaz et al, 1991, 1992, 1993, 1994, 1995).
- Oviedo, studied from 1981-1991, is the second largest municipality population – wise (275,000 inhabitants), and is fundamentally urban (Díaz et al, 1994; López et al, 1995).
- Grado, studied from 1980-1994, is the smallest of the three municipalities based on population (125,000 inhabitants) and is mainly rural (unpublished data).

The highest overall annual rate of suicide was obtained for the municipality of Grado (22 per 100,000), followed by Oviedo (13.5 per 100,000), and Gijon (11.1 per 100,000). The analysis of annual suicide rates clearly reveals that Grado has the highest rates.

The suicide rates for males were high in all the three municipalities studied. In Gijon, the percentage of suicides committed by males was 72% (17.8 males versus 6.8 females). In Oviedo, 63% of all suicides were committed by men (17.9 males versus 9.5 females), whereas in Grado, 70% of all suicides were committed by males. It is important to note that in Grado, no mean rates according to sex were available, but it can be assumed that the rate of suicide among males is higher, based on the male:female ratio in the municipality. The annual suicide rates based on sex in both Gijon and Oviedo show that the rates of suicide are also remarkably higher for men.

When mean suicide rates are compared based on age, we can see that risk increases with age, and, as with mortality in general, adolescents and young adults have the lowest risk. An identical comparison based on age and sex shows parallel results, such that the suicide rate for all age groups is higher for males and the increase detected in the number of suicides after the age of 60 is more remarkable, compared to females.

With regard to marital status, the percentage of suicide was higher amongst married people in all three municipalities (52% in Gijon, 43% in Oviedo, and 52% in Grado). Nevertheless, this puzzling situation is clarified when the corresponding rates are calculated, since the highest rates are observed amongst people who had been widowed, separated, and divorced.

Amongst males, suicide mortality was the highest amongst widowers and those separated and/ or divorced. High suicide rates were obtained among widowed, separated or divorced males in Gijon (78 per 100,000), among widows in Oviedo (155.1 per 100,000), and amongst separated and divorced males in Oviedo (276.6 per 100,000). Likewise, widowed, separated or divorced females committed suicide more often, with hogh rates reported in Gijon (11.4 per 100,000) amongst widows in Oviedo (31.6 per 100,000), and amongst separated and divorced women in Oviedo (13.7 per 100,000).

Married males and females were the least affected by suicide. However, regardless of marital status, suicide rates for males always surpassed those for females.

In the three municipalities studied, the highest percentages of suicides were given for people living with their families (81% in Gijon, 65% in Oviedo, and 77% in Grado).

With regard to place of residence (urban vs. rural), Oviedo and Gijon presented similar results, with a predominance of suicides in urban areas (71% and 72%, respectively). However it must be remembered that due to the fact that Grado is mostly rural, 100% of all suicides are therefore going to take place in a rural setting.

In Gijon and Oviedo, a higher percentage of rates were observed amongst people who had been displaced from their place of birth (60% in Gijon and 59% in Oviedo), with the opposite being the case in Grado (only 30% of displaced people).

The analysis based on occupation points out that in all three municipalities, the highest percentage of suicides occured amongst retired people (26% in Gijón, 41% in Oviedo and 45% in Grado). In the case of Gijon and Oviedo, the group having the second highest suicide rate was made up of housewives (25% and 27%, respectively), whereas in Grado, self-employed workers were the second most likely (40%), and housewives the third most likely (8%) to suicide.

Bearing in mind the urban/rural predominance in each municipality, the leading economic sectors with the greatest number of suicides in Gijon were obtained for the primary sector including agriculture, farming and fishing (35%) and the tertiary sector comprised of services (35%). In Oviedo, the service sector reported the highest proportion of suicide (48%), whereas as expected in Grado, suicide predominated in the agricultural and farming industries (71%).

Spring was the preferred season of the year for suicides in Gijon and Grado (27% and 34%, respectively), whereas in Oviedo, the highest percentages were given in winter (28%). Both in Gijon and Oviedo, there were minimal differences with regard to the season chosen, but in Grado, 65% of all suicides were completed in spring and autumn.

With regard to the method of suicide, despite the wide variety of methods used, some methods were clearly used more frequently. In Gijon and Oviedo, the most common methods were jumping and hanging, with similar percentages in both regions (29% vs. 38% in Gijon and 33% vs. 26% in Oviedo). Whereas in Grado, the most predominant method by far was hanging (75%).

In Gijon and Oviedo, the majority of suicides took place in the home (53% in Gijon and 49% in Oviedo), whereas in Grado, the areas around the home were favoured (40%).

In the three municipalities, there was a clear lack of communication before the suicide was actually committed (72%, 69%, and 54%, respectively), either because such intentions went undetected or because the court files make no mention of it. Moreover, the percentage of suicide notes left behind was less than 15% in the three municipalities.

The percentage of people who made previous suicide attempts was found to be low, with figures of about 20% in the three municipalities.

In each of the three municipalities, more than 30% of subjects who died by suicide had no psychiatric history (41% in Gijon, 33% in Oviedo, and 32% in Grado). In Oviedo and Grado, the leading psychiatric diagnoses were depressive disorders (44% and 35%, respectively), whereas in Gijon, there was a predominance of a loose group of disorders that were not clearly specified, grouped under the heading "off his/her rocket" (44%).

Despite there being a significant percentage of patients who manifested mental disorders, the number of people under treatment was low, around 45% in Oviedo and Grado. In Gijon, only the percentage of subjects that had begun treatment in the prior year was noted, namely 15%, which is why such a percentage is significantly lower.

The percentage of subjects with a prior psychiatric hospitalisation was low in all three municipalities (about 15%). The most probable cause for the suicide was likely to have been the existing psychiatric disorder (57% in Gijon, 41% in Oviedo, and 56% in Grado).

Finally, the percentage of people with a family history of suicide was practically non-existent in Gijon (2%) and Oviedo (1.5%), and slightly higher in Grado (10%).

In Oviedo and Grado, most suicides were committed by people without any kind of somatic or medical illness (69% and 71% respectively), whereas in Gijon, the opposite was observed (41%). In general, respiratory and cardiovascular illnesses and neoplasms were the organic pathologies most frequently found.

Conclusions

1. Suicide rates in Spain are amongst the lowest for Western Europe.
2. In Spain, suicide rates have undergone an increase in recent decades.
3. Asturias has traditionally had and still maintains its position amongst the regions having the highest suicide rates in Spain.
4. In Spain, and in our region, sociodemographic factors associated with completed suicide are similar to those found in the rest of the Western world.
5. In our region, differences are noted between suicides that are committed in rural areas vs. those committed in the urban setting in terms of migration, occupation, method of suicide and place of suicide.
6. In order to lower the risk of suicide on both a national and regional scale, specific preventive programmes must be developed and assessed both internally and externally.

Acknowledgements

We wish to thank Priscilla Chase for helping us in the English translation of the manuscript.

References

Bobes J, Sáiz PA, González MP, Bousoño M (1997a). Suicidio en el anciano. En: J Vallejo (Ed.). *Psicogeriatría*. Biblioteca de Psiquiatría en Atención Primaria. Madrid: Grupo Aula Médica, 75-86.

Bobes J, González-Seijo JC, Sáiz PA (1997b). Prevención de las conductas suicidas y parasuicidas. Barcelona: Masson.

Díaz J, Rendueles G, González MP et al. (1991). El suicidio en el partido judicial de Gijón, 1975-1986 (I). *An Psiquiatría*; 7 (7): 271-278.

Díaz J, Rendueles G, González MP et al. (1992). Suicidios con historia de hospitalización psiquiátrica. *An Psiquiatría,* 8 (4): 128-134.

Díaz J, Rendueles G, González MP et al. (1993). El suicidio en el partido judicial de Gijón desde 1975 a 1986: aspectos clínico-sanitarios. *An Psiquiatría*; 9 (3): 122-127.

Díaz J, López B, Bobes J, Hinojal R. Conducta suicida. En: J Bobes (ed.). (1994). *Calidad de vida y Oviedo.* Oviedo: Pentalfa Ediciones, 165-193.

Díaz J, López B, González MP et al. (1995). Trends in suicide in the elderly in Asturias (Spain). *European Psychiatry*; 10: 339-344.

Instituto Nacional de Estadística (1995). *Estadística del suicidio año 1994.* Madrid: INE.

Instituto Nacional de Estadística (1998). *Estadística del suicidio año 1996.* Madrid: INE.

López B, Hinojal R, Díaz J et al. (1995). Características de los suicidios consumados en el partido judicial de Oviedo. *Orfila,* 7: 351-365.

Soto Loza A, Ruiz Otazo A (1995). Epidemiología del suicidio en España. *Monografías de Psiquiatría* VII (19): 14-20.

World Health Organization (1991). *World health statistics annual.* Geneva: WHO.

World Health Organization (1999). *Figures and facts about suicide.* Geneva: WHO.

Chapter 31

Suicidal Behaviour in Poland

M. Zaluski, B. Weinacker & A. Schmidtke

Description of the catchment area

Up to now there has been no official catchment area in Poland. The Crisis Intervention Centre in Cracow is in negotiations with the Network and is interested in participating as the Polish centre in the WHO/EURO Network on Suicide Prevention. The centre has already delivered some information about its work. The centre was founded in 1991, and is situated in the city centre of Cracow. The total staff of 20 persons included a psychiatrist and a lawyer as consultants, clinical psychologists, social workers, sociologists, and psychiatric nurses.

Sample and method of data collection

Official suicide mortality figures were obtained from the Crisis Intervention Centre and from the WHO in Geneva.

There was no specific information on attempted suicides available.

Results

Suicide

In Poland, about 5,000 people commit suicide each year. In 1999 the suicide rate for males was 26.1 per 100,000 and for females 4.3 per 100,000. The ratio males:females was 6:1. This ratio is higher than the European average (4:1). The age distribution of the raw figures shows the highest percentages for the age groups between 35 and 49 years.

For the period 1951-1998 the total suicide rates increased by 160% from 5 to 13 per 100,000. In the later years of the study the increase has stabilized. According to WHO figures, the increase between 1983-1999 was more pronounced for males (18%) than for females (3 %). In the year 1989, a decrease could be found for both males and females (see figure 1).

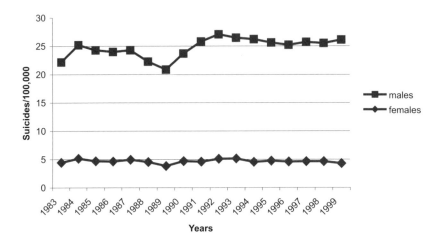

Figure 1. Suicide rates by gender, Poland, 1983-1999

In Poland the statistics distinguish between urban areas (towns) and rural areas (villages). The increase was greater for suicides committed by inhabitants of rural areas than for inhabitants of urban areas.

Analysing the demographic structure, the data shows that the suicide rates increased especially among children and adolescents. The highest suicide rates could be found for children of workers, and the lowest for children of farmers.

Suicide attempts

In Poland, as in other countries, there is only limited data from hospital treatments available, which do not give a "real" estimation of the size of the problem. The crisis intervention centre in Cracow estimated an average of 10,000 cases of interventions per year, however, these are not all due to suicidal crises.

Suicide Prevention Activities

The Cracow Crisis Intervention centre is a joint initiative of Regional Social Welfare and the Jagiellonian University. The centre was founded in 1991 as the first institution of this kind in Poland. The centre is situated in Central Cracow, located close to the main station and is open 24 hours daily. The services are free, and no previous appointments are necessary. In 1995, the centre received an award from the Minister of Labour and Social Policy for the introduction of crisis intervention as a new form of social help in Poland.

The centre offers short-term crisis intervention therapies for individuals and families, crisis interventions at disaster scenes and for schools, as well as police intervention sites. People seeking help include suicidal persons, persons with marital problems or difficulties in contact with children, psychically and physically abused persons, people experiencing a sudden, unfavourable change in life, and people in other stressed situations. Refugees are also treated.

Primary mental health prevention strategies have also been undertaken in accordance with training programmes for students, social workers, sociologists, family physicians, and psychologists. A large-scale program to prevent the abuse of women and children was also launched.

The centre is also establishing a close inter-organisational integration within Poland.

Part III

Future Perspectives

Chapter 32

The WHO/EURO Network on Suicide Prevention

A. Schmidtke, D. Wasserman, U. Bille-Brahe & W. Rutz

Europe's diversity is immense and shows for example up to a 50-fold difference in suicidality for different countries and certain populations at risk. It also shows a 300-fold difference per capita in income and enormous differences in the provision and quality of mental health services – from huge custodial over-hospitalization in some parts of the region to problems with never-hospitalisation and homelessness among the mentally ill in other parts of Europe. This diversity leads to a crucial need of national assessments and mental health audits and individual national planning on developing mental health services, their implementation and their continuous monitoring.

Integrated into this framework, offered to the member states and already started by WHO European task forces, the development and implementation of suicide prevention activities is decisive, together with national action plans against drugs and alcohol – a problem well known to be co-related with issues of suicide and suicide prevention.

However, strategies in suicide prevention in Europe should be integrated into the over-all national planning on mental health. They should also not only initiate and implement suicide preventive programs in various countries but also implement strategies to continuously monitor suicide and attempted suicide in order to assess suicide trends and to determine groups at risk. Suicide prevention programmes also require evaluation, both on national as well as on European levels and in different regions of every European country – again, integrated into the framework of continuously monitoring the overall mental health development in a country.

In recognition of these facts, the WHO Multicentre Study on Suicidal Behaviour has restructured itself into the WHO European Network on Suicide Prevention and Research since the beginning of 2001. The Regional Adviser for Mental Health at the Regional WHO Office in Copenhagen, Dr. Wolfgang Rutz, established this European Network on Suicide Prevention and Research on the occasion of the annual meeting of the researchers of the WHO Multicentre Study on Suicidal Behaviour in Wuerzburg, Germany, in 2000.

The organization of the Network is as follows: The Network was originally chaired by the Regional Advisor Dr. Rutz, WHO, the secretary is Prof. Dr. Schmidtke Wuerzburg. The operative tasks consist of two parts. The first, chaired by Prof. A. Schmidtke, Wuerzburg, Germany, concerns the monitoring of suicide and suicide attempts in different regions of European countries, in order to continue the monitoring of data relevant to suicide. Part two, chaired by Prof. D. Wasserman, Stockholm, Sweden, is the preventive part with the task of developing, testing, implementing and disseminating comprehensive suicide preventive strategies, and developing national suicide prevention programs throughout Europe. These plans should be integrated in national master plans on mental health development. The tasks, therefore, comprise the initiation of national suicide preventive programs in those European countries currently lacking such programs as well as the stimulating of coordination and implementation activities for already existing programs, assisting in the development of new strategies, and developing new tools for evaluating suicide preventive efforts.

A Steering Group, consisting of the chairpersons and five members, is an advisory group to the centres participating in the Network, stimulating and evaluating activities. A publication group is responsible for the publications rules and is stimulating the production of scientific articles.

The network comprises up to now 36 suicide research centres or crisis centres from 27 European member countries, most of them also functioning as national focal points for suicide prevention, to be approved by their Ministries of Health as well as by the WHO (see listing at the end of this chapter). The Network will hopefully expand to all countries of Europe in coming years.

The activities of the Network will hopefully contribute to demonstrating the magnitude and burden of suicidal behaviour in Europe and respond to the need for better services. Within the frame of the Network, several educational programs and information systems are planned to be developed. New research projects will hopefully be generated, especially concerning the testing of different etiological hypotheses for suicidal behaviour as well as projects concerning the evaluation of intervention programs.

The Network has recently started a survey of existing national preventive strategies (see chapter 1). It is already today a forum for exchange of experiences and mutual peer support amongst its members, thus facilitating necessary national adaptations to cope with the huge and in some parts of Europe still increasing problem of suicide in a nationally adapted and individualized way. The decrease of suicides in some European countries with national coordinated suicide preventive programs is here a sign of hope. The new consensus to focus on comprehensive programmes including cultural, sociological, psychological, existential as well as biological and psychopathological factors in the background of suicidality gives hereby new tools and possibilities for powerful synergetically coordinated, comprehensive suicide prevention programmes in the WHO's member states of Europe.

The WHO/EURO Network on Suicide Prevention

Country	National Focal Points

Austria

Hall/Innsbruck

Prim. Univ. Doz. Dr. C. Haring
Psychiatric State Hospital of Tyrol
Thurnfeldgasse 14
A-6060 Hall
Austria

Tel.:   +43 5223 508-2030
Fax: +43 5223 508-2035
E-mail: *Christian.Haring@tilak.or.at*

Prim. Univ. Doz. Dr. C. Haring

Salzburg

M. D. Dr. R. Fartacek
Suicide Prevention Salzburg
Ignaz-Harrer Str.79
A-Salzburg 5020
Austria

Tel.:   +43 664 3371-290
Fax: +43 662 4483-4344
E-mail: *R.Fartacek@lks.at*

Belgium

Gent

Prof. C. van Heeringen
Unit for Suicide Research
Dept of Psychiatry
University Hospital
De Pintelaan 185
B-9000 Gent
Belgium

Tel.:   +32 9 240-4375
Fax: +32 9 240-4989
Mobile: +32 477 39-0181
E-mail: *cornelis.vanheeringen@ugent.be*

Prof. C. van Heeringen

Country	National Focal Points

Denmark

Odense

Dr. L. Zöllner
Centre for Suicide Research
Sondergade 17
DK-5000 Odense C

Tel.:   +45 6613 8811
Fax: +45 6590 8174
E-mail: *lilian.zollner@dou.dk*

Dr. L. Zöllner

lz@selvmordsforskning.dk

Estonia

Tallinn

Prof. Dr. A. Värnik
Estonian-Swedish Suicidological Institute
Vabduse pst. 90
11619 Tallinn
Estonia

Tel.:   +372 56 215580
         +372 65 06188
Fax: +372 67 70489
         +372 67 93154
E-mail: *airiv@online.ee*

Prof. Dr. A. Värnik

Finland

Helsinki

Prof. Dr. J. Lönnqvist
Department of Mental Health and Alcohol Research
National Public Health Institute
Mannerheimintie 166
FIN-00300 Helsinki
Finland

Tel.:   +358 9 47448212
Fax: +358 9 47448478
E-mail: *jouko.lonnqvist@ktl.fi*

Prof. Dr. J. Lönnqvist

Country	National Focal Points

France

Rennes

Dr. A. Batt
Faculté de Médecine / INSERM
Dépt. de Santé Publique
2 av du Pr. Léon Bernard
F-35043 Rennes Cedex
France

Tel.:   +33 223 234553
Fax: +33 223 234533
E-mail: *agnes.batt@univ-rennes1.fr*

Francis Eudier
Rue Henri Le Guilloux
35033 Rennes Cedex
France

Tel.:   +33 2 9928-4304
E-mail: *francis.eudier@chr-rennes.fr*

Prof. Dr. J. P. Soubrier
Union Nationale Pour La
Prevention Du Suicide
25 Rue de la Faisanderie
F-75116 Paris
France

Tel.:   +33 1 4704-6969
Fax: +33 1 4704-9933
E-mail: *pr-jp-soubrier@mail.com*

Germany

Wuerzburg

Prof. Dr. A. Schmidtke
Dept. for Clinical Psychology
Clinic for Psychiatry & Psychotherapy
University of Wuerzburg
Füchsleinstr.15
D-97080 Wuerzburg
Germany

Tel.:   +49 931 201-76670 /-76680
Fax: +49 931 201-76690
E-mail: *clips-psychiatry@mail.uni-wuerzburg.de*

Prof. Dr. A. Schmidtke

Country	National Focal Points

Hamburg

G. Fiedler
Prof. Dr. P. Götze
Center for Therapy and Studies
of Suicidal Behaviour
University Hospital Hamburg-Eppendorf
Martinistrasse 52
D-20246 Hamburg
Germany

Tel.:   +49 40 42803-4112
Fax: +49 40 42803-4949
E-mail: *tzs@uke.uni-hamburg.de*

Munich

Prof. Dr. Ulrich Hegerl
Klinik und Poliklinik für Psychiatrie und Psychotherapie
Klinikum der Universität München
Nussbaumstr. 7
D-80336 München
Germany

Tel.:   +49 89 5160-5787
         +49 89 5160-5540
         +49 89 5160-5541
Fax: +49 89 5160-5542
E-mail: *uhegerl@psy.med.uni-muenchen.de*

Greece

Athens

Professor Dr. A. Botsis   Professor Dr. A. Botsis
University Mental Health Research Institute
P.O. Box 66517, Argurogastrou & Ionas
Papagou 15601, Athens
Greece

Tel.:   +30 210 6170-806   Tel.:   +30 694 4733-630
Fax: +30 210 6927-318   Fax: +30 210 6927-318
E-mail: *abotsis@compulink.gr*   E-mail: *epipsi@internet.gr*

Country	National Focal Points

Patras

Prof. S. Beratis
University of Patras Medical School
Department of Psychiatry
265 00 Rion - Patras
Greece

Tel.:   +302 610 992-996
Fax: +302 610 994-534
E-mai: *stbera@med.upatras.gr*

Hungary

Pecs

Dr. S. Fekete   Dr. S. Fekete
Dept.of Psychiatry
University of Pécs
H-7623 Pécs, Rét u. 2.
Hungary

Tel.:   +36 72 535-900
        +36 72 535-950
Fax: +36 72 535-951
        +36 72 535-954
E-mail: *sfekete@neuro.pote.hu*

Szeged

Dr. B. Temesváry
Szeged M.J.V.Ö.Kórház
Pszichiatriai és Addiktológiai Osztály
Kálvária sgt.57
H-6725 Szeged
Hungary

Tel.:   +36 62 490760
Fax: +36 62 490760 after a voice: +300 or +302
        +36 62 426386
E-mail: *psychiatria@szegedkorhaz.hu*

Country	National Focal Points

Ireland

Cork/Limerick

Dr. M. Kelleher
National Suicide Research Foundation
1 Perrott Avenue, College Road
IRL Cork
Ireland

Dr. M. Kelleher

Tel.:   +353 21 4277-499
Fax: +353 21 4277-545
E-mail: *nsrf@iol.ie*

margaret.nsrf@iol.ie

Israel

Holon-Bat-Yam

Prof. Dr. A. Apter
Chairman,
Dept. of Psychiatry
Schneiders Children's Medical Center
of Israel
14 Kaplan St
49202 Petach Tikva
Israel

Prof. Dr. A. Apter

Tel.:   +972 3 925-3232
Fax: +972 3 925-3899
E-mail: *eapter@clalit.org.il*

eapter@clalit.il

Galilee

Dr. I. Farbstein
Rivka Ziv Hospital
Safed
Israel

Tel.:   +972 4 682-8086
Fax: +972 4 682-70803
E-mail: *farby@netvision.net.il*

Country	National Focal Points

Italy

Padua

Prof. Dr. D. De Leo   Prof. Dr. D. De Leo
GRG-East
Fondazione Zancan
Via Vescovado, 66
35141 Padua
Italy

E-mail: *fz@fondazionezancan.it*

and

Australian Institute for Suicide Research
and Prevention
Mt Gravatt Campus
Griffith University
4111 Brisbane, Queensland
Australia

Tel.:   +61 7 3875-3366
Fax: +61 7 3875-3450
E-mail: *D.Deleo@griffith.edu.au*

Rome

Prof. S. de Risio
Università Cattolica del Sacro Cuore
Facoltà di Medicina e Chirurgia "Agostino Gemelli"
Instituto di Psychiatriae e Psicologia
L. go A. Gemelli, 8
00168 Roma
Italy

Tel.:   +39 06 301-54122
Fax: +39 06 301-6400

Dr. M. Sarchiapone
Institute of Psychiatry - Catholic University
Largo F. Vito
I-00168 Rome
Italy

Tel.:   +39 06 301-6704
E-mail: *m.sarchiapone@libero.it*

Country	National Focal Points

Latvia

Riga

Dr. J. Bugins
Mental Health Care Centre of Latvia
Tvaika str. 2
Riga LV 1005
Latvia

Tel.:   +371 708-0112
Fax: +371 722-2305

Dr. E. Rancans
Department of Psychiatry
Riga Stradins University
Tvaika str. 2
Riga LV 1005
Latvia

Tel.:   +371 9493-336
         +371 7080-131
         +371 7080-133
Fax: +371 7080-132
E-mail: *erancans@latnet.lv*

Lithuania

Vilnius

Prof. Dr. habil. D. Gailiené
University of Vilnius
Traidenio 27
2004 Vilnius
Lithuania

Tel.:   +370 5 2675-254
Fax: +370 5 2675-218
E-mail: *danugail@takas.lt*

Prof. Dr. habil. D. Gailiené

Prof. Dr. G. Zukauskas
Institute of Forensic Medicine, Law
University of Lithuania
Verkin 7/110
2042, Vilnius
Lithuania

Tel.:/Fax: +370 5 272-5049
Mobil: +370 6 861-0984
E-mail: *g_zukauskas@hotmail.com*   *g.zukauskas@delfi.lt*

Prof. A. Dembinskas / Dr. A. Navickas
Vilnius University Psychiatric Clinic
Vasaros - 5
2055 Vilnius
Lithuania

Tel.:   +370 5 261-1043
Fax: +370 5 261-1043
E-mail: *algirdas.dembinskas@mf.vu.lt*   *alvydas.navickas@mf.vu.lt*

Country	National Focal Points

The Netherlands

Amsterdam, Leiden

Prof. Dr. A. Kerkhof, Dr. E. Arensmann
Department of Clinical Psychology
Vrije Universiteit Amsterdam
Van Der Boechorststraat 1
NL-1081 BT Amsterdam
The Netherlands

Tel.:   +31 20 4448-777
Fax: +31 20 4448-758
E-mail: *AJFM.Kerkhof@psy.vu.nl*

Norway

Sør-Trøndelag

Dr. H. Hjelmeland
Regional Resource Centre for Suicide Research
And Prevention in Central Norway
Department of Psychology
Norwegian University of Science and Technology
NO-7491 Trondheim
Norway

Tel.:   +47 73 591-883
Fax: +47 73 591-920
E-mail: *Heidi.Hjelmeland@svt.ntnu.no*

Prof. Dr. L. Mehlum
Suicide Research Unit
University of Oslo & Armed Forces
Medical Service
Box 39, Gavstad
NO-0320 Oslo
Norway

Tel.: +47 22 142490
Fax: +47 22 923665
E-mail: lmehlun@psykiatri.vio.no

Poland

Dr W. Badura-Madej
Crisis Intervention Centre
ul. Radziwillowska 8b
PL-32026 Cracow
Poland

Tel.:   +48 12 4218-248
Fax: +48 12 4216-976
E-mail: *mxbadura@cyf-kr.edu.pl*

Dr M. Zaluski
Crisis Intervention Centre

Country	National Focal Points

Romania

Dr. N. Tataru   Dr. N. Tataru
Private Psychiatry Practice
Neuropsychiatry Hospital
36, Cuza Voda Sta.
3700 Oradea
Romania

Tel.:   +40 745 598866
         +40 259 237885
Fax: +40 259 436577
E-mail: *nicoleta_tataru@hotmail.com*   *nicol@medanet.ro*

Russia

Dr. D. Veltischev   Dr. D. Veltischev
Head Researcher
Moscow Research Institute of Psychiatry
Poteshnaya 3
107076 Moscow
Russian Federation

Fax: +7 095 963-7626
E-mail: *d.veltischev@mtu-net.ru*

Serbia & Montenegro

Novi-Sad

Dr. S. Selakovic-Bursic   Dr. S. Selakovic-Bursic
Institute of Neurology, Psychiatry and Mental Health
Hajduk Veljkova 7
21000 Novi Sad
Serbia & Montenegro

Tel.:   +381 21 423-762
Fax: +381 21 26-520
E-mail: *ssbursic@eunet.yu*

Country	National Focal Points

Slovenia

Ljubljana

Prof. Dr. O. T. Grad   Prof. Dr. O. T. Grad
University Psychiatric Hospital
Centre for Mental Health
Zaloska 29
1000 Ljubljana
Slovenia

Tel.:   +386 1 587-4910
Fax: +386 1 540-2158
         +386 1 540-2278
E-mail: *onja.grad@guest.arnes.si*

Spain

Oviedo

Prof. Dr. J. Bobes   Prof. Dr. J. Bobes
Department of Medicine - Psychiatry
University of Oviedo
Julián Claveria 6
E-33006 Oviedo
Spain

Tel.:   +34 98 510-3553
Fax: +34 98 510-3553
E-mail: *bobes@correo.uniovi.es*   *bobes@ctv.es*

Dr. P. A. Saiz, MD, PhD
Department of Medicine - Psychiatry
University of Oviedo
Julián Claveria 6
E-33006 Oviedo
Spain

Tel.:   +34 98 510-3552
Fax: +34 98 510-3552
E-mail: *frank@correo.uniovi.es*

Country	National Focal Points

Sweden

Stockholm

Prof. Dr. D. Wasserman
The Swedish National and Stockholm County Centre
for Suicide Research and Prevention of Mental Ill-Health
(NASP)
The National Swedish Institute for Psychosocial Medicine
Karolinska Institute
Granits Väg 4
P.O. Box 230
SE - Stockholm 171 77
Sweden

Tel.:   +46 8 728-7026
Fax: +46 8 306-439
E-mail: *Danuta.Wasserman@ipm.ki.se*

Prof. Dr. D. Wasserman

Umea

Dr. E. Salander Renberg
Division of Psychiatry, Department of Clinical Sciences
Umea University
SE-90185 Umea
Sweden

Tel.:   +46 90 7856-323
Fax: +46 90-135324
E-mail: *ellinor.salander.renberg@psychiat.umu.se*

Switzerland

Berne

Prof. Dr. K. Michel
University Psychiatric Services (UPD) Bern
Murtenstrasse 21
CH - 3010 Bern
Switzerland

Tel.:   +41 31 632-4611
Fax: +41 31 632-4604
E-mail: *konrad.michel@spk.unibe.ch*

Prof. Dr. K. Michel

Country	National Focal Points

Basel

Dr. Martin Eichhorn
Oberarzt
Psychiatrische Universitätsklinik Basel
Wilhelm Klein-Str. 27
CH - 4025 Basel
Switzerland

Tel.:   +41 61 325-5182
Fax: +41 61 325-5586
E-mail: *martin.eichhorn@pukbasel.ch*

Turkey

Ankara

Prof Dr. I. Sayil   Prof Dr. I. Sayil
Ankara University Crisis Intervention Center
Ankara Universitesi Tip Fakultesi Cebeci Hastanesi
Dikimevi
Ankara 06100
Turkey

Tel.:   +90 312 362-1292
Fax: +90 312 362-1292
E-mail: *isiksayil@yahoo.com*

Ukraine

Odessa

Prof. Dr. A. N. Mokhovikov   Prof. Dr. A. N. Mokhovikov
Dept. of Clinical Psychology
Odessa National University
POB 270
65026 Odessa
Ukraine

Tel.:   +380 482 326-704
Fax: +380 482 226-565
E-mail: *alexm@te.net.ua*

Country	National Focal Points

Prof. Dr. V. Rozanov
Chair of Clinical Psychology
Odessa National University
Institute of Post-Diploma Education
(Human Ecological Health)
St. Bazarnaya 48, Suite 1
65011 Odessa
Ukraine

Tel./Fax: +380 482 226-565
E-mail: *rozanov@te.net.ua*

United Kingdom

Manchester

Dr. Jayne Cooper
Centre for Suicide Prevention
7th Floor, Williamson Building
Oxford Road
Manchester M13 9PL
United Kingdom

Tel.:   +44 161 275-0718
E-mail: *jayne cooper@man.ac.uk*

Prof. Dr. L. Appleby
Carol Rayegan (Secretary)
Centre for Suicide Prevention and
Centre for Women's Mental Health
Research
Williamson Building
The University of Manchester
Oxford Road
Manchester M13 9PL
United Kingdom

Tel.:   +44 161 275-0714
Fax: +44 161 275-0716
E-mail: *Louis.Appleby@man.ac.uk*
        Carol.Rayegan@man.ac.uk

Oxford

Prof. Dr. K. Hawton
University of Oxford
Centre for Suicide Research
Department of Psychiatry
Warneford Hospital
Headington
Oxford OX3 7 JX
United Kingdom

Tel.:   +44 1865 226-258
Fax: +44 1865 223-933
E-mail: *keith.hawton@psychiatry.oxford.ac.uk*

WHO Europe

Dr. M. Muijen
Regional Adviser
World Health Organization (WHO)
Regional Office for Europe
8 Scherfigsvej
DK-2100 Copenhagen

Tel.:   +45 39 171418
         +45 39 171572
Fax: +45 39 171865
E-mail: *WRU@who.dk*

Chairpersons:

Prof. Dr. D. Wasserman
The Swedish National and Stockholm County Centre
for Suicide Research and Prevention of Mental Ill-Health
(NASP)
The National Swedish Institute for Psychosocial Medicine
Karolinska Institute
Granits Väg 4
P.O. Box 230
SE - Stockholm 171 77
Sweden

Tel.:   +46 8 728-7026
Fax: +46 8 306-439
E-mail: *Danuta.Wasserman@ipm.ki.se*

Prof. Dr. A. Schmidtke
Department of Clinical Psychology
Clinic for Psychiatry and Psychotherapy
University of Wuerzburg
Fuechsleinstrasse 15
D-97080 Wuerzburg

Tel.:   +49 931 201-76670
         +49 931 201-76680
Fax: +49 931 201-76690
E-mail: *clips-psychiatry@mail.uni-wuerzburg.de*

Members of the Steering Group

Apter, A.
Botsis, A.
Henderson, G.
Muijen, M.
Schmidtke, A.
Värnik, A.
Wasserman, D.

Appendices

Suicide Preventive Organisations in Europe
Latest available information

Supranational

International Association for Suicide Prevention (IASP)
Central Administration Office:
Ms Wanda Scott
Le Baradé
32330 Gondrin
France

Academy for Suicide Research (IASR)
Secretary: Prof. Dr. Thomas Bronisch
Max-Planck-Institut für Psychiatrie
Kraepelinstr. 2-10
80804 München
Tel: +49 89 30622-239
Fax: +49 89 30622-223
E-mail: *bronisch@mpipskl.mpg.de*

American Association of Suicidology (AAS)
Central Office: Executive Director
CEO Dr. Alan Berman,
Suite 408
4201 Connecticut Ave, N. W.
Washington, D.C., 20008
USA
Tel.: +1 202 237-2280
Fax: +1 202 237-2282

Befrienders International (BI)
26-27 Market Place
Kingston-upon Thames
UK
E-mail: *admin@befrienders.org*
Several Branches in different European Countries
(Armenia, Austria, Denmark, Estonia, France, Hungary, Italy, Lithuania, Norway, Poland, Portugal, Russia, Sweden, Switzerland, Ukraine, Form. R. of Yugoslavia, United Kingdom, Ireland)

IFOTES
Att: Mark Milton
La Main Tendue
C.P. 161
CH-1010 Lausanne
Switzerland
E-mail: *Milton@bluewin.ch*

World Federation of Mental Health
European Regional Council
Bd. Clovis 7
B-1000 Brussels

Country

Armenia

Trust Telephone Counseling Centre
Grigar Lusavorick
375015 Yerevan

Austria

Austrian Society of Suicide Prevention
Osterreichische Gesellschaft für Krisenintervention (ÖGS)
Kriseninterventionszentrum
Spitalgasse 11
A-1090 Wien
E-mail: *claudius.stein@akh-wien.ac.at*

Belgium

Flemish Suicide Prevention Programme
c/u FDGG
Martelaarslaan 204b
B-9000 Gent
Belgium

Centrum Ter Preventie Van Zelfmoord
Kasteleinsplein 46
1050 Brussel
Belgium

Croatia

Croatian Association for Suicide Prevention
Kispoticeva 12
41000 Zagreb

Denmark

Psykiatrifonden
Carl Nielsens Alle 9
DK-2100 Kobenhavn O

Kirkens Korshaer
Dreyervej 6
DK-2400
Kobenhavn NV

Livslinien
Postboks 1157
DK-Kobenhavn K

Sind-linjen
Landsforeningen Sind
Hostrups Have 50
DK-1954 Frederiksberg C

Finland

Finnish Association for Mental Health
SOS Service
Maisraatinportti 4 A
00530 Helsinki
www.mielenterveysseura.fi

France

Association Suicide – Ecoute
5, rue de Moulin Vert
5014 Paris

Union Nation Pour La Prevention du Suicide
46 Place de Valois
75001 Paris
E-mail: *unps@wanadoo.fr*

Germany

Deutsche Gesellschaft für Suizidprävention und Hilfe in Lebenskrisen (DGS)
Secretariat: Dipl. Soz. M. Witte
Neuhland Berlin
Nikolsburger Platz 6
D-10717 Berlin
E-mail: *gds.gf@suizidprophylaxe.de*

Greece

Hellenic Society for Research and Prevention of Suicide and Violence
106 Kifissias Avenue
Athens 11526
Greece

Hungary

Hungarian Association for Suicide Prevention
att. Dr. Beáta Temesváry
Kálvaria sgt. 5A
6725 Szeged

Ireland

Irish Association of Suicidology
Silver Mind Hospital
St Mary's Hospital
Castlebar
E-mail: *drjfc@iol.ie*

Israel

Inter-departmental government committee
C/o Dr. Dalia Gilboa
Department of Psychiatry
Sheba Medical Center
Ramat Gan
Israel

Italy

Italian Association for Suicide Prevention (A.I.S.P.S.)
C/o University of Padova
Istituto di Clinicia Psichiatrica, III Servizio,
Via Giustiniani, 2
35128 Padua
E-mail: *aisps@intercity.it*

The Netherlands

Ivonne van de Ven Stichting
Paramaribostraat 85 hs
1058 VH Amsterdam
E-mail: *a.n.holstein@wanadoo.nl*

Norway

National Board of Health
PO Box 8128 DEP
NO-0032 Oslo
Norway

Kirkens SOS
Herslebsgate 43
N-0578 Oslo, Norway

Mental Helses Hjelpetelefon
0045-0010 Oslo

Portugal

Hospital de Santa Maria
Nucleo de Estudos do Suicidio
Servico de Psiquiatria
Av Egas Moniz 1649-035
1600 Lisboa

Romania

Anti Suicide Alliance
Cluj-Napoca
Str. A. Muresanu, nr. 11,jud
3400 Cluj
E-mail: *doina.octaviancosman@hotmail.com*

Insitutul de Medica Legala
Assoc Romana Pentru Prevenirea Suicdului
Bv. Independentei nr 1

Spain

Spanish Society of Suicidology
Sociedad Espanola de Suicidologia
Prof. Dr. Ramon Gracia
c/o University of La Laguna
Tenerife
Spain

Sweden

National Centre for Suicide Reserach
And Prevention of Mental Ill-Health
Karolinska Institute
Box 230
S-171 77 Stockholm
Sweden
www.ki.se/ipm

Switzerland

Schweizerischer Verband Die Dargebotene Hand
Zahringerstrasse 53
3012 Bern
E-mail: *verband@tel-143.ch*

United Kingdom

The Samaritans
Central Office
Kingston Road
Ewell, Surrey KT 17 2AF
Tel.: +44 20 8394-8300
Fax: +44 20 8394-8301
E-mail: *admin@samaritans.org.uk*

Contributors

Alberdi M.
Hospital de Guipuzcoa
Po Dr. Beguiristain 115
E-20014 San Sebastian
Spain

Alegría B.
Hospital de Guipuzcoa
Po Dr. Beguiristain 115
20014 San Sebastian
Spain

Andersen K.
Centre for Suicidological Research
Sondergade 17
DK-5000 Odense C
Denmark

Antretter E.
Psychiatric State Hospital of Tyrol
Thurnfeldgasse 14
6060 Hall
Austria

Apter A.
Department of Psychiatry
Schneiders Children's Medical Center
of Israel
14 Kaplan St
49202 Petach Tikva
Israel

Arensman E.
National Suicide Research Foundation
1 Perrott Avenue, College Road
Cork
Ireland

Asherov J.
Department of Psychiatry
Schneiders Children's Medical Center of
Israel
14 Kaplan St
49202 Petach Tikva
Israel

Bale E.
University of Oxford
Department of Psychiatry
Warneford Hospital
Headington
Oxford OX3 7JX
United Kingdom

Barrio S.
Hospital de Guipuzcoa
Po Dr. Beguiristain 115
E-20014 San Sebastian
Spain

Bascarán M. T.
Department of Medicine – Psychiatry
University of Oviedo
Julián Claveria 6
33006 Oviedo
Spain

Batt A.
Faculté de Médecine
Département de Santé Publique
2 av du Pr.Léon Bernard
F-35043 Rennes Cedex
France

Benito R.
Hospital de Guipuzcoa
Po Dr. Beguiristain 115
20014 San Sebastian
Spain

Bille-Brahe U.
Strandgade 46
DK-5683 Haarby
Denmark

Bobes J.
Department of Medicine – Psychiatry
University of Oviedo
Julián Claveria 6
33006 Oviedo
Spain

Bond A.
University of Oxford
Department of Psychiatry
Warneford Hospital
Headington
Oxford OX3 7JX
United Kingdom

Botsis A. J.
University Mental Health Research Institute
P.O. Box 66517 Argurogastrou & Ionas
Papagou 15601 Athens
Greece

Bousono M.
University of Oviedo
Julian Claveria 6
E-33006 Oviedo
Spain

Braeckman N.
Unit for Suicide Research
Department of Psychiatry
University Hospital
De Pintelaan 185
9000 Gent
Belgium

Burke U.
National Suicide Research Foundation
1 Perrott Avenue, College Road
Cork
Ireland

Byrne S.
National Suicide Research Foundation
1 Perrott Avenue, College Road
Cork
Ireland

Chambers D.
National Suicide Research Foundation
1 Perrott Avenue, College Road
IRL Cork
Ireland

Colucci E.
Australian Institute for Suicide Research
and Prevention
Mt. Gravatt Campus
Griffith University
4111 Brisbane, Queensland
Australia

Corcoran P.
National Suicide Research Foundation
1 Perrott Avenue, College Road
Cork
Ireland

Crepet P.
crepet.paolo@flashnet.it

Daly C.
National Suicide Research Foundation
1 Perrott Avenue College Road
Cork
Ireland

DeLeo D.
Australian Institute for Suicide Research
and Prevention
Mt. Gravatt Campus
Griffith University
4111 Brisbane, Queensland
Australia

Dello Buono M.
GRG-East
Fondazione Zancan
Via Vescovado, 66
35141 Padua
Italy

Devrimci-Özguven H.
Department of Psychiatry
University Medical School of Ankara
Dikimevi
06100 Ankara
Turkey

Dunkel D.
Psychiatric State Hospital of Tyrol
Thurnfeldgasse 14
6060 Hall
Austria

Estari J.
The National Swedish Institute for
Psychosocial Medicine
Karolinska Institute
Granits Väg 4
Box 230
SE-Stockholm 171 77
Sweden

Eudier F.
Rue Henri Le Guilloux
35033 Rennes Cedex
France

Fekete S.
Department of Psychiatry
University of Pécs
7623 Pécs Rét u. 2.
Hungary

G-Portilla M.P.
Hospital de Guipuzcoa
Po Dr.Beguiristain 115
E-20014 San Sebastian
Spain

Gailiené D.
University of Vilnius
Traidenio 27
2004 Vilnius
Lithuania

Grad O.
University Psychiatric Hospital
Centre for Mental Health
Zaloska 29
1000 Ljubljana
Slovenia

Groleger U.
University Psychiatric Hospital
Centre for Mental Health
Zaloska 29
1000 Ljubljana
Slovenia

Haring C.
Psychiatric State Hospital of Tyrol
Thurnfeldgasse 14
6060 Hall
Austria

Harriss L.
University of Oxford
Dept. of Psychiatry
Warneford Hospital
Headington
Oxford OX3 7 JX
United Kingdom

Hawton K.
University of Oxford
Department of Psychiatry
Warneford Hospital
Headington
Oxford OX3 7JX
United Kingdom

Hengeveld M.
Department of Psychiatry
Erasmus University
3062 PA Rotterdam
The Netherlands

Hennessy A.-M.
National Suicide Research Foundation
1 Perrott Avenue, College Road
Cork
Ireland

Hjelmeland H.
Regional Resource Centre for Suicide
Research
and Prevention in Central Norway
Department of Psychology
Norwegian University of Science and
Technology
7491 Trondheim
Norway

Jiang G.-X.
National Centre for Suicide Research and
Prevention of Mental Ill-Health
The National Swedish Institute for
Psychosocial Medicine
Karolinska Institute
Granits Väg 4
Box 230
SE-Stockholm 171 77
Sweden

Kapsali A.
University Mental Health Research Institute
P.O. Box 66517 Argurogastrou & Ionas
Papagou 15601 Athens
Greece

Keeley H.S.
National Suicide Research Foundation
1 Perrott Avenue, College Road
Cork
Ireland

Kelleher M.
National Suicide Research Foundation
1 Perrott Avenue, College Road
Cork
Ireland

Kelleher M. J.
National Suicide Research Foundation
1 Perrott Avenue, College Road
Cork
Ireland

Kerkhof A.
Department of Clinical Psychology
Vrije Universiteit Amsterdam
De Boelelaan 1109
NL-1081 Amsterdam
The Netherlands

Küpersepp O.
Estonian-Swedish Suicidological Institute
Pärnu mnt. 104-265
Magdalena Hospital
11312 Tallinn
Estonia

Lawlor M.
National Suicide Research Foundation
1 Perrott Avenue, College Road
Cork
Ireland

Lazarevitch L.
Department of Psychiatry
Schneiders Children's Medical Center of
Israel
14 Kaplan St
49202 Petach Tikva
Israel

Logins J.
Mental Health Care Centre of Latvia
Tvaika str. 2
Riga LV 1005
Latvia

Löhr, C.
Department of Clinical Psychology
Clinic für Psychiatry and Psychotherapy
University of Wuerzburg
Fuechsleinstr. 15
D-97080 Wuerzburg
Germany

Lönnqvist J.
Department of Mental Health and Alcohol
Research
National Public Health Institute
Mannerheimintie 166
FIN-00300 Helsinki
Finland

Lublinsky E.
Dept. of Psychiatry
Schneiders Children's Medical Center of
Israel
14 Kaplan St
49202 Petach Tikva
Israel

Marandi T.
Estonian-Swedish Suicidological Institute
Pärnu mnt. 104-265
Magdalena Hospital
11312 Tallinn
Estonia

Marietta P.
Istituto di Clinicia Psichiatrica
University of Padua
Via Giustiniani, 2
35128 Padua
Italy

Marini M.
Istituto di Clinicia Psichiatrica
University of Padua
Via Giustiniani, 2
35128 Padua
Italy

Martínez S.
Department of Medicine – Psychiatry
University of Oviedo
Julián Claveria 6
33006 Oviedo
Spain

Mc Auliffe C.
National Suicide Research Foundation
1 Perrott Avenue, College Road
Cork
Ireland

McCarthy J.
National Suicide Research Foundation
1 Perrott Avenue, College Road
Cork
Ireland

McCarthy M.
National Suicide Research Foundation
1 Perrott Avenue, College Road
Cork
Ireland

Meerschaert Th.
Department of Psychiatry
University Hospital
De Pintelaan 185
B-9000 Gent
Belgium

Meneghel G.
Istituto di Clinicia Psichiatrica
University of Padua
Via Giustiniani, 2
35128 Padua
Italy

Michel K.
Universitäre Psychiatrische Dienste (UPD)
Murtenstrasse 21
3010 Bern
Switzerland

Mokhovikov A.
Department of Clinical Psychology
Odessa National University
P.O. Box 270
65026 Odessa
Ukraine

Mulder J.
Emeritus, Department of Family Medicine
University of Leiden
P.O. Box 2088
2301 CB Leiden
The Netherlands

Neilson S.
National Suicide Research Foundation
1 Perrott Avenue, College Road
Cork
Ireland

Olsson L.
Department of Clinical Sciences
Division of Psychiatry
Umea University
90185 Umea
Sweden

Ostamo, A.
Department of Mental Health and Alcohol
Research
National Public Health Institute
Mannerheimintie 166
FIN-00300 Helsinki
Finland

O'Sullivan M.
National Suicide Research Foundation
1 Perrott Avenue, College Road
IRL Cork
Ireland

Osvath P.
Department of Psychiatry
University of Pécs
7623 Pécs Rét u. 2.
Hungary

Padoani W.
GRG-East
Fondazione Zancan
Via Vescovado, 66
35141 Padua
Italy

Palo E.
Estonian-Swedis Suicidological Institute
Vabduse pst. 90
11619 Tallinn
Estonia

Parades B.
University of Oviedo
Julian Claveria 6
E-33006 Oviedo
Spain

Perry I.J.
National Suicide Research Foundation
1 Perrott Avenue, College Road
Cork
Ireland

Philippe A.
Faculté de Médecine / INSERM
Dépt. de Santé Publique
2 av du Pr. Léon Bernard
35043 Rennes Cedex
France

Pommerau X.
Unite Medico-Psychologique de
l'Adolescent et du Jeune Adulte
Centre Jean Abadie
89 Rue des Sablieres
33077 Bordeaux Cedex
France

Querejeta I.
Hospital de Guipuzcoa
Po Dr. Beguiristain 115
20014 San Sebastian
Spain

Retterstøl N.
Aker Sykehus Klinikk for psykiatri
Sognsvannsveien 21 Bygning 5
0320 Oslo
Norway

Rozanov V.
Department of Clinical Psychology
Odessa National University
P.O. Box 270
65026 Odessa
Ukraine

Ruiz M.
Hospital de Guipuzcoa
Po Dr. Beguiristain 115
20014 San Sebastian
Spain

Rutz W.
Psychiatry and Health Promotion
Academic University Hospital
751 85 Uppsala
Sweden

Rutz W.
Regional Adviser
World Health Organization (WHO)
Regional Office for Europe
8 Scherfigsvejj
DK-2100 Copenhagen
Denmark

Saiz P.A.
Hospital de Guipuzcoa
Po Dr.Beguiristain 115
E-20014 San Sebastian
Spain

Salander Renberg E.
Department of Clinical Sciences
Division of Psychiatry
Umea University
90185 Umea
Sweden

Sánchez A.
Hospital de Guipuzcoa
Po Dr. Beguiristain 115
20014 San Sebastian
Spain

Sayil I.
Department of Psychiatry
Medical School of Ankara University
Dikimevi
06100 Ankara
Turkey

Schmidtke A.
Department of Clinical Psychology
Clinic for Psychiatry and Psychotherapy
University of Wuerzburg
Fuechsleinstrasse 15
D-97080 Wuerzburg
Germany

Scocco P.
Istituto di Clinicia Psichiatrica
University of Padua
Via Giustiniani, 2
35128 Padua
Italy

Seibl R.
Psychiatrisches Krankenhaus
Primariat B
Thurnfeldgasse 14
A-6060 Hall
Austria

Selakovic-Bursic S.
Institute of Neurology, Psychiatry and
Mental Health
Hajduk Veljkova 7
21000 Novi Sad
Serbia & Montenegro

Simkin S.
Department of Psychiatry
Warneford Hospital
Headington
Oxford OX3 7JX
United Kingdom

Sobol-Havia D.
Department of Psychiatry
Schneiders Children's Medical Center of
Israel
14 Kaplan St
49202 Petach Tikva
Israel

Stefanis C.
Suicide Research & Prevention Unit
University Mental Health Research
Institute
106 Kifissias Avenue
GR-11526 Athens
Greece

Stein D.
Dept. of Psychiatry
Schneiders Children's Medical Center of
Israel
14 Kaplan St
49202 Petach Tikva
Israel

Temesvary B.
Szeged M.J.V.Ö.Kórház
Pszichiatriai és Addiktológiai Osztály
Kálvária sgt. 57
H-6725 Szeged
Hungary

Udrasa S.
Mental Health Care Centre of Latvia
Tvaika str. 2
Riga LV 1005
Latvia

Vaidakis N.
Suicide Research & Prevention Unit
University Mental Health Research Institute
106 Kifissias Avenue
GR-11526 Athens
Greece

van Heeringen C.
Unit for Suicide Research
Department of Psychiatry
University Hospital
De Pintelaan 185
9000 Gent
Belgium

Värnik A.
Estonian-Swedish Suicidological Institute
Pärnu mnt. 104-265
Magdalena Hospital
11312 Tallinn
Estonia

Waeber K.
Universitäre Psychiatrische Dienste (UPD)
Murtenstrasse 21
3010 Bern
Switzerland

Wasserman D.
National Centre for Suicide Research and
Prevention of Mental Ill-Health
National Swedish Institute for
Psychosocial Medicine
Karolinska Institute
Granits Väg 4; Box 230
Stockholm 17177
Sweden

Weinacker B.
Department of Clinical Psychology
Clinic for Psychiatry and Psychotherapy
University of Wuerzburg
Fuechsleinstrasse 15
D-97080 Wuerzburg
Germany

Williamson E.
National Suicide Research Foundation
1 Perrott Avenue, College Road
Cork
Ireland

Zaluski M.
Crisis Intervention Centre
ul. Radziwillowska 8b
PL-32026 Cracow
Poland

Zavasnik A.
University Psychiatric Hospital
Centre for Mental Health
Zaloska 29
1000 Ljubljana
Slovenia